Working Gundogs

An Introduction to Training and Handling

Working Gundogs

Martin Deeley

The Crowood Press

First published in 1989 by
The Crowood Press Ltd
Ramsbury, Marlborough
Wiltshire SN8 2HR

www.crowood.com

New edition 2009

British Library Cataloguing-in-Publication Data
A catalogue record for this book is available from the British Library.

ISBN 978 1 84797 099 2

Disclaimer
The author and the publisher do not accept any responsibility in any manner whatsoever for any error or omission, or any loss, damage, injury, adverse outcome, or liability of any kind incurred as a result of the use of any of the information contained in this book, or reliance upon it. If in doubt about any aspect of gundog training readers are advised to seek professional advice.

Unless otherwise stated, photographs are by the author.

Front cover image by Paul Pederson, Action Snapshot Photography.
Back cover photographs by Jeff Beals (top left and middle right),
Simon Parsons (top right and bottom), and Pat Trichter (middle left).
Front flap photograph by Martin Deeley.
Back flap photographs by *Countryman's Weekly* (top)
and Pat Trichter (bottom).
Page 2 photograph by Paul Pederson Action Snapshot Photography

Typeset by Magenta Publishing Ltd (www.magentapublishing.com).
Printed and bound in Singapore by Craft Print International.

Contents

Foreword

by Cesar Millan

Dog training is first and foremost about understanding, trust, respect, and loyalty.

I first met Martin Deeley at a conference of the International Association for Canine Professionals (IACP) many years ago, after some criticism I had received from people in the dog training industry. Despite this criticism, or maybe because of it, Martin had contacted me, and said he would like me to come on board as an honorary member of the organization – he was excited that I had found a public platform to show dog owners that the responsibility was on them to create a healthy human/dog relationship. He asked me to attend the conference, and I humbly accepted.

At the time, I didn't know who Martin was any more than anyone knew who I was. I'm not the kind who likes to do research on someone before we meet. I prefer to meet people the way a dog would, letting my first impressions and my instincts guide me. I remember when Martin approached me; we shook hands and exchanged a look that to me said: 'Don't I know you?' It was an instant recognition, even though we had never met. He is that kind of person. The kind of man that you immediately feel you've known your entire life.

Even though he's much, much older than me – 100 years older, at least – we established a natural connection on that day. We can look at each other when we are working and know what the other is thinking. We both chose the same career, and we became our own masters. We both work in the same industry, but we have our own styles. It's true that our philosophies and methods are different, but it is our shared opinion that every trainer is different. We all have our own approach and our own methods that come from a lifetime of different experiences. But despite our differences, the goal is the same: to really understand our dogs and build a better relationship with them based on that understanding. Every individual is going to have a unique approach, and will use his or her own words to describe it. By using their own words, they are able to best express what they want with honesty and integrity. That's how you trigger the calm-assertive side that Martin is so in touch with. He will approach a case his way, and I will approach it my way...but in the end, the positive result will be the same.

I was honoured this past year to be able to work with him on my dog training DVD, Sit and Stay the Cesar Way. You don't have to tell him that you're going to do anything: he knows. Organically, he becomes a part of the moment. He knows when to move forward, when to move back, when to change his energy, what body language the animal will respond to – he knows the animal, and that's a rare thing.

I can't think of Martin and not think about dogs (and when I say that, he will know that I say it with reverence and respect!). That is what makes people like Martin so ideally suited for dog training – he lives in that world all the time, and he understands it. He spends much of his professional time with working dogs, and he has embraced their mentality. When it's time to work, he works; when it's time to laugh, he laughs; when it's time to relax, he relaxes. He's always willing to give you everything he has.

When you simplify it, our friendship – like the human/dog relationship – is about the trust, respect, and loyalty that we give and receive. When we feel strongly about somebody, we like to let them know. We're going to make sure they know that we support them in everything they do. In Martin's philosophy, no one

The author (left) and Cesar Millan. (Photo: Neal Tyler / Cesar Millan Inc. & MPH Entertainment)

person is necessarily better or worse than another; we're all just different. We can all accomplish what we set out to accomplish, and we can do so humanely. We both like to share our knowledge with people, and we like to listen to other people share their knowledge with us.

That is the purpose of this book. The knowledge that he has is singularly insightful. It comes from a life spent working with and understanding gundogs – of living and breathing that philosophy of trust, respect, and loyalty.

And he would like to share that knowledge with you.

Cesar Millan

Dedication

To Ben, the best friend that anyone
could have, who taught me so much.

Acknowledgements

Over the years that I have been working and involving myself with dogs there are many people who have encouraged me and helped me to enjoy what has become an important part of my life. In fact, as for anyone who becomes so involved with dogs, these animals have become my life and my teacher.

I have been lucky enough to learn from the best trainers and the best dogs on both sides of the Atlantic. I have also been lucky enough to have been provided a forum and an opportunity to share both my love of dogs, and also what I have learned – and am still learning – about them. Without those willing to listen, share and learn, my work with dogs could never have been as fulfilling as it is.

My family and my dogs have always been the principal motivators for the work that I do, for the enjoyment that I get from doing it, and for the resulting rewards. Without the support of my family, their love, encouragement and teaching, none of this would have been possible. In particular, my wife Pat's belief in this revised book – and in my own abilities – has been an inspiration to me: in writing it, I hope it will mean that more of my experiences in training are accessible to those who wish to work and enjoy their dogs as I do.

To be selected in 2007 by the readers of *Countryman's Weekly* as the 'Gundog Trainer of the Year' was a humbling experience. To have my name set in stone amongst my peers, whom I both respect and admire, was one of the greatest tributes that anyone could have paid to what I have tried to achieve in the dog world.

I hope that this book, and the lessons I have learned, will inspire many to bring dogs into their lives, just as I have done, and to enjoy the pleasures they share with us every day. There is no doubt that, in my life, 'Dogs have been, and still are, my teachers, friends and providers…': may they be yours as well.

Introduction

A well-trained gundog is the best companion that you, as a shooting man, can have. Whether it is to help you find the game, or retrieve it, or both, a day shared with a dog that will work for you and with you, always wanting to help you enjoy your day – and also, of course, himself by doing so – should be the norm, and not the exception. How many days are spoilt for yourself, and for your fellow shooters, by a dog that does not work for its owner, but disappears into the beyond, spreading game far and wide, and well out of shot? If such a dog belongs to someone else you will always be cursing it, and will then threaten never to shoot with the owner again; if it belongs to you, you will be embarrassed by its behaviour, and will risk a coronary by yelling and shouting for it in a temper. Alternatively, do you think that all gundogs are badly behaved, and that everyone around you is ignoring your own and your dog's misdemeanours? I have news for you: they are all being polite.

Training a gundog should not be difficult. To get a dog to a good standard of behaviour, acceptable to any reasonable shooting man and dog handler, is possible for most people. To put the final polish on a dog and win competitions and trials may need that something extra, but that is the same whatever pastime or occupation you become involved in.

This book is not aimed at telling you what to do – although it explains particular exercises and stages to go through – but to get you thinking about training and how to go about it. You are going to manage and train not only a dog but also yourself, and maybe other people around you as well. You will have to spot problems and potential problems, think out solutions for

Hunting tests and trials require a high degree of training and control. (Paul Pederson Action Snapshot Photography)

Make friends with your dog. Build a strong relationship based on affection and respect. (Pat Trichter)

them, and get your dog to achieve the standards of dog work you demand.

I have written about training that works for me, and about experiences that I have had in working dogs. The point to remember is that every person and every dog is different, and that what works for me may not be exactly right for you. You may also develop new exercises and techniques to train your dog, and if they work with no detriment to the finished product, this can only be for the good. If you can get inside the mind of your dog and discover what makes him 'tick', then designing ways of training him can be very creative and rewarding.

A good relationship, with the dog respecting the handler, is the basis of training. You have to create that relationship and manage it. Always remember that a relationship is a two-way thing: how you feel about your dog, and how your dog feels about you.

In training you will go through periods of excitement and a sense of achievement when the dog is learning fast, a 'natural'. At other times

you will go through frustration and despair – what is going wrong, why has the dog changed? I hope that in the book we will share pleasures and problems, and you will realize that everyone goes through these peaks and troughs during training. You are not alone: problems occur for the best dog trainers, and many of them not only accept the challenge of a problem dog, but even enjoy it. You too will enjoy it, providing you overcome it through your own effort. Nothing will give you more pleasure than working with an animal, and handling it in such a way that you can be proud of yourself, and other people admire your dog. My hope is that in some way this book will help you obtain the pleasure that I, and many dog people, have had from training and working good dogs.

I will probably repeat myself a number of times in the course of the book, but I make no excuse for this. Repetition will emphasize a point, and is also the basis of good training, forming habits and responses to particular situations and commands.

Chapter 1

Building a Solid

Foundation of Training

TRAINING AN 'ORDINARY' HUNTING DOG

As a hunting dog trainer I am often told by hunting dog owners that they are 'just hunters' and that all they want is a hunting dog, and not a trials or test dog. This led me to think, what is an 'ordinary' hunting dog? 'Ordinary' relates to the type of hunting and work they are doing, and usually indicates that the owners want no 'frills' on the dog. It becomes 'ordinary' only because they are familiar with the type of work they want their dog to do. But if you really think about the hunter's dog, such dogs are not ordinary at all – they are specialists, they are skilled and precise workers, and there is little that is 'ordinary' about their work.

For instance, the dog that retrieves doves in America or pigeon in the UK specializes at watching that bird fall from the sky, and then going out and picking the one that has just been shot. It also specializes at sitting quietly and patiently in a hide or behind a blind, and not making any movement that would distract incoming birds. Similarly the duck hunter's dog must have not only these attributes, but it must also be highly skilled in water work because it must often traverse difficult waterways, be able to work in poor light, and, in particular, be capable of dealing with diving ducks or large geese. It must also be able to work among decoys, either on the ground or in water. In a number of instances in these situations the dog will not see the fall of the bird clearly because it is in a hide or behind a blind, and it has to learn to locate the fall by other means than marking it down by sight.

On an upland shoot, a flushing dog such as a spaniel or retriever has to keep close, it must

investigate every piece of cover, and after a flush it is expected to wait until it is commanded to fetch, or to continue hunting if the bird were missed. A pointer is expected to hold his point until the handler is within shooting distance and gives the command to flush the birds, or goes in and kicks them out himself. And when picking up shot birds, one of the most important jobs a dog can have is 'sweeping up' for unlocated birds: no one knows exactly where, or sometimes even 'if', they have fallen, and an essential part – and in my experience, one of the most rewarding – of working a dog in the hunting field, is the controlled quartering of the ground by the dog when hunting for dead and wounded birds.

Whatever hunting dog work we look at, each must have a basic foundation of skills coupled with specialist ability. Thus in addition to marking the fall, and then finding and retrieving birds, steadiness (not breaking) is essential, as also is remaining calm and patient, and good manners. If any one of these is lacking, it results in the loss of a potentially good shoot day, and leads to bad tempers, a loss of pride, not being invited back to a shoot, and sometimes a group of very frustrated hunters who have seen a potentially good hunt ruined by a dog.

If we go to dogs of the right breeding from proven hunting lines, the ability to hunt and retrieve should be inherited. We need to develop these abilities as we train, but many owners miss out essential stages in their obsession to create powerful drive and intensity in their dogs (birdiness) from the very early days, usually through repetitive and uncontrolled retrieving. This is done to such an extent that a powerful desire is created in dogs to hunt and retrieve *too early*, making them very difficult for the 'ordinary'

Start with the right breeding: look for pups from working lines.

hunter to train and control. Professional and experienced trainers can usually build up the drive at a young age, and then, largely because of their experience, can introduce and develop control later.

For the everyday hunting man, or even the hunting man who takes over a dog trained in this manner, it can be 'too much dog'. The foundation of a good hunting dog therefore has to be basic obedience and a step-by-step approach to the hunt and retrieve, with control achieved at each stage.

THE PRINCIPLES OF TRAINING

Your dog possesses natural instincts inherited from its wild ancestors. In the wild a dog is a hunter, a killer, an animal which in order to survive has to find its prey, stalk, chase, kill it and then carry it to a safe place to eat, or back to its home for its young. Your job, therefore, is to channel these instincts for your own purposes. You have to bring out and enhance the natural hunting instincts, building a hunting pattern and helping the dog, with your more advanced intelligence, to find what it most seeks – game. The chasing and killing instinct has to be suppressed, and replaced by a different response: the sit and wait until you do the killing. The dog can then be cast off to hunt and 'chase' the dead or wounded game, and bring it ('the retrieve') back to a safe place ('home') – to you, the handler.

Leadership

To help you do all this, remember one important fact: in the wild the dog is a pack animal and has a leader. In domestication *you* have to be that leader: *you* must be at the top of the pecking order, and *you* have to be training the dog, not the dog training you. That is not as strange or funny as it sounds. The dog which taps your leg for a titbit, which brings you the lead to go for a walk, and which returns to you at only the third time of asking instead of the first, *and you accept this*, is leading you and training you. Some dogs are more aggressive in their training methods: you go to pick up their bone and they growl, so you back away, or they whine or yell to be with you rather than in their own bed, and you let them – 'anything for a quiet life': they are training you by force, and you are on the downward path.

Training is all about leadership and building good habits and responses. It is about building a good, strong foundation of basic behaviour upon which you can then develop your dog. Without that strong foundation, make one little mistake and you may not be able to go back to stage one. This foundation can then be built upon gradually with good, well schooled habits. Each training session should reinforce what you have done before, and further develop the dog's ability and experience. Always remember, however, that the dog is only one part of the team. You are the other, and therefore at all times you should be in control of the situation. In your training session take small steps, one at a time. Do not do too much, but ensure that the dog learns and remains interested.

Be Positive

Always try to build on the positive and praise-worthy aspects of performance. Putting the dog in a position where it is always doing wrong and you are chastising it for this, will not create the desired relationship. So think through your exercises and put the dog in a position where it does right. Initially it will not know that it is right, but with praise it will soon learn.

If you put the dog in a position where it does wrong or is tempted to disobey, probably almost always it will not know it done wrong; when you 'tell it off' it then only becomes confused, and in many cases nervous and cowed. In the various chapters I will mention this again, and show some of the ways to prevent your dog doing the wrong thing. Together with being positive and trying to get your dog to be successful each time, you must remember never to give it an instruction or command unless you can enforce it, or show it what you mean. 'Showing' your dog means exactly that: helping, guiding and encouraging. If, for example, you have a dummy hidden in the long grass and the dog cannot find it or perhaps does not understand what you want, guide your dog up to the dummy, encouraging it with your hands and with words until it is successful.

Be aware that things will go wrong occasionally, and be prepared to change what you are doing so that you can put the dog right. It is so easy to overestimate your dog and set too difficult a task; therefore, think through how you are going to react if you do not get the response you require. If you do this, and are prepared for things going wrong, it may avoid the panic reaction that usually results in the dog being shouted at or punished for something it did not realize was a misdemeanour.

Step-by-Step Progress

Training is a step-by-step approach, constantly building confidence and skills, so never take too big a step or attempt to show off or test your dog on something you have not built up to. It

Behave in a way that keeps your dog happy and motivated. (Jeff Beals)

Start building the relationship from the very beginning. (Pat Trichter)

An enthusiastic cocker pup.

is too easy to be tempted into showing a friend how good your dog is, or even trying things out yourself.

One big 'no no' is to enter a competition, no matter how trivial it may be, possibly at a small country fair, and find yourself and your dog faced with too difficult a task. Weeks of good training can be destroyed in seconds. If you are ever tempted and you can see that the tests are too difficult, pull your dog out with a brave smile. Go and win it another day when you are both ready. In fact, it is true of people as well as dogs that they very easily and quickly pick up bad habits, but need considerable praise and encouragement to learn good ones. Don't put your dog in a position where he learns a bad habit or picks up a particular behaviour pattern, which then takes you a lot of time to eliminate, if you ever can.

Training your dog should be enjoyable for both of you. Nothing pleases a gundog more than doing what his instincts tell him, and nothing will please you more than watching the dog use those instincts to your commands, looking to you for help and support, and at the end of the work together 'coming home with the goods'.

PLAY TRAINING WITH A YOUNG PUPPY

Retrieving

Some pups display more of an interest in retrieving than others, but I am always amazed at how many owners are not able to recognize the multitude of opportunities that their puppy consistently presents to them. It's a shame not to take advantage of this natural carrying instinct during the first few months of the pup's life.

When I start 'play training' with a young pup I have a preference for using a puppy bumper: a tennis ball, a knotted handkerchief or especially a 'parcel' of old smelly socks (they are very popular), and unless the pup is having problems I do not retrieve with anything else. If he is not interested in a particular retrieve 'object' then I find something that he is fond of carrying and use it as the 'special' retrieving 'bumper'. Something else I do that might be helpful to encourage your pup to retrieve is to put scent on to the retrieve object by spitting on it and rubbing the spittle into the fabric.

Initially, so as not to be overwhelming and to encourage a good return, crouch down low or sit on the floor with your legs outstretched. Have the pup by your side or between your legs, held lightly with your hands. Tease it with the bumper, and throw it only a short distance – three or four yards. Little tugs of war with a small object can encourage the pup to hold and carry, but be careful not to do this too much as the dog may refuse to let go when you need it to. (I only play 'tug' with a dog that is not good at carrying and holding.) When you throw the bumper, immediately let the pup go, saying the word 'fetch' to introduce the command. Then as soon as the pup becomes keen, you can begin to restrain him gently for one to three seconds before allowing him to go for the retrieve, thereby introducing the beginnings of steadiness.

Maintaining a crouched or seated position,

encourage your pup to come in close to your body with the bumper by tapping the inside of your thighs. Stroke under his chin, on his chest and down his back, but do not take the bumper, and absolutely do not reach or grab for it. One reason I stroke under the chin and not on top of the head is to help the pup to hold the object longer, and lift his head at the same time. Keep in mind that sitting and presenting nicely is not necessary at this stage of training.

Developing Control and Obedience

After pup has held the bumper next to you for a few seconds, put your hand slowly under it and say 'drop'. Gently take the bumper and hold it yourself for a few seconds, before returning it to pup once more to hold. Don't let him leave, but continue to gently restrain and pet him before taking the bumper again. This technique teaches the pup that you are *sharing* a retrieve, and to stay with you, and to trust you. In time he will become confident and happy to return to you with his retrieve.

Because retrieving is the big reward, I use this to develop many of the controls and basic obedience I demand in a hunting dog, and encourage this interest in my young puppies from the age of seven weeks. What I *do not do* is keep throwing bumper after bumper. If I get two or three nice retrieves I stop there. I teach 'sit' before I throw a bumper, and the little dog learns this so much more quickly because it relates it to the fun reward of a retrieve. I call the pup with a bumper twirling in my hand, and crouch down to greet it before going through a retrieve routine. Pup quickly learns that the commands mean that fun begins once he does them.

As soon as I have a pup wanting to retrieve and bring it back to me, I begin to introduce memory retrieves. A memory retrieve is where I drop a bumper and then take the pup away from it on a leash before turning around, sitting him, and then sending him back for the retrieve with a clear signal. Initially this may be only a few yards, but the distance can be quickly built up. In this way the pup learns not to go immediately for the retrieve, and it certainly helps to build his memory and focus. I then begin to introduce more control by holding the pup for longer periods of time and not allowing him to just run and chase the bumper — I crouch down or hold pup on a leash and make him wait for a few seconds before sending. Never send when he is struggling to go for the retrieve, but gently restrain and wait until he is sitting still and calmly.

Creating Good Habits

I keep my retrieving bumpers and tennis balls away from the dogs unless we are in a training session. They are not left around for the dog to

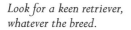

Look for a keen retriever, whatever the breed.

play with, and no one is allowed to go out and play 'crazy' fetch with anything. If we want to create good habits in our dog we have to ensure that they are related to the good fun times we have together training. I also begin to teach a dog to stay for longer periods of time, and will go myself and pick bumpers I have thrown. Again the aim is to get the little fella waiting for your command, increasing control and building patience, and especially not anticipating what comes next.

Early Training of Flushing Dogs

With flushing dogs, initially I like to keep them close: the closer they are, the more likely you are to be listened to and to be in control. To keep them close, as I walk along behind them, I drop tennis balls or bumpers unseen, for them to find. Sometimes I have to stand still and encourage them back to find them, but after a few successful finds they begin to realize that a recall whistle means there is a bumper down and that the 'treasure' they seek is not fifty yards away but close to me.

Once a dog has experience picking birds such as pigeons, this becomes an even bigger reward as they find pigeons close to you. Some hunters may feel that the dog will then always stay close and never cover the area they need to find wild birds. However, my experience has been that as the dog gets real hunting and scent in its nose, it naturally begins to take in more ground. But by that time it should understand the commands you have taught and be far more responsive.

In the early days of training with a young spaniel, retriever or pointer I do not let them relate the retrieve to the find. In other words, I teach the point or encourage a good flush, but do not allow them the retrieve immediately. I keep retrieve training and flush training separate until I am confident I am in control of both. If there is a constant sequence of find, shot, fetch, then very quickly a dog will begin to anticipate and chase the moment a shot is fired, or even worse, before; and a pointer may begin to move in to the game too quickly as its natural enthusiasm takes over, and the controlled point then disappears. To reduce the chance of breaking I teach my dogs to sit not only to the 'sit' command and a single whistle blast, but also to the flush of a bird, and to a shot going off.

SPECIALIZATION TRAINING

As I mentioned previously, all hunting dogs are specialists, and some will require more specialization training than others. Training a hunting dog is not just a matter of obedience and control, but preparing them during training for the main jobs they will be expected to perform. Although the basics of gundog training may be the same for all dogs – to gain the foundations of control and obedience while developing their natural instincts – there are ways in which an owner can give their dog experience, which will help both of them in their hunting partnership.

Water Retrieving

I learned one specific skill with the first spaniel I ever owned many years ago. We were in Scotland on holiday, and I had taken Sam with me. We were doing water retrieves as I had some duck hunting at the time and wanted him to be good in water. One of the bumpers I was using must have had a puncture because after a few retrieves it became waterlogged and began to sink. Sam had been sent for this, and as it went down just under his nose he put his head underwater and picked it.

I found this amazing and amusing, as you can imagine, so I used the bumper again and this time made him wait a little longer before sending him. The water depth was just enough for him to swim, I would guess about two to three feet deep. The retrieve was short, but again as he got to the spot where the bumper had disappeared he put his head under and went down to bring it up. Through this lesson we learned by accident he became one of the best retrievers of diving wounded ducks I have ever had.

By using an anchor of some nature and a light line attached to the bumper, you can pull a bumper underwater as the dog reaches it, and thus teach him to look below the water surface. By bobbing it up and down you can simulate a duck diving and then resurfacing. Be sure the line you use is light, and let go of it the moment the dog has the bumper in its mouth to avoid his legs tangling in it. Alternatively, as I did accidentally, use a sinking bumper and start very near the shore, building up distance and depth as your dog gains experience.

Duck hunting in a blind / hide.

Working with Decoys

Owners who want their dog to go dove / pigeon or duck hunting should introduce a blind during training, and have decoys out in a field or on the water to accustom their dog to working with these accessories. By doing specialized training in this way your dog will become familiar with decoys and the hide, and the first time he is taken out in the field will be less likely to take blind and poles with him on the first retrieves, or frustrate you by checking out each decoy as the wounded bird hobbles away. The same is true of duck hunting where a platform or special boat is used. A dog has to be trained to be calm and to wait on a platform or in a boat, as well as knowing how to get on a platform or in and out of the boat.

Developing Gun Sense

Working often in heavy woodland or in poor light, I found that my dogs needed to mark the fall of a bird by sound as much as sight. To provide experience, a friend and myself go out together and take turns at firing a starting pistol and throwing a bumper into woodland or over rushes and reeds into the water. Firstly we do it so the thrower can be seen, but we then progress to firing a shot and throwing bumpers so all the dog hears is the gun and a splash or a crash in cover. Some dogs learn to mark the fall by sound very quickly, and it also teaches them to hunt on their own initiative once they think they are in the right area.

A dog does not always see a bird shot, especially when the cover is tall grass or heavy

---

Training Points to Remember

- It is easier to establish good habits than to change bad ones.
- Take training in small steps, at the pace of your dog.
- All dogs are different and learn at differing rates.
- Even clever dogs can encounter difficulties.
- We are always training.
- Help your dog, and put it in a position where it can do right.
- Avoid situations where your dog can easily go wrong.
- Guide and show, and always give your dog the benefit of the doubt if it goes wrong.
- Even dogs have off days.
- Be patient, take your time, and keep calm.
- Be confident, positive and clear in all you do.
- Stop on a high when your dog is doing well.
- Do not be tempted to 'test' your dog in situations he has not yet learned about, even when encouraged by friends.
- Spend time with your dog, and create a relationship of trust and respect.

- Training is exercise.
- Short, successful sessions are more effective than long, tiring ones.
- Train first, allow a free run afterwards.
- Be as positive in your approach and rewards/motivation as possible.
- Corrections should fit the crime. But always ask yourself first, is your dog wilfully disobeying, or does he just not understand yet?
- Without a good training foundation the advanced work will fail.
- Never be too proud to go back to basics
- Watch and learn from everyone, but make your own decisions.
- Be fair, be firm, but always *have fun*.
- If you have to correct your dog, show it immediately what is required and get it to do it right, even to the extent of making the exercise less complicated. Praise and make friends with your dog.

---

undergrowth. What your dog needs in these situations is gun sense, the ability to realize that in front of the gun that fired is the bird. Some dogs quickly develop the skill, others have to be taught when he hears or sees the shot being taken, to observe the direction the gun has been pointing, and upon command make for that place. Done enough times a dog begins to realize that the retrieve will usually be no further than thirty-five yards in front of the gun.

A dog that has been taught to go to the gun that has been fired, and which understands that following the gunshot scent results in a retrieve at the end, makes gun sense look second nature. This can be taught by using live cartridges during training to fire along the ground to where a bumper has been seen to be thrown, and then progressing to unseen retrieves where a bumper is lying there previous to the shot being fired, and the dog is encouraged to retrieve it by following that line of shot.

Always remember to follow the same safety codes when training with live cartridges as you would be expected to observe at a shoot. There is no doubt that this form of training is very beneficial: a dog that works for, and to the gun, is a jewel to behold.

IN CONCLUSION

There are therefore so many ways in training that you can prepare the ordinary hunting dog for his specialized task, and have lots of fun doing it. I am certain that dogs also enjoy the special challenges and variety these training situations present. I have mentioned only a few here, and briefly, but do think about what you expect from your hunting dog, think about what it will need to do, and then be creative in training and preparing him for these 'ordinary' tasks. But throughout, never ignore the basic and essential foundation of obedience: if you do this I have no doubt he will be no ordinary hunting dog in other peoples' eyes, or even in your own, from the first day you take him out. I will be explaining how you can achieve a great hunting dog through being creative and following general guidelines in training: but the end result lies in your hands – so go out and enjoy the times with your dog.

In this book my aim is to provide you, the reader, with ways I have found successful to build a solid foundation of training with your dog for all forms of gundog work in the field and on water. Work with your dog, help him and enjoy him – the more you do this, the 'luckier' you will be with him.

Chapter 2

The Qualities of the Trainer

Although I have said that anyone should be able to train a gundog up to an acceptable standard, experience has shown that this assumption was wrong, and there is no doubt that some people cannot do this. They have failings, weaknesses, habits and mannerisms which make it difficult for them to build a good enough relationship with a dog to train it. So are *you* really up to the long-term task of training, and then maintaining the training, of your dog?

ESTABLISHING TEAMWORK

Training and handling a dog is built around teamwork, which must involve respect and affection for each other. To create that team, that respect, you have to realize that the dog is a fairly simple-minded creature with a lower level of intelligence than yourself. He can, however, learn to be crafty and sometimes even dishonest, but only if he gets the responses he wants from you.

How Intelligent is Your Dog?

Like me, you have probably heard dog owners claim that their dog is highly intelligent and understands everything they say — but this level of intelligence or reasoning power is debatable.

There is no doubt that some dogs are cleverer than others, and that some can solve problems encountered. Generally, however, these dogs have had experience of similar situations. For example, the bird that falls on the opposite side of a rabbit wire fence creates a problem: the dog can see this and can take many courses of action, but many a young puppy will run up and down the fence not knowing what to do. When shown how to jump, the dog will then attempt to jump

the fence for the retrieve. Some dogs have experienced finding holes in fences, even gates, so will look for a hole as an easy way through the obstacle. I have seen others, even with a low fence, try to burrow underneath, or try to reach the bird with their paws and then pull it through the holes in the fence. But I have yet to see a dog that runs up to the fence and then stops to think out which would be the most efficient and energy-saving method of retrieving.

When sent for a retrieve across a river, a dog can be carried downstream a little before leaving the water. This may result in the dog losing his mark on where a bird has fallen, and therefore he has to be handled to the fall, which could be a considerable distance from where he left the water. The moment the dog gets the bird and wishes to return, very often you will see him re-enter the water at exactly the same spot he left it, even though it may not be the best point of entry or produce the speediest return. It is possible that the dog feels it was a safe route on the way out, therefore it is the best risk on the return. Some dogs will run a long distance to find a bridge across the river, rather than swim. Is this intelligence, experience, or reasoning? I suppose it is what we want it to be.

Certainly dogs do understand what we say, but they learn the words by repetition and association. Repetition of a word together with praise when carrying out the appropriate act, and disapproval when doing the wrong thing, is bound to bring results. Words such as 'dinner' and 'walk' are always part of the dog's understanding, as those words are always followed by something pleasurable.

What you have to do, therefore, is to use the skills and resources available to you to bring out the best in your dog, utilizing his natural instincts and reading his level of intelligence and rate of learning. But remember that you, too, will be learning, and that your dog will have to live with your rate of learning, so do think before you act. To utilize your dog's abilities and all the available resources to the full requires experience on your part, and you may not have that yet. For instance, are you sure you can tell when your dog really doesn't know what you want, or is just 'trying it on'? And are you sure your dog understood that signal, or did you give it wrongly? Does your dog know why you are punishing him, or are you causing confusion and further problems? Do think about specific situations before acting or reacting.

What Do You Wish to Achieve?

You must have a clear idea of what you wish to achieve – the end result. In your mind you can build up a picture of the ideal dog you require, and the job he has to do. You can then develop short-term aims: what you and your dog have to achieve at different stages of the learning process. What you want to achieve is very dependent upon the job your dog is going to do. If you are not sure what to expect from your dog, or the precise level and standard of skills he should possess, then don't be afraid to ask others, and watch how other dogs work in the field.

Wildfowlers often require a dog that will run in to a falling bird (not to shot) because the flow of the tide or river can carry a bird out of reach very quickly – yet this tendency is, of course, unacceptable for a gun at a driven shoot. Equally, some rough shooters will quite happily put up with a dog that yips, and will even encourage him because then they know when it has found something; sometimes they will even know from the level and type of noise whether it is bird or rabbit. If, however, your aim is to work your dog in the beating line, this behaviour may be frowned upon, and certainly in field trials your dog will be disqualified for giving tongue.

I would always recommend that you only work a dog that is obedient to your commands, that you can be proud of, and people around you are pleased to have working around them. Even the wildfowler *who wants* his dog to run in can train him to go only when given the order!

The two main uses of a dog in the field are for hunting up game and as a no-slip retriever for the standing gun. The hunting dog must hunt within shooting distance, sit to shot, whistle and command, or flush and retrieve gently to hand when given the command. The no-slip dog (one without a lead attached) must sit calmly but attentively by the side of the gun, walk to heel when ordered, and retrieve gently to hand at the end of the drive when commanded to do so.

Unfortunately, my experience has been that some trainers have set and achieved too low a standard. Sometimes this is because they have not seen a really good dog and handler working together, or because they have tried to rush the finishing process. Impatience to get the dog into 'the real thing', and giving him too much 'real work', can be the downfall of many a good dog. Take your time training your dog, and remember that he is going to be working with you for the next eight to ten years or more. Time spent now instilling all the good habits and responses will pay dividends, because your time spent with your dog can be pure delight and enjoyment, or hell and frustration – so don't rush it! Read your dog and your own performance at each stage, and adjust your training as necessary.

At one time the trainer adopted the 'boot and stick' approach, where a dog was allowed to do what he liked using his natural abilities, and any action a trainer did not want was punished. But this is a very negative approach, and one which can create either a very nervous dog or a very hard one. The sensitive dog, which often has a higher degree of intelligence, could not be brought to a good standard using this method.

Some people have been very lucky in achieving a good standard with their dog, but don't really know why. They have created a bond with their dog, whose personality matches their own, and together they have become an acceptable team, but they are not sure what the 'magic' potion was. If you have a natural ability with a dog, then try to analyse as you go along how you are achieving it, and build on that. There is no doubt in my mind that although there are certain techniques and skills which can be learnt, some people do have dog sense, and dogs like working with them.

Today's good trainer works with the aid of dog psychology – what makes them tick, what pleases them, what stimulates a particular reaction and, in particular, what goes into creating the team where you are the leader. As you can imagine, this does not involve a couch, but observation and constant awareness of what your dog is doing, and why. By using a knowledge of dog behaviour, and by having a clear picture in your mind of the standards you require, you should be able to mould your dog's personality and his way of working.

PERSONAL QUALITIES OF THE TRAINER

What about the characteristics *you* have to adopt? You are the animal in the team with the highly developed intelligence and reasoning power, so it is up to you to use it. Sometimes you will have to act a part and not show your true feelings. The dog may see through this act, but you have to do things that will produce the results you require.

Be Patient

Patience is a virtue which is tested in all of us from time to time. I would be very surprised if your dog did not try your patience sometimes, but the important thing is not to show it, even if the dog has done wrong and has to be punished. Punishing a dog with a loss of temper often means that you over-punish, and the dog then loses sight of why he is being punished.

Don't rush into situations; if you haven't got the time to train your dog one day, then it is better not to try. If you are in a bad mood from work or you are upset about anything, then sit with your dog and share your feelings, but don't try to train. You will find that stroking your dog, and talking to this friend who understands and loves you, can calm you down. But if you train while you are 'up tight', your dog will notice and you may create not just an undesirable reaction, but a habit which may be difficult to remove. In fact, some problems that have been created 'in the heat of the moment' have lasted a lifetime.

A calm, quiet and patient approach is the best one to adopt. Your dog will learn at different rates: thus on some days he will be excellent, and everything will go so smoothly that you

Let a pup come right up initially, and then patiently show it what is required. (Jeff Beals)

will believe there is nothing to this dog-training game – on others you will wonder why you ever started. The thing to realize is that everyone has these days. You will find that your dog will learn some exercises very quickly, while others create real problems, your dog seeming to have a mental barrier against what you want to achieve. The only solution is to think through the problem and develop exercises that will gradually overcome that barrier – a patient approach will get you there in the end.

Be Firm and Fair

Patience is one thing, but allowing your dog to get away with actions both you and he know are wrong should not be tolerated. Be firm in following up commands. If you say 'sit' the dog should sit. Even if you give a wrong command, it is sometimes better to make sure the dog does it, rather than apologizing and letting him get away with not doing what you commanded. You can then put your dog and yourself right afterwards. Firmness but fairness with your dog is essential: if you ever lose your temper and are unfair with your dog, it is no use apologizing afterwards, because unlike people, he cannot understand and forgive.

Be Consistent

Your dog is going to learn through repetition, therefore it is important that the commands and actions you take are consistent. You will have habits and mannerisms your dog will recognize, so make them good clear ones. Your words are often the 'trigger' for action from your dog; therefore think carefully, and be consistent in how you use them.

One big problem that can occur is associated with the positive action of praising your dog, which of course you must do. When your dog does things right you praise him with 'good boy'. You may also say 'good boy' when you let him go and play, which is a very enjoyable part of the day – but very quickly he will associate 'good boy' with the more pleasurable action of running off. The number of times I have seen a handler take their dog off the lead and then send him for a retrieve, or even to play, immediately – and yes, you have guessed right, the next thing that happens is that every time the dog is let off the lead he runs away – which is not always what is required. This action, which the dog believes is right, is then punished, with the result that you have a confused dog. Therefore consistent, simple commands, carefully used, are the way forwards.

Creating Respect

By being patient, consistent, firm but fair you will create a respect in your dog, which will show itself in the way the dog looks to you and is willing to work for you. If you have achieved this respect and things start to go a little wrong, it is more likely that you are trying to move too fast and that you have not shown your dog exactly what you require. Exercises that you carry out successfully close up may go wrong when the distances are increased. Your dog may sit quite happily to the whistle up to twenty yards away, but ignores you when thirty yards away or while he is searching for a dummy. Build up the complexity gradually, reinforcing the learning process at each stage. Help your dog when he looks to you for guidance, but do allow him to develop a little initiative and hunting ability. You are trying to create a very delicate balance between a dog that has plenty of drive and resourcefulness, yet is with you and under your command.

Handler and dog working together, the latter even as a pup. (Pat Trichter)

Concentration

In any job that you do it is important that you concentrate. With a dog it is essential not only that you concentrate, but also that he knows you are concentrating on him and giving him your full attention. By making the dog your centre of attention and building the essential relationship, you should also become the dog's centre of attention.

If you are finding concentration difficult or there are other distractions for either yourself or your dog, it may be better not to train at that time. The most obvious loss of attention occurs when someone talks to you when you are out with your dog. Not wanting to be rude, or maybe not thinking, you start to talk and forget about the dog, who then does his own thing; you thus lose the mental contact with him. Depending upon the dog, many things can happen, from him sitting by your side and faithfully waiting, to wandering off, free hunting and getting lost.

If your attention is distracted, or you no longer wish to be training (you need a break), then put the dog in 'neutral' and slip the lead over his head. In that way you will maintain the physical contact, and the dog will not be able to do anything he feels like.

Not only must you concentrate on the dog, but you must get him to concentrate on you. Create interest and enjoyment, and attract his attention when it is wandering and should be on you. Develop a little insecurity in the dog by hiding behind something when his attention is distracted, so that he has to look for you. If he walks up one track – leading you – you walk up another and catch his attention so that he has to follow. Only issue commands when your dog is watching you and concentrating. When the dog starts to 'feast' you with his eyes and watches your every movement in order not to miss anything and to obey your command, then you know you are becoming the 'centre of attention' – the leader.

Concentration by a handler can, however, sometimes create tension, which a dog will sense. Always concentrate in a 'relaxed' manner. If you watch top professionals in any sport, and particularly dog trialling, they look relaxed. Inside they may have nerves, but they do not show it. The slightest movement or reaction of their dog does not go unnoticed, and they are quick to react when necessary, encouraging when the dog is uncertain, and checking him when he may or does go wrong.

Looking relaxed should not mean that you are slow to act when required, or lacking in concentration. In fact, that concentration should never be relaxed totally until the dog has been put into 'neutral' on a lead. Many is the time that handlers have completed the main job with their dog, such as a retrieve, then relaxed when the dog is finishing off the work. I have seen dogs change birds on the way back to the handler (a serious fault in a trial) – they have put down a bird and begun chasing another – all because the handler has relaxed. Keep that concentration and do the job well.

Knowledge and Experience

Why is it that the less we know, the more reluctant we are to ask for help and advice, and if given any, then ignore it? The more we know, the happier we are to listen to other people's experiences and methods, to try out their ideas and learn from them. I have often wondered whether I should really be writing this book, because although I have been training and handling dogs for over thirty years, I have never found the 'magic key' to making it all happen. I never stop learning new things about dogs and training, and the more I learn, the more I realize that there is still so much more to find out and experience. The reason is probably that although there are guidelines to training, because we are dealing with two animals – human and dog – there are no scientific equations that work every time. Training and handling a dog to me is an art more than a science, as dogs differ dramatically from one to another, and their behaviour does not always appear to conform to the basic theories and principles.

Gain knowledge through reading books, watching films and videos, experiencing situations, talking to people with appropriate knowledge, and watching others train and handle their dogs. In all cases, however, acquire the knowledge and identify the techniques, but do not apply them without thought. What works for someone else and their dog may not work

Get down to the level of your dog and show him that your hands and body are friendly. (Pat Trichter)

for you and yours. You should build a pool of knowledge of dogs, training and handling. Then, by watching and working with your dog, getting to know his character and temperament, apply the knowledge you have gained to achieve the results you are aiming for. You can learn from every minute you are with your dog. How often have you heard the saying that there is no substitute for experience, and agreed with it?

So gather knowledge and tuck it away for future use. Listen to people's advice, and take it if you feel it is of value. I suppose it should be said that some people give advice when they would be better advised themselves to keep quiet, as they show their ignorance by their own words. I have often found that the most knowledgeable comments and advice come from those you have to ask, the people who have been in the business for some time and have learnt not to give advice freely because it has not been accepted correctly. I have learnt a tremendous amount from trainers and handlers I respect simply by talking to them and listening. Maybe it is my age, but I find it easier to listen these days than when I first started.

Acting the Part

Your dog, except when he is feeling ill, will generally be himself. He will, however, interpret your actions, noises and mannerisms, and react to them. You therefore have to do things which are not in your character, not your normal way of doing things. In order to get the best out of

your dog you have to act a part which gets the results you require.

With most puppies and young dogs you need to exaggerate your actions, and use all the tones and volumes available in your voice. Many novice handlers find this difficult. Whether they are shy, think it silly or are embarrassed, whatever the reason, it is difficult to get a very manly handler to use a high-pitched encouraging voice or to exaggerate a hand signal. Some people do find it difficult to change their voice naturally, but it certainly does help, so practise it and use all your body and voice to communicate what you want to your dog.

If you ever listen to dogs, when they are showing pleasure they use a light whine or moan, if they are angry they growl, and if they wish to attract attention they bark. Your voice can communicate in the same way. Your dog cannot understand sentences and will need short commands, but will quickly learn to read tone and volume because that is how they 'talk' to each other. Again it reminds me of what my wife often tells me when I say something wrong: 'It's not what you said, it's the way you said it!' If you say 'good boy' in a growling voice you shouldn't be surprised to see the dog look a little concerned. And how often have you heard dog owners say 'Oh, you *are* a naughty boy!' in such a sweet voice that the dog wags his tail – useless!

In giving directions and commands you are going to be using your arms and hands. Make sure these signals are reinforced with your whole body. Accentuate the hand signals by leaning in the direction of your hand, or lift yourself to your full height when giving a stop and sit signal. Maybe even stamp your foot to reinforce the signal.

A handler uses the hands not only to direct the dog, but also to praise him. Don't be afraid to have contact with your dog, by stroking, holding, shaking or cuddling (if he's that type of dog). Your dog will get many messages from your hands; make sure he gets the right ones. I often wonder if your dog can sense your emotions from your hands. Most dogs will sniff your hands and quite often lick them; I wonder whether they can taste whether we are happy, angry, nervous, bad-tempered or just normal. I must admit that if a dog has disobeyed me and has had a bit of a telling off, it pleases me when he comes up and licks my hand – an apology, subservience, or finding out whether I am still upset with him, who knows?

The other part of your body you need to bring into play is your face, and particularly your eyes. Eye contact, as I have mentioned before, is essential in building a good working relationship, but you must use your eyes correctly. Watch animals that are aggressive with each other: their eyes are open wide and they stare at each other, their lips part showing some teeth, and their necks arch.

Now think about yourself watching your young dog bringing back a retrieve. You are concentrating intently, as I have advised, so you are probably staring, your mouth is slightly open, not smiling, and your neck is arched waiting for the dog to come below you at your feet with the retrieve. If you are in the presence of other people or have experienced a few problems with your dog, you are probably also exuding tension. What picture has your dog got of you as he returns? Are you surprised therefore that he runs around you, shrinks to the floor, drops the dummy, or does a variety of things which compound your problem, because you are not communicating the right messages? Animals, when they are showing affection, partly close their eyes, the corner of their mouth lifts in a smile, and their body relaxes. If you wish to encourage

your dog, create this image and use your voice in an encouraging tone.

Play the part that will get the desired response from your dog, but beware of two things. Firstly, do not play a part which, because of your mood, you cannot carry through. This is particularly true if you are in a bad temper. It is better to leave the dog in the kennel or house, because however clever you are at acting, the dog will sense that things are not right, and will behave out of character; you will then end up doing something you will probably regret. Secondly, if your dog does something wrong, particularly running away from you, and in order to get him back you adopt a sweet encouraging tone but then punish him on his return, do I have to say you have created a problem? In future you will not get your dog to return, no matter what tone you adopt.

Therefore, act the part that communicates to your dog what you mean and what you require from him. Again, be consistent in the way you communicate, and act to create confidence in the dog, so that he knows what to expect.

Becoming a Leader

Your dog is a domesticated wild animal, which was predominantly a pack animal. In fact, if dogs are put together without any human influence they will tend again to 'pack'. A leader of the

Create an interest in what you are doing, so your dog looks to you for the pleasures in life. (Pat Trichter)

pack will emerge, and a pecking order instituted where the more dominant dog takes priority. A good example of this is in areas where there is a preponderance of stray dogs who come together to 'hunt' the district.

Your dog therefore has a natural instinct to be part of a pack. Your family becomes the 'pack' that your dog belongs to: he recognizes the members of the family as part of the group that he feeds, works and plays with. What has got to happen, though, is that you must become the leader of that pack, and particularly of your dog. Even if you feel that you are well down the pecking order in your family, your dog has to be below you and look to you for leadership. Becoming the leader of your dog is not always easy, particularly if he is of a dominant nature. The gentle, subservient type that looks to you for protection and guidance, and will not let you out of its sight, is an easy one. The independent, dominant dog is the one to watch for: he will start to compete for leadership, and once you give an inch, he will start to take much more.

I will be talking about dominant and subservient dogs later, but the way you become the leader is to make sure that your will is the strongest. Any command you give must be obeyed, and once the dog understands the command, it must be obeyed immediately.

DEMANDS ON YOUR TIME

Training a dog takes time, and therefore you must set aside time to do this. What you must realize is that your dog is learning all the time he is around you, and although the training sessions may take place at a specific time, *what you do at other times is just as important as what you do during the training session*.

The main guidelines in terms of time spent training are that it must be done when the dog and yourself are alert and in the right frame of mind. The time taken must be long enough to make an impression, but not so long that it risks boring the dog. For a puppy or young dog, five to ten minutes will be long enough; for an older dog, generally fifteen minutes to half an hour, twice a day if possible, would be ideal. It is very dependent upon yourself and your dog,

and it is surprising how much you can do over smaller periods of time in the house or even when you are out for a walk with the dog. If you do take your dog out for walks and train him during the walk, be careful that the dog is not tired from walking, and so cannot concentrate on the training session. You will find that although your dog physically seems alert and ready for work, mentally he may have done enough. Your dog's brain will tire long before his body gives in.

If your dog has a special place, either in the house (perhaps a corner of the kitchen) or a kennel, then it can 'switch off' in that place. Train the dog to go to his own area and stay there. It isn't cruel: a dog, if left alone, will sleep a large amount of the time anyway. He will feel comfortable in 'his' place, and you can both relax knowing he is out of harm's way.

Your dog does not need a lot of free running; in fact, I would recommend that your dog never feels 'free' but is always in contact with you, either through the lead or a mental link. If your dog does not come when called, or does not want to stay around you, then do not allow it any freedom unless it is in an enclosed space, where you can still maintain a contact and obtain control. I have found that dogs do not need long walks or long periods of freedom. Periods of freedom can create independence and a will to go hunting alone.

You can maintain your dog's fitness through food control and exercise during the training periods. I will mention some training exercises later that will give your dog the running it requires, while you still maintain control.

Organize your training sessions to be little and often. A number of short periods are better than one long one, and five minutes in the house or garden whilst waiting for dinner can do much to progress your dog's learning. A little relaxation under control before and after the training session will also help your dog to look forward to, and enjoy the training sessions with you.

I will talk a little about formal training classes later, but it is worth mentioning at this point that the time you spend in a training class is not sufficient to train a dog. In fact, the class is to train you to train your dog. So spend the time gaining knowledge and then apply it in your own training sessions.

Lack of time should not be an excuse for not training a gundog; it is the weakest of excuses. Most professional trainers will spend no more than about half an hour to an hour per day with any dog, at the most, and this for only six to nine months of 'intensive' training.

TRAINING YOUR FAMILY

A dog that is around the home will be trained as much by your family as by yourself, and it shouldn't be hard to realize that the dog can be just as easily *untrained* by the family, and in fact even spoilt as a gundog.

No one expects your dog to be completely isolated and have contact only with the trainer; I personally do not believe that it is important for *only* the trainer to feed it. Although advantageous, the main link between dog and trainer comes from working together and enjoying life out in the field as a team. So you give your dog things to do that he enjoys, satisfying his natural instincts, and you will be the one he wants to be with. Hunting, retrieving and generally working together will create a bond that food alone can never do.

Other members of your family may take your dog out for a walk. The dog may live indoors and be part of the family, and why not? Your family likes the dog, so what can go wrong? The things that can and do go wrong are many and varied. If you have children, the dog may become a plaything for them, and all children have seen dogs fetching sticks that have been thrown for them. So the odd ball or stick gets thrown, and very quickly the puppy starts to run in, and then run about with the retrieve. Children, not knowing any better, chase after the pup, and very quickly you have a dog that thinks this is where all the real fun lies – chasing after things and then being chased itself. What happens, though, if the object the dog picks up and runs away with is a favourite doll or Action Man? The chase then degenerates to one of anger, and when the dog is caught, punishment follows. So then you have a dog that is frightened to come back with a retrieve, or may refuse to retrieve anything.

Imagine another scene which is not uncommon, where the dog picks up a personal object – clothing, toy or whatever – which is then either taken roughly from his mouth, or causes a tug of war. In either case, a problem is created which can easily result in the dog holding a retrieve too tightly, and if it is a bird, damaging it. A hard mouth can be brought about in this way: the dog has not inherited the problem, but been taught it.

These are only examples, but they illustrate some of the problems that must be avoided. Train your family to handle the dog the way you want it done; in other words, to be consistent. If you do not allow the dog to come into other rooms than the kitchen, make sure that no one else allows it at times when you are absent. If a member of your family gives a command, the dog must obey, but children must not play at training. The dog must not be teased or encouraged to do things which can affect the training process. If your dog is excitable, don't allow others to over-excite him, and train them in how to keep him calm and sensible. If you give the dog a command, don't allow other members of the family to overrule it, or encourage him to do the opposite.

This may sound like common sense – in fact, dog training is common sense – but too many people do not apply common sense to their

If you want a family dog, familiarize him with members of your family from an early stage.

dogs. I have found that families that have well behaved, polite children also have well behaved dogs. This may seem rather a sweeping statement, but the rules that apply to 'training' children apply equally to training dogs.

PRAISE AND REWARD

Praise must have meaning to a dog, it has to *know* that it is being praised, and is being recognized and rewarded for doing something right or well. If, however, a dog is fussed and praised to the same degree all the time, it becomes nothing more than a sound like background music: it is there, but not really noticed. Some dogs will need a lot of encouragement and praise in the early stages; others will require little, and may even need 'calming' praise, as their enthusiasm not only carries them through the training sessions, but can overexcite them to the extent of losing control and forgetting what they have learned.

The handler must also be very careful in the way a nervous dog is praised. Sensitive or nervous dogs may be quite reticent, and in order to 'hype them up' or encourage them to perform I have seen trainers go almost into excited hysterics – but all they are doing is making the dog even more nervous. Praise should not be given to such a degree that it distracts the dog's thinking: it must not clear the dog's mind of the command that has been given or the job it is working on. I have even seen dogs avoid behaving in a certain way so as to avoid being praised, because they thought it was more punishment than reward.

Praise comes from the voice, hands, eyes and body posture, and to be effective you have to mean it. A dog quickly learns when you do not mean what you are saying: watch someone who is calling a dog and saying 'Good boy' in order to get it close enough to catch it! The dog certainly knows that what the handler is really saying is 'Wait until I get my hands on you!', and that he doesn't mean 'Good boy' at all – in which case, this expression is no longer praise. If you have a problem with praise, smile at the same time, even put a laugh into your voice, and not only will the dog recognize it, but you will also relax and feel better.

COMMUNICATING THROUGH THE VOICE

Your voice produces the praise sounds; it is the main 'vehicle' of praise. As such it should be played like a musical instrument, sometimes enthusing, other times calming, often encouraging and occasionally commanding – but always communicating so that the dog understands. The voice is also the main communication 'vehicle' of reprimand: warning and punishing. Tone, pitch, volume and the words used all help in that communication and understanding.

The timing of praise is essential to achieve maximum effect. If you want a dog to pick up an object, praise it gently as it is investigating that object, giving the command to pick. Then the moment the dog has picked the retrieve, praise more triumphantly. Praising too excitedly when the dog is investigating can often, with an inexperienced dog, put it off picking and make it return to you. So timing and the type of praise has to be thought through and practised. At all times read your dog, its concentration level, emotions, concerns, lack of confidence and even its enthusiasm, and balance your praise accordingly.

COMMUNICATION THROUGH THE HANDS

As I have already mentioned, some dogs do not like being touched too much. However, in the majority of cases not only do dogs enjoy being praised with the hands, but they almost insist on it once they know that it means the handler is happy with the way they are doing things. Over the last few years there has been considerable discussion and practice in the art of 'hands off' training. In many instances this has been brought about because some people cannot use their hands correctly: they may frighten or excite the dog, or make it nervous, and provoke a multitude of other emotions because they presume the dog knows that what they are doing is acceptable.

Unfortunately many owners do not know how to touch or handle their dogs, and this is one of the reasons we have obedience commands taught with food treats, to guide them into what we want. But what is more pleasurable than having a partner that you can touch, that wants – even demands – to be touched, and shows attention, affection and willingness by either touching back or initiating the touch?

It is argued that a dog that initiates a touch is not just demanding attention, but is also showing leadership. This need not be the case if other control training has been put in place, and a command from you should stop him touching you if it is not what you want. I have to emphasize here that I do not mean you should be deafening the dog with vocal praise and endless chatter, or constantly running your hands over the poor animal. But I believe controlled, guiding communication through voice and hands will bring out a more loving and understanding, obedient dog when used as part of a learning programme.

In using your hands it is essential that you 'read' your dog at each stage of the training process. Some, as I have explained, will expect and accept only minimal hand contact, while others will take as much as you can give. Some will need a lot, and used in a particular way, in order to get the results required; others will need to be taught that it is enjoyable. But one of the most important things to teach a dog is to respect and accept your hands, and to pay attention to them, so it is watching for signals when you want it to. With some dogs, too much contact is a distraction, and simply doing the job is sufficient reward; with others, it is the motivation for obeying. No two dogs are the same, and like humans, we need to know what 'handling' makes them tick, gives them praise, and pleases or annoys them.

Teaching a Pup to Enjoy Hand Contact

So how do we encourage a pup to enjoy hands, and teach him to realize that firstly they are nothing to fear, and also how they communicate praise? When holding a young pup, find out what it enjoys: generally a calm, stroking motion with the flat of the fingers under the chest or chin, along the back and side, and certainly a light scratching at the top of the rear end, always gives pleasure. On the chest the pup will usually enjoy a backward and forward motion with the fingers, gently penetrating through to

the skin, and the same is true when rubbing the rear end; on the back, however, stroke only in the direction of the coat, otherwise it tends to be irritating and will make the dog shake.

A useful erogenous zone is under the ears: start with rubbing backwards and forwards under each ear in turn with the tips of your fingers, whilst the cheek and side of the nose is nestling against your palm. When the dog begins to find this enjoyable, do both ears at once so that your palms form a cradle for the dog's head, and lift its eyes towards you. Encourage your dog to look at you, and smile whilst it is doing so, making a face which is not threatening or concentrated, but one which is calming and friendly; laughing gently helps to relax even the concerned dog. The smile, the laugh, the touch now becomes a totally positive reinforcement of verbal praise.

Another pleasure-giver is to cup floppy ears in your hands, the dog facing towards you, and then use the side of the knuckle of your first finger to rub behind the ear. Both hands doing this together bring an ecstatic reaction. With the dog sat by your side, a calm rub under the ear with the flap cupped in your palm encourages it to come that little bit closer, maybe to rest a head against your leg. I have also used this to build closeness and calmness in heel work. Discover what your dog enjoys, what gives it pleasure, and let it perceive your hands as 'friends' that provide enjoyable rewards.

Building a Relationship with the Hands

Your hands are sensitive instruments which can be used in many ways to work with your dog, and not only to give praise. That calm, slow stroke from the back of the neck to half way down the back, the short strokes over the head, the deep finger-probing scratching on the rear end, the flat of the hand up and down the chest, the upward-lifting motion as you stroke the chin, and rubbing under the ears can be staccato, strong, gentle, manly, loving and bonding. Think how to use your hands, and read the reactions from your dog.

With all dogs, make the early days of hand socialization easy, calm and consistent. Make the dog feel as though your hands and arms

Ways of Praising with the Hands

There are several different movements you can make with your hands to touch, praise and caress a dog:

- The **stroke**: a common movement, where the flat of the hand glides down with slight pressure over the dog's body.
- The **circular rub**: where the flat of the hand describes a circular movement on the front of the chest.
- The **pat (percussion)**: a 'drumming' action using the flat of the hand, with varying degrees of intensity on the dog's body. Usually the best place to pat a dog is on its withers or its side, and occasionally under the chest. Never pat on the top of the head.
- The **scratch**: as it infers, a scratching action using the tips of your fingers under the chin, behind the ears, on the rear end towards the tail, and sometimes on the top of the head. Once your dog accepts being handled and 'massaged', two-handed scratching deeply up and down the body does release tension and body stiffening. Generally this is not something you want to do for too long a period of time.
- The **grip**: a kneading motion where the hand takes a gentle grip of hair, loose skin and sometimes even muscle tissue. The shoulders, the chest, and the base of the back respond to this movement.

In all these actions the emphasis in the early stages has to be on calmness, and a meaningful pressure, but not one which is annoying or painful: it should range from a light caress to firm. The size and type of dog has to dictate this, and it is important to consider your own strength when handling the dog, too. In most cases, once a dog gets to trust and accept the handling, and sees it as part of pack grooming, and acceptance, praise and also subservience to you because you initiate it, then pressure can be increased – but never to pain levels, of course. So when does a *pat* become a smack?

The most effective way of showing hand praise is with either the **pat** along the side of the dog, the **circular rub** on the chest, or the **stroke** and **pat** along the dog's side together, whilst verbally praising the dog.

are the protection that 'Mum's' legs and paws provided when it was suckling at the milk bar. Make movements easily, confidently, and in a way that does not excite or frighten the dog, and don't expect everything to go right from day one. Some dogs have to learn in very small stages just how pleasant hands can be. Explain to guests, and especially children, just how they should handle, stroke, caress and reach for a dog. Doesn't everyone know to reach forwards towards a dog, palm upwards with their hand under the dog's head height?

A sensitive dog with an inherent fear of strangers and their hands should be ignored by the stranger, who should let the *dog* do the initial investigative greeting. Often a sniff of your hand will be enough to let the dog know whether it should be friendly, or just stay away. I have had a number of dogs of my own that not only sniff my hands when we are working, but also lick them. I often wonder whether they are tasting my mood: a look at my face, a deep search into my eyes, and a lick of my hand, and they know how I am feeling.

Hands: A Tool of Punishment

Hands not only convey praise and build a relationship, they are also a tool of punishment. A shake of the scruff, or a smack over the nose or rear end, are ways in which we punish our dogs. Again, many modern theorists believe that all training should be positive, but the occasional reprimand for an action the dog knows is wrong is not cruel providing it is not abusive to the dog, and more importantly as long as the dog does know *what* it has done wrong. A bitch will hold a naughty pup down by the scruff or will put a paw on it; a dog will put another 'in its place' by a quick shake of the scruff, or by lifting its paw or head and placing it across the shoulder of the other. With verbal reinforcement it is generally enough to say, 'That's all I will take, thank you! Now behave yourself.' The hand placement, holding the scruff, the stare into the eye, and the growl of the voice, is enough to reinforce your displeasure. The pressure and intensity depends on the dog and the degree of naughtiness.

A dog should understand the communication from the hands, whether they are rewarding, punishing, calming, encouraging or just showing 'togetherness'. If I were to generalize with hands, I would say that men don't use them enough, and ladies tend to overuse them in praising their dogs. Make love with your hands to your dogs, and receive their love in return. As a handler you can initiate actions with your hands, and you can refuse them. By giving the right actions at the right time, you will show how pleased you are with your dog, and how you are thinking. In return your dog will know he is part of your 'pack', and will want to do

Hands used to guide and praise. Here both hands are used; one rubbing the chest while the second is stroking under the chin to reward also, and in doing so lift head up for good delivery. (Jeff Beals)

more to gain your 'hands on' attention, which to him is praise and motivation.

COMMUNICATING PRAISE

If your hands communicate praise through touch, your eyes should reflect it and your body show it. If you have a tense body and staring eyes, a dog will sometimes receive the wrong signals. If you believe that your dog is trying to please you at all times and when it goes wrong it is due to lack of understanding, poor communication or misplaced enthusiasm rather than disobedience, then you will approach training in a better frame of mind. When your dog fails in its attempt at an exercise, or does something not quite as well as you require, it will only realize this if you bring it to its attention.

Sometimes a reprimand at the wrong time can do untold damage, which could take a lot of time to put right. It is often better not to make an issue of a problem, which could reinforce it, but to look for ways of avoiding it, or even waiting for a moment when the dog improves even a small amount and then you can praise it. Look for opportunities to praise, bringing the action to the attention of the dog, and letting it know that you approved. Always give your dog the benefit of the doubt unless it is obviously showing wilful disobedience.

The more advanced a dog's training, the less frequently should praise be required, and emphatic praise is best kept to times when something new or improved has been achieved. The strongest stimulus for a dog which likes praise is intermittent praise or reward, when praise is not given every time, but only when it does really well or completes a complex series of tasks. Even then, the quality of the praise should be tempered to the task and the dog.

When your hands and voice communicate praise, your eyes, face and posture must reflect this. So smile and communicate togetherness — remember, your dog is watching you!

Chapter 3

Your Dog and His Basic Needs

WHAT BREED FOR YOU?

The choosing of your dog is something you should not take lightly. Too often an impetuous decision is made, sometimes based on the wrong requirements. I have seen dogs that have been bought for fashion, to ensure that the owner 'looks right' at social gatherings. I know of owners who have bought a less popular breed of dog such as a Brittany spaniel, Italian spinone, Welsh springer spaniel or gordon setter just to be different from the rest, without giving any thought as to whether the dog is from working stock or can do the job they require it to do. Please do not think that I am condemning any of these dogs, which, if bred from the right stock, can do an excellent job in their own area of expertise. The emphasis has to be on the job they are expected to do and can do, plus consideration for the pool of working blood from which you can choose.

When considering the breed of dog, think first about the type of shooting you intend to do. The rough shooter who has to work hard for his sport needs a 'hunting' dog, one that will search out every piece of cover, helping to find that elusive rabbit or bird that will give the owner a chance of a shot. The most obvious choice in this case has to be a spaniel, the most popular and numerous of which is the English springer. Other spaniels, particularly the cocker, clumber and Welsh, have their followers, and good working blood can be found in these breeds. In particular, the working lines of the cocker have improved tremendously over the years, and I have seen some excellent cockers working at trials and in the shooting field.

Whatever you do, do not consider the Irish water spaniel as a spaniel-type dog. His thick, curly coat makes work in the undergrowth very difficult, and is more suited to water work, as his name implies. However, this spaniel does make a good retriever, and is classified as such in competition work. The English springer has earned its nickname 'the maid of all trades', and as an all-round dog takes some beating. However, it has a reputation for being more difficult than a retriever to train, although I would disagree with this – it all depends on the particular dog and trainer.

For water work and driven shooting, the retriever breeds come into their own, the most popular being, of course, the Labrador retriever. The golden retriever is also a very popular dog in some parts of the country, and I have many friends who not only work their dogs in the field, but also show them, which gives them double satisfaction. Other retriever breeds you may consider are the flatcoat, the curly coat and the Chesapeake Bay retriever, the 'Chesie' in particular being thought of as a good water dog.

You might think that what you would really like is an all-round gundog of continental breeding, known as the 'HPR' (hunt, point, retrieve) breeds: the German shorthaired and wirehaired pointer, the Weimaraner, Munsterlander, spinone, Brittany spaniel or Hungarian vizsla. These dogs were introduced quite recently into this country, and although increasing in number, there is only a limited choice. Enthusiasts of the HPR breeds have worked hard to raise their standard and trainability, and although I have yet to see an HPR dog enter thick cover as readily as a spaniel, or enter water and retrieve as well as a Labrador retriever, I have enjoyed a good day's shooting over them, where their pointing and general all-round ability helped to bring game to the bag.

At the end of the day the decision is yours. What do you really fancy? I have seen and trained spaniels to be driven shooting dogs. Retrievers can be trained to hunt close, like a spaniel, though they were never as good as one. I have even seen spaniels and retrievers pointing game; in fact, when I was training one of my early spaniels in a rabbit pen, I developed a pointing instinct in him by mistake which lasted a number of years until old age and enthusiasm took over! Your only restriction on breed could be whether you wish to enter competitions with your dog. Trials are run for a specific breed of dog, therefore obviously you would need a retriever to run in retriever trials.

If in doubt about breed, do go to tests, trials and breed clubs, ask questions and watch dogs performing. Get to meet the dogs, and not only their owners who generally, if naturally, are biased, and see whether the character and personality of the dog suits yours.

I started off my working dog relationship with English springer spaniels, for which I have great admiration and affection. They are fun characters who live life to the full, and when well trained will work with an optimism and enthusiasm that will 'make' your shooting day. I have used my springers for all types of shooting work, from trials to pigeon shooting, in the beating line, picking up (at which they excel when you want a good 'hoover'), wildfowling and duck flighting. However, although good swimmers, they do feel the cold: on cold winter days, after being in the water, my spaniel would look wretched, his body would curl up, and he would be shivering uncontrollably; even wrapping a sack around him brought only temporary relief. I am sure that many spaniel lovers will say they have no problems with theirs, but that was my experience – and it wasn't that he wanted to stay at home.

It was with this in mind that I obtained my first Labrador retriever. The Labrador has an oilier coat, which makes water absorption more difficult, and they will enter water time and again without showing the same degree of discomfort that my spaniel experienced. So now I run both spaniels and retrievers, and when asked which I prefer, I find it difficult to answer. I enjoy both and get on well with both. They have different characters and temperaments but they both suit

me, and the thrill of working a good dog is far beyond thinking about which breed I prefer.

FINDING THE RIGHT DOG

Finding the right dog for you and your family is never easy. Many people expect the dog to play two roles – that of family pet and that of gundog. So where do you start? If you are lucky you all like the same breed; if not, then have the breed of your own choice and don't compromise.

One important factor that must be considered is whether you and your family are willing to take on the responsibilities of dog ownership together with some of the ties and expenditure that it demands. Feeding, grooming, exercising and training all take time and effort, and the enthusiasm and interest shown by members of the family when the dog is just a puppy can soon fade as the dog matures. If you make the decision to have a dog, it is a responsibility for the rest of its life, and should not be taken lightly.

What Do You Look For?

So, you have decided on a dog – what do you look for? The most obvious answer is 'one that meets your requirements', but it should also be one that meets your temperament and skill. Some advertisements in the sporting press emphasize that the puppies for sale have a field trials champion (FTCH) sire or dam, or both; others state they have a number of field trials champions in their five-generation pedigree, leading the reader to believe that the more FTCHs in the pedigree, the better the puppy. The one thing these qualifications do indicate is that their ancestors have reached a particular standard of gundog expertise. These puppies should have the natural instincts you require, they should be quiet while working, and should have a good mouth, and thus be gentle in their handling of birds. It also indicates that their ancestors were trainable – but how easy was it? Remember that a FTCH is often handled by someone with a fair amount of experience, and in some cases may even have been a professional, who can get the best out of the most difficult dog.

So, read the pedigree, understand what it is saying, and then start to ask questions about the

Keen and calm, yet alert-looking, yellow Labrador.

ancestors of the prospective puppy. The further back in the pedigree, the more people's memories of that dog may be 'coloured'. Memories are wonderful, but do tend to exaggerate what they want to. One man's meat can also be another man's poison – what *you* like may not be what your adviser likes.

The best guideline is to get to know the immediate ancestors of your prospective pup. The dam is usually accessible as she is generally with the pups, but the sire may be a considerable distance away. You should bear in mind that many breeders will travel long distances to obtain the right stud dog.

Choose a Working Line

Ensure that the parents are working dogs, and that they come from dogs that have been worked in the field. In some breeds the inclusion of a show dog is accepted, particularly flat-coats. However, in general, avoid show blood unless the dogs have been dual purpose, for both working and showing; indeed, in some breeds there is such a difference between the show and working lines that I would avoid show blood like the plague. The English springer spaniel is one good example where the working dog is a completely different animal – in build, natural characteristics and often ability – from the show dog. If you go back far enough through the bloodlines of the spaniel there are bound to have been dogs that were shown, but today I would not wish to have any show lines in any of my springer pedigrees.

Stud dogs can become 'fashionable', and many owners wishing to breed from their bitch will look for a FTCH to service her. This does not mean that you will end up with a good pup, but it should be easier to sell them. Many experienced breeders I have talked to think that the bitch puts a stronger 'stamp' on the puppies than the dog, as much as 70 per cent of the pup's make-up coming from the dam. If this is the case, perhaps it is more prudent to get a puppy from a FTCH bitch. My own experience is that there are sires that can put a 'stamp' on a litter of puppies regularly, and there are those that don't. In fact, some of the best quality sires may not produce the best quality puppies, but those puppies when they become sires may do so; it can therefore be worth considering getting a puppy not sired by or out of an FTCH, but sired by a dog that has already produced FTCHs.

Study the Pedigree

The pedigree can give you a considerable amount of information if you know the dogs that are on that pedigree, and their particular abilities and temperament. The general rule is to look for a puppy that shows evidence of thoughtful, systematic line breeding. This is where the breeder has brought together, on both the sire's and dam's ancestries, dogs that are the same or have a close relationship. Care is needed to ensure that the relationship between the sire and dam is not too close, or that the line breeding, instead of magnifying the positive qualities, does not magnify the adverse ones. In a five-generation pedigree I saw one dog's name appear nine times. Whether this high injection of one dog's blood is good or bad can be debated at length, but it is a factor to be considered.

In the past I have seen and worked with dogs that have been perhaps too highly bred, one particular parent or line being very strongly represented in the pedigree, which has created neurotic, nervous animals. Now and again a breeder who has been breeding close relations in his or her lines will go for an outcross — a dog where there is no common blood, or very little. The aim is basically to maintain good working ability by using the right dogs, and to bring some stability into the line.

Breeding is a science, a skill and an art. The potential owner of a puppy should seek out the breeders who have the ability to produce

Look for a pup that enjoys carrying.

consistently the type of dog they require. The occasional breeder may be lucky and produce the right pups, or may have done some research to find the right sire for their bitch. Find out before purchasing.

There are occasions where you may know of, or see, a good dog or bitch working which matches the type you are looking for. Make enquiries and see if they are to be bred from. If they are, and you can see a potential mate that you also like, then they may produce the ideal puppy for you.

Check Against Physical Defects

Wherever you obtain your pup, check, as far as is possible, that the parents are free from defects that could be hereditary. Physical defects such as retinal dysplasia in spaniels, progressive retinal atrophy (PRA) and hip dysplasia (HD) in retrievers, can be inherited, and if you wish to avoid heartache, try to ensure that your dog will not suffer with any of these by checking on the physical condition of the parents. Retinal dysplasia causes varying degrees of sight weakness; progressive retinal atrophy eventually causes blindness. Hip dysplasia may not show itself until the dog is well over a year old, by which time you will have developed a bond with it, and also spent time training and building the necessary skills. HD can be crippling, and although in some cases the dog can be operated upon to relieve the main disability, in most cases it will not be able to carry out a full day's work. It may not even be able to work at all, or at worst will have to be destroyed.

If ever you have the misfortune to purchase a dog with HD or any other physical defect, never be tempted to breed from it, no matter what the circumstances. Retinal dysplasia and PRA can be tested for at a very early age, and many dog owners who wish to breed now have their dogs tested by approved veterinary eye experts before they proceed.

Dog Or Bitch?

Today the demand is for bitches, but not so long ago it was for dogs. Whether this is due to fashion or good reason, your choice should be based on logic and preference.

A bitch will come into heat twice a year, and you can gamble that one of those heats will be during the shooting season! An old saying is that a bitch may be a problem twice a year, but a dog is a problem all year round. Many owners choose a bitch because they feel she will be softer, more loyal and easier to train, but this is not

Three pups from the same litter, but their personalities will probably be different. (Pat Trichter)

necessarily so. Dogs are claimed to be harder, bolder and better in cover – again this is not always true. The owner who buys a bitch in order to get a little income from breeding later will be surprised at how much it costs to rear good puppies; the profit margin is small, if there is any at all. If you wish to continue a particular line from a litter, then this is an admirable reason, but make sure that you are not bringing pups into an already over-pupped market-place.

To make generalizations is difficult. No two dogs are the same, and different strains within particular breed types can contrast greatly. I even know litter brothers and sisters that have differed dramatically. Personally, I have always preferred dogs, but I have also had many excellent bitches. The main factor to consider is, what do you like? If you are looking for a second dog, however, it may be prudent to get one of the same sex, particularly if they live in the house.

CHOOSING YOUR PUP

Choosing your pup is not easy; in fact, it is downright difficult! Some trainers who have bred a litter wait until everyone else has had their pick, and then work with the one that is left – not very scientific, but as good a way as any. If you can tell how a puppy of six or seven weeks is going to develop, learn and finally work, you have a marvellous ability. Provided you have carefully selected the line of dogs that interests you, have chosen a reliable breeder, and decided on dog or bitch, you are nearly there.

If you can, leave the selection of the pup until the sixth week, when they should be moving about quite well. Look for puppies that are clean, alert and well developed. No one can guarantee the future make-up of the puppy, either physical or in temperament, but there are a few guidelines that may help. If you are a novice it may be worth taking along a more knowledgeable friend, and certainly after you have chosen a puppy, make sure that you obtain agreement that in the event of an unfavourable veterinary examination you can return it. This should take place no more than a few days after you have taken the pup.

The first thing that you should look at is the breeder and the kennels. Are the kennels clean? Are other dogs happy in the company of the breeder? Are you allowed into the kennels? Can you see the bitch and, if possible, the sire? Puppies are sometimes bought in, and may not be from that particular kennels.

Puppies seem to spend their time in bursts of energy, followed by eating and sleeping. So judge what state they are in before jumping to any conclusions. If you have decided on the sex of your pup, remove the puppies of the sex you do not want. Spend some time watching the chosen sex, holding them, and playing with them. Judge their temperaments and characters: there will be the cheeky one, the bully, the timid one, the comedian, the thinker – they will all be there. Throw a knotted handkerchief, and see which one rushes out and picks it up. But most of all look for the one that appeals to you, the one where the 'chemistry' is beginning to work.

Once you have an idea which pup you may like, check it over. A healthy puppy has bright eyes, a glossy coat, and it is plump and soft to touch. The bones should not stick out, and it

A cute mum and attractive pups makes selection difficult… (Pat Trichter)

…but do not be tempted to take two.

should not have a pot belly, which could mean worms – a puppy should have been wormed before it is six weeks old. Check the eyes and the ears for discharge, and that the teeth meet evenly at the front. Don't accept excuses for faults: the discharge from an eye could be entropion (ingrowing eyelash), uneven teeth could result in an undershot or overshot jaw. So if in doubt, and if you really like a pup, get the advice of a vet. Check for signs of diarrhoea, and make sure there are no abnormalities in the form of lumps, particularly in the region of the navel, as this could be a hernia – rarely serious, but a problem that may only be resolved with an operation.

Have the dew claws been removed? Did you want them removed? I personally have no strong feelings either way, although I do appreciate there are advantages and disadvantages to each. If you are looking at a spaniel pup, to what extent has the tail been docked? If it has been given the traditional short (very short) tail, then you are at a disadvantage in competition, as the true style of the dog will not show through. My own preference is for a tail that has been docked by approximately one third, leaving two-thirds of the tail to do all the 'flag waving' with a white bit at the end, where possible. There is a move towards no docking of the tail, but this can mean it will get damaged when working in heavy cover, and does affect the style of the dog.

Although you may have taken along an adviser, use him or her to look mainly at the condition of the pups and the kennel to spot any potential problems. The choice of pup should be yours – it is to be *your* future partner. My own feeling is to think with your head and then, in the final selection, choose with your heart. Your new puppy will change as it develops, and it is almost impossible at this stage to determine how it will turn out. So, if you pick the one for which you have an affinity, you are more likely to forgive and overlook any failing.

Buying Your Puppy

Buying your puppy is a commercial transaction, and as such should be businesslike. The breeder may be a good salesman, so resist all pressures and psychological sales techniques that may be thrown at you; if you have bought a number of pups, you will probably have met them all – for instance, the challenge: 'That one is really too good for you, I don't think you could handle it'; the flattery: 'How did you pick that one out? I thought you didn't know too much about dogs'; the false resistance: 'That one over there? – no, it isn't for sale. It's the best one I have had for years, and you really couldn't afford to pay what I would want!' Techniques are numerous, so don't be swayed and sold a pup, but make up your own mind, and go out and buy the one you want.

Prices can vary, but often you will find that the difference in price between a top class dog and a mediocre one is small; moreover, if you consider that difference spread over the lifetime of the dog, the cost per annum is negligible. Therefore do not let cost be a major factor in your decision. If you have to think about the cost with some degree of concern, then I would advise you not to have a dog at all. The purchase price is only the beginning – injections, housing, feeding, and kennels whilst you are away on holiday make the purchase price appear only a small percentage of the overall cost of owning a dog.

To sum up, follow the basic rules of going to a reliable breeder with a good dam and sire from the line you like. Look for a healthy puppy with the temperament that potentially will suit you, and most of all that you feel attracted to. Use your instinct if all else fails – it can work out to be the best way of all.

Rules are Meant to be Broken!

When I first started in dogs and was looking for a puppy, I had read all the books, and understood all the rules; after selecting a quality breeder, I went along to look with my wife (it is not a bad idea to involve the family, as they may have more contact with the dog than you). I wanted a dog, so when the litter was shown to us I picked out all the dog puppies and set to work watching them, playing with them, throwing a knotted handkerchief and identifying the ones that wanted to be with me, the ones that watched my hands and face. It was difficult to choose; they were all good. After a while I said to my wife that I just didn't know.

'I like that one,' she said, pointing to a dark-headed, soft-eyed fellow sitting watching us as we talked. That was the one we took, and he turned out to be one of the most honest, hard-working dogs I have ever had. As a companion he is second to none, and his willingness to be trained and to work with me has always been a delight – just the right type of dog for me to start on. But I did not choose him.

Only last year a similar opportunity occurred. My Labrador had sired a lovely litter of puppies from a very nice, well-bred bitch. So when the pups were six weeks old I went across to view and choose my pup as pick of the litter (the stud payment). I wanted a bitch this time, so out came all the bitches and away I went with my usual routine – all very scientific. After quite a while I selected one little bitch which I thought would suit me down to the ground.

During this time my daughter, who is pretty good with dogs, had been playing with the dog pups, and one in particular had taken her fancy. When I got up to leave, the inevitable question was posed: 'Can we have this one as well?' It was a good litter and, as there is always someone ringing me and asking if I know of any good pups or dogs, I did not see any reason not to buy it too. A week later we picked up the pups and back home they came, where they settled in very well together. Having two at once can be good in that respect, but problematical in other ways. It wasn't long before I realized that of the two, it was the dog that was becoming part of me. He was attentive, followed my every step and responded promptly to every call.

The little bitch, on the other hand, was a leader: in the kennel she led him, and outside, because she thought that she was in charge of the 'pack', tried to lead us, but only when her brother was out as well. This is not an endearing trait, and I could sense that although we could work together, the 'chemistry' would be missing. When she was five months old I had a telephone call from a shooting man wanting a bitch puppy to start training. He came along, saw and liked the young lady, who was now retrieving and doing basic obedience, and immediately they 'clicked'. So off she went to a home where she will be the only dog, with someone she liked and, more important, someone who really felt an affinity for her. As for her brother,

he is still with me, and always will be. We have that special relationship that says we can live and work together as a team.

Thus, sometimes someone else's choice can be better than your own. It just highlights the fact that choosing a puppy is one of the most difficult jobs, and that even though you have chosen what you feel is right, as it grows and develops the pup may change from the one you thought you had bought.

There are times when you may not have a choice of pup and therefore the decision is easy. Some of the top lines of gundog are booked well in advance from the breeder, and it may be that if you are lucky enough to get one you take 'Hobson's choice' – meaning no choice at all! I had one puppy sent down to me from the north of England. I knew the line well and had seen the sire working, so I asked the breeder to make a choice for me and to send a bitch down with a friend who was visiting him. The result is I have a superb little bitch, which again has fitted in with my ways and my character. We enjoy each other's company and work well together. Perhaps I ought to let other people select my dogs for me – rules were always meant to be broken, I am told.

WHEN TO COLLECT FROM THE BREEDER

The age at which you acquire a puppy can be critical, and some important and practical scientific studies have been carried out on this subject. Konrad Lorenz, who was honoured with a Nobel prize for his studies in animal behaviour, introduced the word 'imprinting' with regard to animals learning a behaviour pattern from the animals and other environmental factors around them – social awareness. Imprinting can be very fast in some animals: geese, sheep and cows are animals whose social awareness occurs quickly.

In dogs, the senses are not so well developed at birth, and their social awareness is delayed. The main period of awareness is from four to about fourteen weeks, when the senses develop quite rapidly: they learn to recognize their own kind, they begin to play a role within their group, and during this time they will learn to accept other creatures as part of their pack or 'society'. Man must therefore become part of this social awareness and be prominent during these weeks.

If we take this situation to the extreme, a puppy that is hand reared and therefore has little contact with the mother will have difficulty recognizing itself as a dog. This has been known to cause problems: for example bitches will be aggressive with other dogs, particularly if they show a sexual interest, and some dogs reared in this way may also show no interest in mating.

The converse can also cause difficulties. Puppies that become part of the pack, with little or no human contact during the social awareness period, may find human contact stressful. They may be nervous and very wary, and winning their confidence and creating that willingness to work can take a lot of patience. Even when the owner has won that confidence, they may still show a reluctance to meet other humans, and be nervous in their presence.

Your puppy needs to have had contact with both humans and dogs during this period to develop a balanced social awareness. If your dog is to be more humanized because it has to work as part of your 'pack' and not degenerate into being purely a dog, which can happen if it is left in the kennel too long with other dogs and has limited human contact, then six to seven weeks would be the optimum time for you to take ownership. If it is left until later, do make sure that the puppy will have human contact until you collect it, so that it looks to its owner for guidance and leadership.

Some breeders are very good at this, and if a dog you are interested in is older than fourteen weeks, this does not mean that you should discard it. Watch how it reacts to the breeder, and particularly to yourself, who will be a stranger. If it is friendly, looking to be part of the human pack and responding to commands, then you should be all right; if it is sensitive, shy, tail down and wanting to go back to the kennel, look again.

KENNEL OR HOUSE?

You must decide how your puppy is going to fit within your family circle. A puppy around the house can get into all kinds of mischief and trouble, and it can be chastised in the wrong way and inconsistently. These early months are formative ones, and the puppy can develop a personality and habits which could create problems for you in the future.

Children in particular can create a multitude of problems without ever realizing it. Playing with, and teasing the dog in what most people would consider a normal way can develop serious problems for a gundog. Objects thrown continually for the puppy can overexcite it, and snatching objects from its mouth can create a tendency to hold tight or run away with the object. Chasing the dog is a common fault, which results in the dog thinking that being chased is a great game. The 'circling' dog that you cannot get near can test even the most patient of trainers.

This is where a kennel really comes into its own. In a kennel the dog is out of harm's way. My own first three dogs started their life in the house with all the ritual of house training. This was acceptable; what was not acceptable was that the third arrival decided it would be great fun to take up the kitchen flooring, not once, not twice, but three times. The third time resulted in a kennel being built, and outside they went. In hindsight it was the best move I made, or that my wife forced me to make. In the kennel they could not destroy the furniture; when they came out of it they were happy to be with me, and looking for things to do which they enjoyed – training. It helped me to become the centre of their attention. If we went out in the evening, we knew what they were not doing – destroying the kitchen – and we did not have to rush home from social occasions to check up on them.

I also found that they grew thicker coats, which must have benefited them when they were out on a cold winter's day, particularly in water. I don't know about you, but I would find it quite a shock to the system to be one minute in front of a warm fire, and then the next being asked to swim for a duck in near freezing water. Yet that is what we sometimes ask of our dogs, and although some breeds have coats that shed water, others are not so lucky.

When I first built the kennel, I came home one evening to find my wife sitting in the living section, which was made of wood. Worried because the dogs had been turned out in the winter months, she wanted to convince herself that they were comfortable. The comment that was mumbled from the depths of the kennel was, 'It's quite warm in here!' It is surprising how much heat a dog will generate, and if housed sensibly the heat will be retained and he will be comfortable.

Always make sure that your kennel is dry, and free from draughts and damp. Wooden kennels are warmer than concrete, but can be 'eaten'. Ensure that the sleeping area or bed is raised above the floor to stop any cold striking through. A raised wooden pallet is also very acceptable in the run, to enable the dog to lie outside without being in contact with concrete. The floor of the kennel should ideally be made of concrete and sloping to the front so that it can be washed off. Grass runs can get very messy and contaminat-

ed, so unless you can move the kennel to fresh ground regularly, avoid them.

If you accept that a dog is a demolition expert with four legs, then you will plan to build the kennel with a strength to defy all efforts at reducing it to match-sticks. A roof over the top of the run as well as the living area will help keep out the weather and, more importantly, stop your 'Houdini' from getting over the top. It is not just the large dogs that can jump – I have had little dogs that run up the walls like monkeys. Most of my kennel runs are made of weld-mesh panels, which are far stronger and safer than wire trellis fencing. Weldmesh is square shaped and welded, whereas wire fencing is diamond shaped and interwoven; a small break in wire fencing can result in a big hole, and if a dog jumps up at this structure the V-shaped holes can trap a leg, with disastrous results.

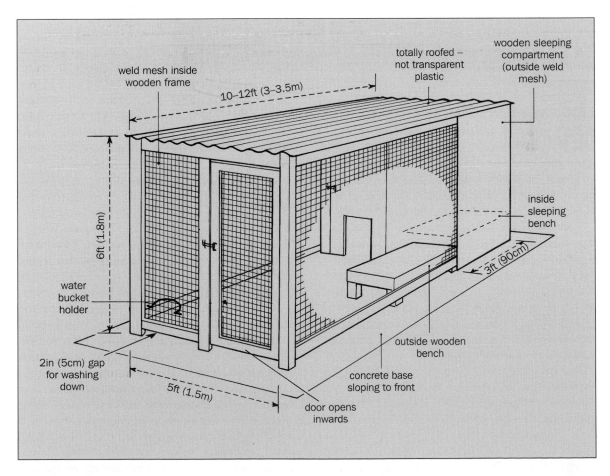

Example of kennel construction.

A crate becomes your dog's own bedroom or den.

A kennel does not have to be of any particular design provided that it has the space for a dog to exercise and sleep in, and is comfortable and safe. To make your job easier, the living quarters should be easy to enter and clean.

If you are kennelling your dog, do not forget to clean it out daily; in fact, if there is a mess in the kennel, clean it up as soon as you see it – I am sure the dog appreciates this. For dogs that do soil their kennel I use fresh, clean pine sawdust on the floor; it smells clean, provides a mild disinfectant, and is easy to sweep up with the mess. The kennel should also be washed down regularly with a good quality, approved disinfectant. If your dog reacts to sawdust (it may irritate the eyes), then you will probably just have to wash out daily.

For bedding I prefer wood wool, a packaging material that can be bought by the bale from packaging wholesalers. Wheat straw, if changed regularly, can be acceptable, but it does harbour parasites and becomes quite dusty, and again, a blanket or rug can be ideal. However, I regularly find that no matter what bedding you provide, most dogs kick it out and prefer to sleep on the wooden bench, even when it is cold. Maybe the bedding makes us feel better, rather than the dog! Nevertheless, it does help to dry a dog that is still damp after a day's work.

Using a Crate

It wasn't until I began training in America that I was introduced to a crate for my dog. I had used a dog box in the car, which my dogs had stayed in overnight when I was at trials or staying at friends, but my main choice at home was a kennel, and then in my home. However, many dog owners do not have enough room for a kennel, and would in fact prefer to have their dogs in the house – which is where a crate can be invaluable, especially with a young dog in training.

Dogs seem to like the idea of their own den; my own house dogs will even go in their crate when the door is open, and sleep in it by choice. It provides a secure area for them, their own space where they feel confident, and somewhere they will not be disturbed.

A crate is one of the best ways to tackle

many of the problems that we associate with young dogs, and can help us to train our pup through them, and even avoid problems altogether. Housebreaking (or housetraining), where the dog is taught to go outside to urinate and defecate, is so much easier using a crate. In the crate he cannot chew furniture or the carpet; small children cannot annoy him, and even undo much of the training we have devoted to him; when friends come he can be safe if they are afraid of dogs, and again they will not be able to spoil all the good training and habits we have instilled into him. Friends are great at creating problems and then leaving them behind for you to deal with.

It also familiarizes your dog to being in a crate so that when you travel he is happy in one in the car, or even at someone else's home or in a hotel, and especially if ever he has to stay at a veterinarian's. But most of all when he is in a crate he is resting, and thinking about the training you have done, and will then be more pleased to come out and work with you. In a crate he can learn no bad habits, and 'out' time can be quality time, where you can concentrate on what you want him to learn, and in doing so build a true relationship.

Start using a crate the moment you bring your pup home. I even put a crate in my whelping pen for the pups to explore, and many begin to sleep in there without being encouraged, simply because it feels secure.

In the home there is no problem with having more than one crate. Sometimes people like to have their pup in the bedroom at night so they can hear when he needs to go out, so a crate in the bedroom for that is a good idea. However, during the daytime, have the crate in a place where there is plenty of human traffic, so that he can become familiar with sounds and movement. It is also a big advantage if it can be near the door he has to use to go to the yard or garden for his toilet; when housebreaking, if he shows signs of needing to 'go', from here you can get him outside quickly before he has an accident. So the best position is where there are people, and he is close to an outside door but out of draughts and away from heat such as a radiator. I also like to add an old towel or bedding so that he is comfortable; this can always be washed.

As well as bedding, I like to put a good chew-type toy in there for him to work on as he wishes: my favourites are a good bone, a hard bone-type nylon toy, or Kong-type toys; this is especially useful for pups when they are teething. But always take off any sort of collar when your pup is in the crate, as it can easily get caught on the bars, and may even choke him.

As part of your training programme, the crate, like the kennel, can provide structure, security, and a place where your dog can think about what he has learned, and concentrate it into his memory cells. I have found dogs very happy using crates, and at times relieved to be in them when the home becomes very busy, especially if there are children flying about everywhere.

Types of Crate

There are two main types of dog crate: the airline plastic one, and the wire cage. I like the wire-type crate, so that the dog can easily see what is happening, and I can also see him. The plastic crate is more suitable for travelling, and very useful in a car when a dog is wet and dirty as it keeps most of this inside the crate, which can then be washed. Make sure the crate is large enough for your dog to stand up and move around comfortably.

Crate Training

If you decide on a crate – and I particularly like them now after using them for many years in the USA – establish a routine for using one as soon as pup moves into your home. Teach him a command for crate. You can call it 'kennel', although some owners do give it a cute name – one with a sense of humour I know calls it 'jail', and the dog happily goes in on this command. Also teach the dog to wait before coming out. While waiting, you can put on his collar and leash, and then invite him out. I teach the 'wait' command here by saying 'Wait', then I gradually open the door, and as he tries to come out, close it again on his nose with a gentle flick. Do that a few times until he stops trying to come out and looks at you, then gently praise him and put him on the leash.

I use 'wait' rather than 'stay' as a means of informing my dog that he must not come over a particular threshold until invited. 'Stay' means 'freeze in the position you are in until given another command'. 'Wait' is very useful when you are going through a door or into a room where the dog is not allowed, but he is still free to walk around in the allowed area.

Thus a crate provides a very economic way of providing a safe haven and den for your dog; it becomes his indoor kennel and bedroom, and when in it he cannot get into trouble and learn bad habits. You can set routines to have him out and teach the good habits, and time together then becomes quality learning time. Gradually, as the good habits are learned and training advanced, you can allow your dog more and more time outside the crate and in your home. But guess what: if you keep the crate and he has adopted it as his bedroom, then he will constantly be going back to it and getting his 'security blanket' naps whenever he is allowed.

FEEDING YOUR DOG

There is such a wide selection of dog foods on the market now that you really are spoilt for choice. Your young puppy should come home with you together with a list of foods that the breeder has been feeding it; this will enable you to continue feeding the same, and then to introduce gradually the food of your own liking.

The market place is full of different brands, many of which specialize in food for puppies, for different stages of growth and different sizes of dog. It can be quite confusing deciding which to select. I always go for a 'premium food' from a leading manufacturer, where you know the quality and consistency will remain the same. Some owners still prefer to feed raw food, while others choose the convenience of kibble. This is up to the owner, and all I would say is, look at the condition of your dog. Look at his coat, skin and eyes, and observe his energy levels.

Young puppies up to four months old should have four meals a day; I then reduce this to two meals a day. Some owners prefer to give one large meal a day, and this can also be acceptable, although I have found that one large meal can be too much at one time for some dogs. In my experience, two meals of half the daily requirement each time seems to create better condition on a dog. In addition, I do not feed a large meal prior to working them.

If at any time you decide to make changes in your dog's food, make it a gradual process. In general, dogs like consistency, and although they will eat most things, a change in diet can cause a violent reaction. A good indication of a healthy, well fed dog is a firm stool. Crude maybe, but dedicated stool watchers find it a good way to judge the condition of their dogs, and therefore to assess the way they are looking after them.

Most owners tend to overfeed their dogs; in fact, the amount that should be fed can vary at different times of the year. When deciding how much manufactured food to give, always note that the manufacturer's guidelines are exactly that – guidelines. Every dog is different, and the amount can vary slightly from one dog to another of the same weight and breed. During the winter months when the dog is working and needs to generate more internal heat, a larger portion or a higher protein diet may be necessary. The summer months may require a reduction in food intake. Keep an eye on the physique of your dog: if he is putting on a little fat, cut back; if he is looking lean, feed a little extra. Weighing the food helps you know exactly what is happening, and how much to give.

The condition of the coat will also be a good indicator of your dog's health. Be aware when it is in moult, since then you cannot expect the peak of condition; however, if the dog is a little dry in his coat then he could benefit from a tablespoon of corn oil or a knob of margarine in the food. If the coat looks generally out of condition, then a course of vitamins may be in order, and be sure you worm your dog regularly.

Vegetables, either cooked or raw, are always appreciated. Cooked greens, and the water used with the meal, and raw carrot always seem to go down well with a dog.

Your dog can only give his best when he feels at his best. I never leave food down for dogs, even puppies; they quickly learn to eat it when it is given to them, and a healthy dog almost always eats its food immediately. If your dog is generally a good eater, but begins to show a reticence to feed, then take this as an indication that he is off colour. Get to know your dog, and by knowing him you will then be able to tell whether he is feeling 'under the weather', or, even more important, is seriously physically ill. If ever you are in any doubt, consult your veterinarian.

TRAVELLING IN THE CAR

When you go to collect your pup from the breeder it would be advisable to pick it up in the morning and ask for it not to have been fed. The majority of puppies will not have experienced a car journey before, and therefore may have a tendency to car sickness. The new environment, noise and movement all contribute to stress, which can lead to profuse 'dribbling' from the mouth and possibly vomiting. This does not endear the dog to car travel, as you can imagine, and also does not provide a good start in your relationship.

Go prepared with paper (kitchen roll is very useful), a towel, some clean water and a polythene bag (to put any 'nasties' in). If the journey is only a short one, there may be no problems, but on a long one, expect the worst. On a long journey don't worry about the dog being fed during the trip; if he has been reared well and is healthy he will be able to last for a day without food, but a drink of clean water may be required.

Although my dogs usually travel in a special travelling box, which helps protect the car and stops them being thrown around, I prefer to have a companion with me when picking up a pup, to hold it during the journey. In the arms of someone who knows how to hold and handle a pup, I have generally found that they relax and fall asleep. Your companion, however, should be prepared for the worst, dressed suitably, and armed at the very least with a large towel and paper. Long journeys should not be made without allowing the pup to answer the calls of nature regularly, and to enjoy a little exercise. This should avoid accidents and tire the pup, so that it will relax and sleep once more.

Some dogs never get used to the car, but this tends to be the exception. Once a dog realizes that at the end of a car journey there is enjoyment in the form of exercise, training or shooting, any travel problems tend to disappear.

The best way to avoid any problems with car travel is to assume that they will happen, and make moves and plans to avoid them. Spend time sitting in the car with the dog without going anywhere.

You may encounter difficulties getting the dog into the car until he learns to jump in. Lift him into the vehicle when he is small, but as he grows, teach him to jump into the car by putting the front feet in first – encouraging all the time – then lift the back ones in if they have not automatically followed.

Dog boxes are ideal for transporting your dogs, whether in the car or, as here, while training. (Jeff Beals)

A commercial trailer, which is ideal for transporting more than one dog.

The first journeys should be short, if possible. This will build confidence and the dog will be thinking about the 'good things' to come, which are not too far into the future. An older dog that is already used to the car will often lead a puppy into the vehicle and, as long as he is the relaxing type, will provide an example to the younger dog to do likewise.

A dog guard in an estate car is a must, to my mind. Even though your dog may not jump over the back seat, in the event of an emergency stop a guard can prevent a flying dog hitting you in the back of the head, which would do neither of you any good. My own preference is for a travelling box. Well ventilated, these boxes provide a secure place for your dog, they help to protect the car, and keep it clean. In my own case there is usually more than one dog in the box, and so they tend to be well packaged and comfortable.

If you have a saloon car, the safest position for your dog is in the front passenger footwell; if he is trained to stay in this position he is not able to cause a distraction to the driver, and will tend to curl up and relax. Unless you have a special safety belt for your dog, travelling on the seats must be avoided for the comfort and safety of all concerned, and particularly the dog. Personally I think that is only common sense.

Chapter 4

Understanding Your Dog

PUPPY OR PART-TRAINED DOG?

When I first started shooting I had to get all the 'gear' – boots, Barbour, shotgun – and thank goodness, part of that 'gear' was a gundog. Although I had owned dogs before, I had never had to make a decision on a dog that would work in the field for me; however, I was lucky in that near to where I lived there was a breeder of good, hard-working field-trialling spaniels, and I started off with a great dog. I say 'lucky', because that is what started me in dogs and enjoying dog work to the extent I now do. Dogs change your life, and unless you realize that you have to make changes for your dog, you should not take on the responsibility of one – and there is no doubt in my mind that dog ownership is a responsibility.

Over the years I have bought and sold puppies, and both part-trained and fully trained dogs, the latter for clients in both Europe and America. During this time I have realized that there are advantages and disadvantages of each, but the most important factor is that the dog must match the owner. Although everyone wants a good hunting dog, in order to achieve a true working association, the dog and owner have to like each other, and their personalities have to fit.

Personally I love puppies, and bringing them on: that is the big plus for me. Again I have been lucky in that I have been able to select my dogs from the best working lines due to my friendship with top trialling people. Going to the best dogs reduces the risk of getting one that has a problem, and dogs with proven trialling ability and awards are more likely to produce pups that are of the required quality. Occasionally I

have had pups that, as their training progresses, I realize will not make the grade for trialling, and these I have sold on as shooting dogs: they have no faults, they just do not have the style and pace I am looking for in a trials dog. Such dogs are also available from other trainers for the everyday shooting man as part-trained or even fully trained dogs.

The big advantage to a pup is that it is a pup, together with all the joy it brings; plus, of course, there are more of them to select from than trained dogs. I enjoy training and am willing to spend time doing it; first it was a hobby, and then it became my livelihood as well as pleasure, so a puppy gave me a multitude of gratification. However, training a pup to be a good hunting dog does take time, commitment, experience and ability, plus having the facilities

These pups follow and are all delightful, but how will they turn out?

Buy the best — over the years the difference in price is negligible.

available to be able to train him — and not everyone has these.

We can all learn, and can make time, but for some owners it is not in their motivation. Time and commitment are the most important factors in training, together with the ability to solve problems that arise. Every dog has problems at some stage, and that is when we need help from experienced trainers; without this help the problems can last a lifetime. Also, of course, a pup will not be ready for the shooting field for at least a year to eighteen months, and even then the amount of work he can do will be limited by maturity and the training that has been put into him.

Housetraining (for a house dog), destructiveness in the home, family intervention and behaviour problems all have to be dealt with to ensure the right habits are built into the pup to make him into a dog you can work with. But the big advantage of having a pup and training him is that you learn with the pup. You will know the dog and build a good relationship through the training programme, and there is no doubt that working with a dog is not just dependent upon its own ability, but also the handler's.

Although pups may come from healthy and good working parents, there is no guarantee they will turn out the way you want, either

workwise or physically. Even pups from parents that have a clean bill of health can develop eye and hip problems.

Costs and Relative Benefits

The actual cost of buying a pup is not high when you consider that he is to be with you for, on average, ten years. So with this in mind, my advice is usually not to compare prices from different breeders, or even to let this come into the equation. I have always been willing to pay over the odds for the right pup from the lines and parents I like. It is difficult to give an actual figure, as this can vary and certainly does so from breed to breed — and of course that is only the start, with food, vets' fees, kennel (if you want to use one), plus training equipment, books and videos doubling the amount. But all this becomes minimal when compared to the costs of the destruction a puppy can wreak, and the emotional upheaval within the family with all the problems it can bring.

There is no doubt in my mind that a young puppy has to be a family decision. Some owners buy a puppy and then decide that it should go to a professional trainer for training, but this can prove to be the most expensive option. Most trainers want the pup at about six to nine months of age, and will then keep it in training for between three to six months, depending on the level the owner wishes it to be taken to. Three months will only give a dog the very basics, and even with six months' training its experience and ability will be only at beginner level. Remember these dogs are still only a year to fifteen months when they return: they are still pups requiring a lot of experience.

The Part-Trained Dog

Often the most economic way of obtaining a gundog is to buy a part-trained one from a reputable trainer. The price of part-trained dogs can vary dramatically, but again, market pressures come to bear and also, of course, the quality of the dog. I cannot emphasize enough how imperative it is that you go to a reputable trainer, one who has built his or her reputation on providing quality dogs and services. If you do not know the market place, get the help of someone who does, and who knows what a good dog is — and that is someone who *does* know, and not just *thinks* they know. It's surprising how many are impressed just by the fact that a dog will stop and return on the whistle, or if it is a spaniel, will hunt within twenty yards of its handler, and this in a field that it knows like the back of its paw.

Many prospective buyers who are concerned about the cost, or perhaps feel they can introduce a dog to game themselves, will opt for a part-trained dog, one that has been dummy trained but has had little experience on the real thing. However, getting a dog on to game can be quite difficult, and full of problems for the unwary and inexperienced, and a lot of good training can be quickly undone. Where this is the case it is often advisable to buy a dog that has been fully trained with considerable experience on game; in that way all the good habits should have been learnt under the guidance of an experienced trainer. The cost of a fully trained dog? Well, how long is a piece of string?

With both part-trained and fully trained dogs you have the advantage of seeing what you are getting, provided you are given a full demonstration. A quick run with two or three retrieves and the word of the trainer is not enough. With one dog I had trained, we spent a weekend at the client's shoot working with the guns on a 200-bird day before he decided to buy. This is excessive, but a good trainer will want to show you everything the dog can do and be sure that he is the dog for you, and the best place for this is in the actual shooting field. Don't be too shy to ask for special requirements such as water work or, with spaniels, work in heavy brambles, if that is what you require. Also, of course, these older dogs will be fully grown, and you can see whether you like their look and style.

With a part-trained dog, what you see should be what you get.

A part-trained dog should demonstrate his abilities before you decide whether to buy him.

Part-Trained and Finished Dogs

Both part-trained and finished dogs should have had their eyes and hips checked, and have a clean bill of health from a veterinarian. Insist on this, and look at the general condition of the dog and where it has been kept. The big advantage, of course, with the part-trained and fully trained dog is that time has been given to their training by a trainer who has the experience and facilities to do this, and they can show you what the dog can do and guide you in handling it. The big disadvantage is that the dog may know far more than you, and you need to learn how to handle it so as to avoid potential problems. Dog behaviour does not remain static, and faults will occur if you do not keep up the training and good handling – the most obvious being unsteadiness to gun shots.

Often the part-trained and fully trained dog has been kept in kennel, and if your requirement is now for it to be in the home, there is the problem of housetraining. Most dogs take to this quite easily, but some can be a problem. Again, a look at the trainer's approach and the condition of the kennel can give you a clue. One

fallacy concerning trained dogs, and one that should be quashed, is that an older dog will not bond with you: on the contrary, treat him well, work him, spend time together and provide the pleasures you both enjoy, and he will quickly become 'your' dog.

Most potential part- and fully trained dog buyers begin looking in about July and August so that they have the dog for a couple of months before the season starts, but the best time to buy, in my opinion, is between February and April. This is not the peak period for buying, and trainers will be looking to sell on dogs that have not made the grade in field trials but are ideal shooting dogs. Generally these are well trained beyond the needs of the ordinary shooting man and they can make first class gun dogs, plus if they have had minor awards in field trials their ability and mouth has received positive recognition. In July and August the availability of good, fully trained dogs is sometimes limited.

Future Running Costs

I have found that potential owners often look at the price of the dog and rarely consider future running expenses. Food costs are dependent upon the size of the dog, but good quality premium food is not the cheapest, one bag lasting about a month per dog. A kennel, if required, will be as much as you wish to spend. Vet bills are a normal annual expense provided you have no accidents, which can bring in the big bills. Dog beds, a travelling crate, and training equipment and all the accessories add to the costs.

But none of these are the big costs once you get a dog – well, not if you are like me. The big costs for me included a new house with plenty of ground to train and run a dog, cars purchased with dog in mind, or a second car for when you take him out working, a dog trailer (when I moved up to more than one dog) – and the list goes on. The costs I have incurred with my dogs I have never, and will never, regret; I have had – and still have – wonderful dogs that have filled my life with much happiness and unforgettable experiences – they have made my life what it is today. But I would never recommend anyone buying a gundog unless they are willing to shoulder the responsibility a dog requires, and to give it the attention it needs in its life. A gun-dog is a wonderful companion, but unless you are willing to bring it completely into your life and family, then you should not have one, but should hire a dog person to work their dogs for you in the field – the costs to you and the dog could be too great otherwise.

UNDERSTANDING YOUR DOG

How often do you hear the phrase 'There is no such thing as a bad dog, only a bad owner'? How often do you agree with it, and then realize it is not a totally true statement? There are dogs that are difficult to train to the standard required for the field, and dogs with a problematic personality, which makes them difficult to work with. There are some dogs that are bad for their owners because their temperaments do not match. Perhaps I ought to say there are *some* bad owners, as many potentially good dogs become bad due to poor training, bad handling or lack of training – and a good dog can easily be turned into a 'bad' one. Therefore, you must not only ensure that you go about choosing a puppy correctly, one that matches your temperament and character and with the potential to do the type of work you require, but also you must make the effort to understand your dog and the changes that he will go through during his development.

Get to know the type of dog you are in partnership with. Look for particular traits, strengths and weakness. The behaviour of a dog will change depending on the environment and the people or other animals around it, so study the way in which your dog acts and reacts in differing circumstances. I have known dogs that will jump up excitedly, wanting to be with you, when they are in kennel, only to act nervously and be extremely submissive when they are near you outside the kennel. Only by watching your dog and trying to 'read' what is going on in his mind will you be able to determine ways in which to act to overcome the problems.

Dogs generally like routine, and feel confident in familiar places. They will remember areas where they have been in trouble, and have been punished or frightened. As an understanding handler you need to be able to recognize these fears, phobias and personality traits, and work patiently either to overcome them, or to avoid situations that can create them.

Your dog will give you signals of affection, attention and obedience. Look for those signals – the eye contact, the lick of the hand, the immediate response to a command. He will also give you signals of independence, arrogance, downright wilful disobedience. Notice these also – the cocking of a leg and the scornful look, pretending not to hear you, waiting until you have given a command a number of times rather than obeying immediately.

A kind eye and a soft expression: learn to read your dog at all times. (Pat Trichter)

Managing Characteristics

A dog, like all animals, has been born with characteristics and a personality that can be developed through the correct upbringing and training. Some characteristics may be so dominant, though, that you cannot suppress them – and the advantageous ones you should not want to suppress. The most problematical characteristic I have found is that of independence, which can lead to dominance and the inability of the dog to become part of your team. If the independent dog also acts in a very sensitive way to any form of pressure or discipline, then you really do have a very difficult job indeed.

One of the sure signs that your dog is with and part of you is the way it 'feasts' you with its eyes. Good eye contact is a real benefit in training a dog. I find myself reading a lot of the dog's character from the eyes. Perhaps I have been lucky, but I think it is because I have worked at creating the situation, that I have dogs that look at me. By 'look at me' I mean not just a glance but a look full of interest, enthusiasm, affection and togetherness. A look that says, 'I'm waiting for your next command, what do you want, boss?' The eyes of your dog will convey a lot of meaning, and from them and from his body posture you will be able to recognize feelings and emotions.

Learn to recognize lack of understanding, fear, panic, excitement, aggression, lack of interest and sickness. When you read these signs, act accordingly; for example, a dog that is showing a lack of understanding needs help, not shouting at in the hope that the louder you shout the more likely he is to get the message. What usually happens in these circumstances is the look indicating lack of understanding then becomes a look of fear, followed by you getting even angrier and creating a problem, a negative fixation in the dog's mind, which you have to work hard at to overcome.

No two dogs are the same, even if they are from the same litter. They will each have individual characteristics, strengths, weaknesses and mannerisms. You have to learn how to read these, and interpret what the dog is thinking and how he is feeling. Communication is a two-way process, but your dog cannot talk to you, so learn to read the communication through the many other signals you will receive. Only by understanding your dog will you be able to play a role that will bring about the desired results.

MOTIVATION IN A DOG

When I talk to other trainers or watch them working with their dogs I often realize how lucky I have been with most of the dogs I have had the pleasure of owning or working with – lucky, in that most of them have been motivated dogs, or easy to motivate. They have the drive of a hunting dog. Maybe it is the choice of breeds that has made the difference, or the lines of a specific breed, or maybe it is because I have always looked creatively at ways to use their natural motivation and drive in training.

I was brought up as a hunting dog trainer, and the 'golden rule' was not to give food treats during training – the word more commonly used was 'bribe'. The main reason was that a dog could quickly learn to drop a dummy to collect a treat at the end of a retrieve exercise, and as any good 'hunter' will tell you, we want a dog to hold until asked to release. The lack of food treats never seemed to be a problem. When one was given, it would be at the end of a training session, and was merely a 'feel good' action, not associated by the dog to the training.

So I used other ways to reward my dogs for what they did, and developed techniques to encourage them to perform as I wanted them to. I learned to provide a reason for doing things – a motivator, a stimulus, an influence, and an incentive to do what I was asking. As an ex-university management lecturer, I find it interesting that motivation in people is often discussed, but it is a word I rarely hear discussed in connection with dogs.

Willingness and Trainability

When training dogs we often talk about willingness and trainability; some people talk about a dog wanting to please, others state that a dog is only pleasing itself. Whatever the interpretation, all I am interested in is providing training

OPPOSITE: Enthusiasm and drive. (Simon Parsons)

Courage and determination. (Arno Brosky)

where the dog performs in a way that pleases me, and in doing so gains pleasure itself. Knowledge of breeds and breeding has to be a prerequisite of anyone who wants a dog for a specific purpose. Some breeds have a natural learning and intellectual ability, others may be willing but have no aptitude for the task required; some will have the ability but no willingness, no desire to learn or to please, and a few will have neither. Of course there are varying degrees of willingness and aptitude, and that is what makes dog training so interesting and a challenge: every dog is different, and will require differing approaches.

Where both willingness and ability is high, you will find dogs that want to learn and are easier to train – they almost demand training and work, and perform best by introducing variety and new challenges. We may train through repetition, but with the 'high fliers' you need to recognize early their abilities, and balance the repetitive training with a variety of challenging games, exercises and problems to stimulate their intelligence and motivational needs.

But be careful, because these positive motivations can sometimes work against you. I had a very good example in a male Labrador puppy called Roper that I bred from two dogs I brought over from England. These both had excellent working pedigrees and good temperaments, and their litter of pups were great hunting, training and companion 'raw' material. By the time Roper was fourteen weeks old I had done a few little retrieving exercises in confined areas, but nothing too difficult, and then decided I would start giving a few longer retrieves in the garden, and begin to introduce 'sit' and 'stay' while I threw the retrieve.

Roper took no time at all in deciding that this was what life was made for. Because he was so willing, he was easy to do things with, because he had already realized that by doing what I asked or guided him into, he got to chase, to carry and to enjoy the experience. There is no doubt that because of his breed, much of what I did was self-rewarding, retrieving being the obvious self-rewarding action.

Now my problem was that every time we went out, he walked by my heel watching closely and expecting to train. Now why should this have been a problem? Because sometimes I wanted him to go out to eliminate, and although he had been taught to eliminate on cue, unless he was bursting, the drive to work with me made him overlook this fact. So I adopted the policy of waiting, and not even attempting to train until he had at least urinated, and he gradually got the idea that the quicker he did so, the quicker we began training. If I hadn't done this, the potential for accidents in the house, or stopping for a 'pee' in the middle of a training exercise, was guaranteed to increase.

Rewards and Motivators

If we consider what a dog wants from life, and what motivates it to behave in certain ways, we can then recognize what it will consider to be a reward for doing what we show it or ask it to do. Most of my other dogs have been hunting dogs – English springer spaniels and cocker spaniels – but I have found that even with my occasional terrier, German shepherd and poodle, retrieving, carrying and 'killing' an object have been very strong motivators.

So often many of today's dog trainers rely on food, and when ordinary kibble is not tempting enough, some trainers will ensure the dog is hungry or will try even tastier morsels. But food is only one motivator, and we should recognize that. Dogs are motivated to behave and perform in different ways by varying stimuli, including fulfilling natural instincts, safety and security, avoiding discomfort, being part of a group or partnership, and doing things better than they have before. The most powerful ones are when a dog is fulfilling natural instincts (self reward), such as hunting, finding game and retrieving. Using this as the primary reward, good behaviour and performance is accelerated as a motivator if, following the successful action of the dog, you as a trainer heap on the secondary motivating rewards – giving praise and showing pleasure at a job well done.

In human activities I have found that when athletes are pushed to the limits by coaches, and workers are pushed to their limits by managers and colleagues, they give their best when being correctly 'driven', and rewards come in a form very acceptable to them. A good coach and manager will create a sense of achievement, and they want to do it again in the way that created that success. I often find that dogs are very similar, in that a fair correction or a motivating pressure, followed immediately by a recognizable reward, will increase the willingness of the dog to do that action again in the improved way. The amount of pressure applied must always be relative to the dog and the situation, as too much pressure can be just as demotivat-

ing as it could be motivating, and could also, of course, create the wrong behaviour change.

Equally, the same can be said of applying too strong, or sometimes too frequent a reward motivator. I have seen retrievers become retrieving 'fools', and very difficult to control because the motivation to do the activity is higher than the willingness to obey related commands; an obvious result is unsteadiness – dogs that lack control and do not wait before being sent for a retrieve.

Creating a Balance

Therefore in training we are always working to create a balance between motivation, which includes drive to do the work, and control to ensure that the dog does the work correctly and safely. At certain times and stages in the training process we may have to build up the motivation and not concern ourselves about control. At other times and stages we may need to institute more control to ensure that the motivation and drive does not go 'over the top' and we actually lose control of the dog. There has to be a balance.

Attentiveness, enthusiasm, motivation and control all in balance. (Paul Pederson Action Snapshot Photography)

UNDERSTANDING YOURSELF

This partnership of you and your dog is exactly that: a partnership, and as such has to be worked at. Many partnerships between humans fail because we do not see all our faults – only the ones we do recognize can we apologise for. Dogs, however, don't understand apologies; they can, however, often recognize our weaknesses and take advantage of them. So it becomes necessary for the trainer to do a little self analysis, and also to take some advice on how best to train a dog. Some of your shortcomings you may not have noticed, but they may be obvious to others. When you ask for advice and opinions from others, don't take their comments personally, otherwise friendships are lost and help will not be given in the future.

I mentioned earlier some of the human aspects of gundog training, which verge on the qualities of a saint. To these we can add certain skills that you must develop if you are to be at one with your dog and in constant control.

Concentration was one of the training qualities I specified earlier, but together with this must be the ability to read what is happening, and to react promptly. Understanding what is happening will come from experience, but reacting as promptly as necessary is something you must develop and do. Be attentive to all the dog's movements and attitudes: notice when he is on scent, or not trying, when he is pretending to do something else instead of what you want, or if he really is doing his own thing, and act accordingly and as it happens. Notice particularly when your dog is confused and looking for help, when he is really trying hard for you but not getting it right.

If you leave your actions too late, the dog will not know why you have acted in such a way, or will relate it to the wrong action – the one he has just carried out. As you gain experience from the different situations associated with working your dog, you will be able to foresee problems and also opportunities for getting the best from him. So look ahead, see what could go wrong, and also how you could make it go right. This ability to be one step ahead of your dog, or the situation he might find himself in, is a skill you may not always notice in others, because the people who do it well rarely get into difficulties. They also make the opportunities look so natural that you just accept them.

While we are on this subject, think about what makes you 'tick': what gives you pleasure, what makes you angry? Are you moody, are there certain little things that really annoy you and get on your nerves? Some of these feelings you may have to control for the benefit of training. Don't train if you are in the wrong mood: count to ten, and then still do not lose your temper. Think whether that annoying little trait of your dog is worth getting upset over: showing irritation to the dog may cause even worse problems. Get to know a bit more about yourself, and without having a nervous breakdown, be a little self critical. Find ways of improving your character, and the abilities that will enable you to create a good, lasting relationship with your dog. Remember that you are not only training and developing your dog for the gun, but also yourself as a handler. So don't be afraid to learn.

PRAISE AND PUNISHMENT

Both praise and punishment of your dog take many forms and are applied in varying degrees. The key is to match the praise or punishment to the action, and also to the temperament of the dog.

One of the main skills of good gundog training is being able to put your dog in a position where he does things right and can therefore succeed. By getting the dog to succeed, you can then praise him, and this reinforces the success and the action carried out. By developing the dog's training in small stages, and ensuring through a positive approach that he always succeeds, your dog will grow in confidence – as you will yourself – knowing only what is right. Make sure that the difficulty factor associated with a piece of training or dog work is only increased gradually, and is always within the ability of the dog. You are building in small stages on what has gone before, and success will only come from success. Then you can communicate praise in a way your dog will appreciate.

The character and nature of the success must dictate the level and method of praise. Some dogs, because of the way in which their owners give praise, never even realize it is being given: thus a 'good boy' in a dull, monotonous tone may not even be noticed. On the other hand, if you praise your dog lavishly, for example by patting it with much too heavy a hand, it may become nervous of being praised. An excitable dog might need calming as it is being praised, to ensure that it does not become too carried away by the praise and then proceed to do something silly that will result in punishment, thereby destroying all the benefits of success and praise.

Some dogs, when praised over enthusiastically, get so excited that they will then dash about in a wide circle, sometimes rushing at their owners and avoiding them only at the last minute. To make matters worse, I have seen owners encourage them to do this by making silly noises or 'threatening' gestures in play. I call this 'having a mad turn', and although it seems to be a natural action of a dog enjoying himself, it can lead to problems. When he does it with a dummy in his mouth you begin to realize the error of your ways.

Uncertain, shy dogs may need motivating, or 'pepping up' with extra praise. Don't be afraid to use your voice and hands in such a way that the dog knows he is pleasing you.

One word your dog should learn from a very early age is 'no'; once he learns this, he can be stopped from going wrong, and then praised immediately he does right. The word can also be used as a mild reprimand or a reminder that you are watching, and what was going to be an action against your wishes should not be made.

Sometimes you may have to punish your dog quite severely. The best way of doing this is by picking the dog up, with your hands gripping either side of his throat, lifting him off the ground, growling, or speaking in a very threatening manner and staring forcefully into his eyes. Give the dog a shake to reinforce your domination and the punishment, then put him down and finally make him wait to let the punishment, and the realization that you are not pleased, sink in. With this form of punishment you are acting like another dog, which grabs hold of an adversary by the scruff of the neck, gives him a good shake with plenty of noise, and then stands over the vanquished to show who is boss. The emphasis should be on contempt and not anger – dogs do recognize the difference.

Anger can also lead you to too harsh a punishment, and one that will not produce the required response.

Pups that have a dominant streak can easily develop into dominant adults. When playing with your pup, do ensure that it does not get carried away and the play degenerate into 'beating' you in a contest. With a dominant pup I will sometimes hold it to the ground if it begins to show an aggressive attitude, as the mother of young animals will often do if they are beginning to be more than playful and are 'pushing their luck'. She holds the youngster down by placing a firm but gentle paw on top of it, or by using her mouth to hold it to the ground until it stops struggling and admits who is boss.

A dog must realize who the leader is, and what is right and what is wrong; a look, a word, a quick shake of the scruff may be all that is required. There are no hard-and-fast rules other than those I have stated previously: punish or praise at the time when the act is committed. (As a young boy I knew that when my mother said, 'You wait till I get you home', I would remember what the crime had been! Dogs, however, do not remember.) Punishment and praise have to be given within one and a half seconds of the act for the dog to understand what it is related to; after that time he will not know, and could relate it to a different action, which is not what you want. Match the punishment or praise to the action and the dog, and know your own strength.

Too harsh a punishment can cause a nervous dog to become cowed, and regular punishment can 'case harden' a dominant dog so that he will accept anything you can give, and still continue doing wrong. Gradually increasing the punishment level can do exactly the same. It is much better to design ways of avoiding the misdemeanour so that the dog will forget the bad habit, or at least temptation is not put his way. One of the more regular faults I hear of is where a dog will ignore the owner and run off to chase or play with other dogs. Why give the dog the opportunity? Don't train where there are distractions: if other dogs are around, keep your dog on a lead until you become the centre of attention, and keep him close enough to maintain control through your presence and leadership.

What you see is not necessarily what your dog sees.

Praise and reprimand show the dog that you are concentrating and are in the 'driving seat', so when developing a young dog do not be afraid to give praise the moment he does right. A quick growl 'Aah!', or 'No!' or 'Oi!' when things go wrong, followed by praise the moment he does right, can work wonders.

UNDERSTANDING THE DOG'S WORLD

No matter what your feelings are for your dog, you must realize that he is an animal with a much lower level of intellect than yourself. As such, he will interpret situations differently and, also, because of his height from the ground, will see situations and actions from a completely different angle.

Try to put yourself in your dog's 'shoes' and see the problems he comes up against, and try to use this visualization to avoid the problems. That small hump in the ground ahead to your dog is a hill, which stops him seeing where a bird has fallen. The retrieve that has fallen the opposite side of the fence is on the near side for an inexperienced dog. At first, heavy cover is just prickly and hurts, and doesn't hold the opportunity of live game in the mind of your dog.

You may have experienced the situation where a dog sees a bird fall out in the open, is sent for it, but then runs all around the bird without picking it. You know where it is, and often you can see it, which tends to test your patience, particularly if others are watching. What has happened is that your dog has marked with his eyes and sometimes his ears, but once in the area of the fall he switches to his nose — he 'looks' through his nose, obtaining a picture by the scent he picks up. But if scent is bad, or the bird is lying in a 'dead' scent area such as a hollow in the ground or an area particularly well known for scent problems, a gateway for instance, then he will not 'see' it.

Feel for, and be sympathetic towards your dog. In the majority of cases, with few exceptions, he is trying his hardest to do what he really enjoys doing: finding game. A little help in these situations will help build the bond between your dog and yourself, and he will realize that, when in difficulty, a look towards you will result in the guidance necessary to bring success.

Believe that your dog is working for you, and develop an understanding of the world of your dog; without this understanding it is so easy to build up stress in your dog. Stress shows itself in many ways: licking the lips, showing the whites of the eyes, droop of the tail, uncertainty of action. If your dog becomes stressed its concentration will diminish dramatically, and you may as well forget training. The causes of the stress can be varied: other dogs, unfamiliar places, inconsistent actions from you, strangers. By understanding your dog you should be able to calm him, and overcome these stresses. Stress does cause a dog to misbehave, but punishment of this misbehaviour creates more stress, and a downward cycle begins. This must be avoided at all costs. By getting to know your dog, and thinking like him, you should be able to appreciate some of the problems and stresses on him, and react accordingly.

BEAUTY AND STYLE

The beauty of a gundog lies not only in his physical conformation but also in the way he works. The style with which a dog works, picks up scent, and carries out the retrieve creates beauty and pleasure to the watcher, which for most gundog *aficionados* is more important than the pure physique of the dog.

Drive, pace and style are three things that we look for in a good gundog. Drive is the will to do the job no matter what the adversity. In a spaniel it will relate particularly to hunting any cover with a determination to find game. Pace is controlled speed. No one wants a potterer, but raw speed, which often shows itself in a young dog, is also undesirable. So a fast dog working within the conditions of the day and his own ability, showing drive and determination, will not only bring game to the gun but also be more pleasing to watch and work with.

But style is an additional feature. Not only can it please the eye, but it is a great communicator. The style of the dog will communicate feelings, thoughts and intended actions, for example the presence of game and therefore the chance of a shot. The tail action will score highly in the style of a dog: this is a great communicator, which together with the body movement and the dog's bearing will speak volumes in a stylish animal.

There is no doubt that most dogs will have a style of their own; whether it is pleasing to watch is very dependent upon what you, as a handler, prefer. Style in competition from the beauty angle can become a 'fashion' feature, and in a spaniel trial where there is a run-off for a placing, judges will not only assess how the dog works the ground, but also its style. A long-bodied 'snaking' dog may have an advantage over a more 'cobby' competitor because the movement is more attractive to watch, in the eyes of the judge. Small trials spaniels

A dog has difficulty marking a fall through natural obstructions such as long grass and undulations in the ground.

Dog training is a partnership. Can you and your dog create the right relationship? (Pat Trichter)

became fashionable for a time in certain parts of the country because they looked more exciting in action, and so caught the judge's eye. My own preference is for small dogs, be they spaniels or retrievers, because I get great pleasure from watching them work. But then I have seen very stylish big dogs working – I just happen to prefer small dogs at the moment. I must also add that this does not cloud my judgement in competition – well, not knowingly anyway.

A further aspect of style is not purely the action of the dog, but the way in which he deals with ground while hunting for game or a retrieve. Systematic hunting – a thoroughness in covering an area where game may be found – is natural in some dogs, but in many has to be developed. This skill, which will contribute towards the style of your dog, must be developed by you and your dog during the training sessions. At the end of the day we are looking for a dog that has natural style, pace and drive, developed and honed through good training. This dog will not only do the job well for you, but will also give you great pleasure in watching him do it.

BUILDING A RELATIONSHIP

Up to now we have talked mostly about the dog and yourself as individuals who have particular characteristics and behaviour patterns. When you come together to train and work, you have to be a team, working together with one aim. My own personal feeling is that in order to work with a dog really well, you have to like him, and also he has to like you: your temperaments and characters have to 'fit'.

I am sure you have met people whom you know you don't like and won't get on with, even though they have done nothing to harm you and may never really have talked to you. This can happen with dogs, too. Your dog might also develop an annoying habit, nothing important maybe, but it could build up into a barrier that stops the development of a good relationship. If the 'chemistry' is wrong, the best thing for both of you is to part; let someone have the dog who will like him, and you find another partner. I am sure that some people consider they will be disapproved of by others because they sell or give their dog to someone else, who then trains him up to a good standard. However, it is not a weakness or sign of defeat to admit that you don't get on with a dog: you can't get on with every dog, and they may not all match your character.

My own feeling is that it is also wrong for the dog to suffer, because there is no doubt that it will. We are all different animals and cannot expect a relationship to 'gel' in every instance. If you feel that you just cannot get on with the dog, then don't be too proud to let someone else have it, and don't be too conceited to accept that they may do a better job of working with that dog than you could. Your next dog could be the one that responds perfectly to you and creates a partnership that is unbeatable.

I have had dogs that I knew I would constantly find fault with, and therefore would not enjoy working with, because we did not 'fit'. These dogs in other owners' hands have come good, and made admirable companions and gundogs. At the time of writing this book I have a dog that I bought from a friend because they just did not hit if off at all. This dog came very good for me, winning tests and trials as well as performing to a very high standard in the shooting field.

I could do with that dog what my friend could not do, because I liked him and therefore I did not magnify his faults. Our personalities also match, and we work together as a team. This does not make me a better person or trainer than my friend: he has been successful with dogs I could not have been successful with.

You and the dog have to 'fit'. You will be 'married' for maybe ten to fourteen years or more, and if the chemistry is wrong, do not make it a lifetime of unpleasantness for either of you. I'm not one who believes that you will learn to love each other.

In the first early months with your pup the most important aspect of your work with the dog is to build a relationship that will result in respect and a liking for each other. Some people find it difficult to admit that they 'love' a dog, but they will admit to liking it a lot. But as I have said already, like it you must, if you are to put effort into the work and get enjoyment out. If you like your dog and can show it, there is no doubt that the dog will respond and in return will like you, and through training should learn to respect you more. However, if you don't like your dog, then you will find it difficult to understand its actions and accept its weaknesses.

Spending time with your dog, training it and enjoying working together, helps to build a good relationship. I have heard it said many times that if you want to build a good relationship, then you should always feed the dog yourself. I certainly do not believe this to be true. It may help, but true respect and a bonded relationship comes from working and achieving together, where you give a dog the training and the work that it really wants to do. With a gundog, that is all aspects of gundog work, and particularly going shooting.

When you can read your dog accurately, and in return it reads you and your wishes, that is when a real relationship has been formed. You work together as a team, a partnership which, almost silently, performs a job as natural as wild animals hunting in a pack. A glance at each other, a hand signal from you, a cock of the head and glance from your dog, a change in body action as the dog picks up scent and tells you to be ready: you know each other, and are working with the same objective in mind. A relationship is formed and bonded – but behind it is a lot of

training and hard work from both of you, mixed with a fair amount of affection.

Always give your dog time to learn; some learn quickly, others are not so quick – and the speed of learning can change as your dog progresses. Thus a dog that developed quickly in the early days of its life can slow down as it gets older, whereas a slow developer may learn much more quickly once things begin to 'click'.

Don't try to show off with your dog to friends, and don't try to advance in big steps, but take it a little at a time: let the dog be successful in easy stages, and in this way, as you both succeed, the relationship will grow.

If at six months old your dog will sit and stay on command, come when called, walk on a lead comfortably, do a simple retrieve and hunt for a hidden one, then you are setting the foundation upon which a good gundog can be built.

During these first formative months that you are creating habits, make them good ones – they are the foundation upon which the rest of your training can develop. Moreover be sure not only to train your dog, but also your family to treat the dog correctly and not make problems for you. By making your times with your young dog happy and enjoyable, you will create the foundations of a relationship that will last a lifetime.

Help your dog to succeed. (Pat Trichter)

Chapter 5

Creating a Partnership

The relationship between yourself and your dog is being built the moment you pick him up as a pup and take him home: from then on, everything you do and say will have an effect on him. The car journey on the way home may make him sick, and therefore not only will he see the car as a most unpleasant experience, but also the person who put him in it as not a nice person. So reassurance and kindness may be the first signals you have to give your dog, and understanding and comfort when things are going wrong.

You are going to replace mum and the other members of the pack as the provider of leadership, companionship and the basic necessities: food, water, exercise, and most of all fun. I have already said that I do not believe that you have to feed the dog in order to become the centre of its attention, although it may help; most important at this stage is to play with it in a constructive but enjoyable way. Exercise, and training to bring out its natural instincts and mould them to your requirements, are what will build the partnership. If your dog enjoys the things you do together, it will enjoy being with you, and will look forward to those times as the highlight of its day.

Constantly watch your puppy to get an understanding of its character and personality. While playing and 'wrestling' with you, it may start to get a little aggressive – don't allow this, but firmly show it that you are the stronger. With the pup that is nervous and shy, encourage and introduce it to everyday objects and situations. All the time look for ways to encourage it to want to be with you and watch you. If it is a little independent and wanders too far, hide or walk down an alternative path to the one it has taken. Call it once and make it look for you – don't follow it and do what it wants or expects you to do. Vary

what you do, so that it looks to you to find out what is happening next.

Training is the art of creating particular patterns of behaviour in your dog, and, as it is developing from the moment it is born, you must start to train as soon as you bring it home. Good breeders will have started this 'training' sometimes without even knowing it. Thus the puppies are called or whistled, or the bowl is tapped at feeding time, and they respond by coming to the call – and so a habit or behaviour pattern is created. Some breeders encourage their pups to do their toilet on a piece of newspaper, which is gradually moved out of the house or kennel into the garden, and so a housetraining routine is established. I remember a poodle we once had that was trained in this way, but we had to be very careful not to leave the current newspapers lying on the floor.

Spend time with your dog, enjoying his company and letting him enjoy yours. He will not require hours of endless running; in fact, I would not recommend long periods of free running at all. If you are in an area where he can have some freedom, then let him run by all means, but never let him think that he is not under control or being watched. I regularly call a puppy to me and praise it for coming. With a spaniel pup I would encourage it to hunt rather than run, and in hunting keep it very close to me. There will be times when your dog will be distracted by other dogs or people, and will run up to them to investigate. However, if you have developed a good relationship and have established in him the habit of coming when called, it should be an easy task to continue your exercise period with the minimum of disturbance.

Many dogs are allowed to run, and only called when either they are in trouble, or the time has come for them to be put on the lead and taken home. Ask yourself how you would feel: you are enjoying running about without a care in the world, you have met some rather nice friends who are fun to be with, and then you are called back to someone who will probably tell you off for having fun. You are put on a lead or into the back of a car and, in an atmosphere of bad feelings, taken home. If this is the general routine, then it is no wonder that when you call your dog, the last thing he wants to do is return. So by calling him up, praising him, and then allowing him to run again, you will develop a habit that will make life much easier.

PLAY TRAINING

As previously mentioned, training starts the moment that you get your puppy, but don't put any pressure on it until you feel it is mature enough to take it. Generally, you will find that as it matures and your training develops, there is a natural progression to more complex and controlled exercises. You never really make that conscious decision to start training; it just happens.

Play with your puppy, using games that will encourage the habits and characteristics that you will need to produce a good gundog. Spend time enjoying each other's company, and help it to become accustomed to a variety of sounds and experiences. Other animals, cars and aeroplanes can be very unsettling to a young dog, and it should be introduced to cattle, horses and sheep so they become part of its everyday life, and nothing to be frightened of or chased. I very rarely take a young dog where there are pheasants or rabbits until it has a degree of obedience and loyalty. Many keepers I know take the opposite view, however: they have no alternative but to let their dogs see game of all types, because it is all around them – but when it becomes part of the everyday sights, the dogs take no notice at all. Mind you, they soon learn when it is a shoot or working day, and then any game is considered with a different eye altogether.

When your pup shows suspicion or fear of anything, reassure it and help it build confidence; even fallen trees, stones and ordinary objects in unexpected places can create problems, so be understanding. When it shows aggression or chases

Play with your pup and create an interest in working with you. (Jeff Beals)

other animals, stop it from an early age with the word 'no'. A dog that growls at another should not be gentled and told 'Don't do that – there's a good boy' in a kind tone, or he will believe that you approve; he should be told firmly that you do *not* approve. In playing we often tell a puppy too kindly that we are displeased, and the tone of voice therefore communicates the wrong message. 'No' should be one of the first words your puppy understands – it will stop it getting into all kinds of trouble. And praise should be given only when the dog is doing right, again with the appropriate tone.

A young puppy does not need lots of exercise; short spells of play usually tire it, and then it will return to its bed. But during those short spells you need to be creating the relationship. Sit on the floor with your pup – get down to its level. If your pup is going to become a large dog, it is probably not advisable to let it enjoy sitting on your lap, and get into that habit, and you will look less daunting sitting on the floor; like that you can easily get the pup to sit alongside you, and can touch and rub its chest. This type of contact can calm a pup and instil a habit of sitting correctly, which will help in its training for the delivery of a retrieve. Also, by getting

(1) Create an interest in the dummy.

(2) Interest aroused, pup is sent for the retrieve immediately.

(3) Puppy returning at a good pace.

(4) Puppy allowed to hold the dummy as he is being encouraged into the body.

(5) Puppy guided in close to the body; the dummy is not taken.

(6) The dummy is eased out of the puppy's mouth. The sit is not emphasized at this stage, but encouraged if it happens.

(7) When the pup is really enthusiastic about the retrieve, hold him a little longer.

(8) Even pick him up and walk away a little before turning around and sending him, to build memory. (Jeff Beals)

down to your puppy's level there is no need for it to jump up to reach you.

I must admit that I encourage my dogs to jump up. I believe it creates a bond, and it has helped me in developing some good retrieving habits. However, jumping up is not everyone's idea of a good habit, particularly if you or your friends are in good clothes. So sit on the floor, praise the puppy for coming up to you, and encourage it to sit as it greets you. In time you will find that as it greets people it will sit, which will be reinforced by people praising it and petting it while it does so.

Instil the habit of wanting to be with you by never chasing the puppy, but walking away from it if it is distracted. Initially you may have to catch its attention by clapping your hands or calling, but you should stop repeating the calling once the puppy notices and knows what you are doing, and what is expected. By walking out of sight or running away the puppy should want to chase you – a natural instinct, with you being the quarry. Other people and dogs can be too much of a distraction, so play and be with your dog in isolation to start with.

Of course, you will not always be able to be on your own, and it is better then not to give a command if you feel it could be ignored. We humans are sometimes prone to feelings of jealousy, and when this little pup, which is the apple of our eye, ignores us and talks to someone else, we can show that emotion in a rather aggressive manner. The pup will then see you as someone who is to be feared, rather than enjoyed, and you are creating a rod for your own back. You may hide that jealousy by stating that the pup should come when you call it, but depending upon the nature of your dog, you can create all sorts of problems. Some puppies will hide when you call them, some will look for protection from the other person, some will quickly learn that the safest way is to stay with the other person because you will not punish them if they are in company, some will return but reluctantly – whichever way you look at it, your relationship with the pup has been compromised.

Make this play training a happy time, and if you are restraining your pup it should not realize it. It is learning without pain that certain actions on its part get positive reactions from you: thus, it comes when called, you are pleased and make a fuss; it sits when told, it gets fed or praised; it brings you something it is carrying, and you show delight, maybe throwing the object for it to fetch (which it enjoys). But all the time you are developing a bond based on pleasure, fun and enjoyment, and this is the most positive form of training.

During all this play training you should be studying your puppy and analysing its character and personality. Excitable pups may need to be calmed, quiet ones to be motivated. Watch also for the changes as your dog grows up. It never ceases to amaze me how the quiet and sensitive dog can become bold, and the bold dog nervous. This does not happen very often, but enough times for me and other dog people to notice it. So look for the different stages of your dog's development, and react accordingly by adapting your handling methods.

CREATING THE RIGHT HABITS

Training is the art of creating the right habits and behaviour patterns. Good habits are created by repetition associated with pleasurable experiences. The dog sits before he receives his meal, sits to have a lead on, waits to allow you through a door first – the repetition becomes automatic. Your routines and good habits bring about good habits in the dog, in the same way that it will pick up sloppiness and careless thinking.

In my experience the dog is an animal that likes routine because it provides him with a secure and confident feeling, a knowledge of what is expected, and what will happen next. He has a body clock that lets him know what should be happening and when, much of which revolves around his stomach; therefore I believe in feeding at regular times, and exercising and training at regular times also. Your dog will look forward to these occasions, and will enjoy them and your company all the more.

Another good practice that instils confidence and a belonging, relaxed feeling in your dog, is for him to have his own place where he can go to sit and sleep. In the kennel this is no problem, but if you keep the dog in the house it is advantageous to provide him with his own bed or lying area. I once had a bench seat that I built in my kitchen. The indoor dogs had their bean bags underneath; this was their 'place', where they felt secure and more important, and could keep out of the way when visitors were in the house, work was being done in the kitchen or they just wanted to relax. A 'place' can be movable, of course, and many dogs are trained to sit or lie wherever their bed is placed. In this way many pups have been taught to 'sit and stay' long before serious training commences.

THE LEARNING PROCESS

The learning process is a continuous one, where your puppy learns through doing things: when it does things correctly, it gets praise; if it does things wrong it gets a rebuke. It is much better if you can plan and arrange actions so that the majority of the time the puppy does things right and gets praise. This is by far the better method, and is a very positive approach to training.

The best way to organize this is to think through what you want to achieve, and then how you could achieve it without allowing the pup to go wrong. Take the learning in steps, small ones at a time. A lot of little steps make up a long distance. If each step is taken carefully, and the next one not made until the previous one has been completed successfully and learnt, you will be surprised and pleased to notice how quickly your puppy develops. The basics are important, they are the foundation upon which you will build; a weak foundation and the whole lot could crumble, leaving you the difficult task of picking up the pieces.

Take your dog through playschool before primary, then secondary before university. Some dogs will learn quickly, others more slowly. Some habits will be quickly assimilated, others you feel will never be absorbed. Don't despair, but work patiently at each of the steps until you find that you are able to progress.

Although I prefer to take my dogs out on a training session each day, this is not possible on some days when the weather is bad or other commitments intervene; however, I have found this can be advantageous, because providing you have instilled the good habits and routines, not only will your dog have remembered them, but in many cases will have improved on them. Whether it is because they have gone into the kennel and thought about their exercises and the results that have pleased their owner, or are more keen and attentive because they have not had a training session the previous day, I don't know. What I *do* know is that it happens. I certainly do not advocate leaving your dog for long periods without training, but on the other hand, don't worry if for a short while you can't fit in a training session – and don't fall into the trap of lengthening today's session because yesterday's was missed.

It is important to mention that if you cannot train and someone else takes your dog out, make sure they train only if they know what they are doing. To be safe, they should know what is allowed and what is not allowed, even if they are only walking the dog. A bad habit is easy to pick up and difficult to remove.

READ YOUR DOG

During all this play training you will have the opportunity of 'reading' your dog. You will be able to assess the dog's character, and from this you should decide the best ways of making yourself the 'pack leader', the centre of attention. The early months are constructive play months, and during this time you must be developing the relationship that will last a lifetime, a relationship built on trust and respect, where you will have confidence in each other. You will be able to read each other and know what is expected. Look for the good signs and strengths that you can build upon, observe the weaknesses, and work out ways of overcoming or minimizing them.

So in these early days, get to know your dog, and likewise let your dog get to know and believe in you as the provider of all that is fun in life, and in doing so, the one who is obeyed.

THE TOOLS OF THE TRAINER

In training your dog you will be carrying out exercises to create habits and responses that

A variety of whistles.

will prepare him for the job ahead. You will be communicating through voice, hand signal and whistle, and will need training aids to help you not only with the basic exercises, but also to simulate what may occur in the field in the future.

Whistles

The fewer vocal noises that are made in the shooting field, the less chance there is of disturbing game. Little will frighten a wild animal away more than the sound of the human voice, and it will certainly annoy other shooters and dog people around you. A whistle will not disturb game and is far more acceptable to the shooting man's ear, provided it is not played like a massed pipe band. A dog, once trained to the whistle, will often react more quickly and be more attentive to its shrill sound; his ears are attuned to a higher frequency than our own, and the whistle sound carries over longer distances than our voices ever could. It will help you communicate with your dog, and will build a responsiveness to your commands.

The market place is full of a variety of whistles – some plain in looks, some smart; some plastic, some metal, and some stag horn or other types of horn such as buffalo. The 'Thunderer' and America Roy Gonia whistle are very loud, football referee's type of whistle with a cork 'pea', while at the other extreme the 'silent whistle' has a high frequency that can be regulated, but certainly isn't silent. In between there are whistles of varying tones and frequencies,

some with a pea and some without. I have found that some attract the dog's attention more than others, and also, although it sounds strange, I have found that a high frequency whistle works better with a more energetic, highly charged type of dog than a low frequency one.

My own preference is for the plastic type of whistle, because you can always carry two that sound exactly the same; carry just one, and it is sure to get blocked or lost at the wrong time! Although stag horns may look attractive I have found some of them very 'dead' in sound. I also like a whistle you can grip with your teeth so that you can walk around with it ready in your mouth, and still talk. Silent whistles are made of metal, and most of them have a metal mouthpiece; if you cover this with a small piece of plastic or rubber tubing you will find it much easier to grip, and in cold weather your lips will not stick to it.

One whistle should be enough for training your dog. Some people advocate the use of the 'Thunderer' as a whistle to stop your dog, but I have found it just as easy to stop the dog on the one whistle that I use for other signals.

Put the whistle on a lanyard or piece of cord around your neck; at least you will know where it is, and if you let it go from your mouth you will be able to find it again easily. Carrying a whistle in your hand can work, but I have found that it can get in the way, and if you are giving hand signals, putting a whistle to your mouth and giving signals at the same time can create problems. That is why I like one that will rest comfortably and securely between my teeth.

Whatever the whistle, blowing it well and consistently needs practice. Whistle blowing is an art, and the good gundog handler can communicate very effectively using variations of the main signals. To whistle well, hold the whistle between your teeth, close your lips around it, put your tongue over the end and 'spit' blow to produce a sharp note. Practise generating rising and falling notes, long blasts and short 'pips'. This may all sound rather silly, but the whistle is the first main contact with your dog when it is working away from you, therefore knowing how to blow it spontaneously and well is essential.

If you are a natural whistler, which I am not, then you may be able to dispense with the artificial whistle, the natural whistle having the advantage that you cannot lose it or leave it at home; it makes a useful back-up if you do forget the proper whistle.

With a young dog, I do whistle between my teeth to attract attention. With many spaniels I have developed their hunting technique simply by using this method of whistling, keeping the artificial whistle for longer distance work and emphasized commands such as 'Sit'. It may therefore be practical to apply both the natural and the artificial whistle, but as is often the case, it depends on you, and how comfortable you feel doing it.

Dummies

The dummy is the main tool for training the dog to carry, and as such it has to be well designed and adapted to develop your dog through the stages of training. To train on real game or rabbits would be too difficult; even cold game stored and used when required would prove quite inconvenient and sometimes unpleasant. The real thing, even cold, can also be quite exciting for a young dog, which could create problems with control, and also start the dog whining or barking (giving tongue).

So in place of game, the trainer uses dummies and balls, or items that the dog will happily carry, but which will not damage his natural soft mouth. Some dogs may not like the commercial dummy initially, in which case a rolled-up sock or old glove can make an ideal first dummy; I usually find that the older and therefore smellier these first dummies are, the better the dog likes them. Remember that you have been adopted by the dog as mother, father and hopefully leader, and anything that smells of you is comforting and brings confidence. So the first retrieves should be small, light, easily held without gripping tight, and should smell of you – the boss.

There are some excellent commercial dummies on the market, the best known being the canvas range, but you can make them yourself or adapt the commercial varieties by adding certain 'decorations' such as feathers and rabbit skins. If you decide to make your dummies, then you need to provide weight, buoyancy and bulk. I would recommend mixing sand and sawdust together to provide the right weight, packing the mixture into a strong polythene bag well

A variety of traditional dummies.

Dummies to simulate real birds.

Plastic American dummies or bumpers.

sealed with a waterproof glue, and then wrapping this in a strong material; canvas, denim, strong cotton or corduroy provide ideal coverings. Some trainers use washing-up liquid bottles to contain the sawdust and sand mixture, covering them in cloth or rabbit skin. These are particularly good for water work – but don't cover them in a rabbit skin if that is where you intend using them!

Make or buy a range of dummy sizes and types. Your dog will not be carrying the standard shape and size of object all through his working life, and in this way, you will accustom your dog to picking up and holding a wide variety of retrieves. Generally, a combination of made, bought and 'tailored' dummies will provide you with the retrieves you need to give your dog the experience required. When you do start to fix rabbit skins or wings to the dummy, make sure that they are attached firmly; a loose skin, in particular, can cause a young dog to start playing and 'mouthing' a retrieve. Once your dog has become familiar with wings tightly attached, you can fasten them, sown only at the 'shoulders', to the dummy; they will thus be able to flap, simulating the wing movement that the dog will experience when retrieving a real bird. The general rule is to start using skins and feathers only when your dog has accepted the habit of always retrieving a normal dummy cleanly to hand. I say this as a general rule, because I have known some dogs that do not retrieve enthusiastically unless the dummy is covered in a rabbit skin or feathers.

I am often asked whether the new commercial dummies have any artificial scent on them. As far as I know they do not, and yet dogs will retrieve them with delight, at tests and in training, the moment they are taken from their polythene bags. I presume that the act of pulling them from a bag puts human scent on the dummy, or the dummy scent has been mixed with human scent on old dummies so that dogs associate one with the other. Whatever it is, it seems to work, and thank goodness it does, because to train a dog that dislikes dummies is very tedious and difficult. I have known dogs that will not take to dummies, or quickly become tired of dummies, but they are the exception rather than the rule.

In addition there are the American-type plastic bumpers. These are great in water, and can be obtained in black, black and white, white, and orange, so you can use whatever makes the retrieve simple, or creates the right exercise for your dog. For most dogs, orange is not so easy to see and is therefore ideal for blinds where you want the dog to learn to use his nose. The dummies that are shaped like birds are also of great benefit in teaching a dog how to balance a bird.

Another useful 'dummy' is a ball: because it bounces and rolls it can be used to simulate a variety of situations. It is usually more exciting for the dog, and if used correctly can help to develop steadiness by bowling it in front of him while he is sitting, or in the case of a spaniel, while hunting, to simulate running game. Tennis balls are good for hitting long distances with a tennis racket, and hard rubber balls can be used to create a line, which the dog will then have to work out and follow. Make sure that when you start using a ball your dog is fairly steady, or at least that you are more attentive and can hold him on the 'stay', as it provides an added temptation to move, which can cause problems. A slow dog can be speeded up with a ball, but beware of 'mouthing'. Because a ball is small and spongy a dog may develop the habit of biting on it; if this happens, use the ball sparingly.

The other problem is that because the ball is small and held well back in the dog's mouth, it is difficult to extract, and, in addition, because he likes the ball, he may be reluctant to give it up. However, while keeping the dog's face towards you, if you place a hand at each side of his mouth, like a sandwich, you can gently take hold of the ball. Furthermore, the exercise can develop the right habits, because it is often the feel of the material and the scent it holds that the dog prefers, and once he enjoys tennis balls, there are commercially made dummies that are manufactured from tennis ball material, so a dog can progress from a ball to dummies. These are very popular with all dogs, especially puppies that are teething: they help them grip more easily, and are soft to carry.

Commercial retrieving balls are available, but I have found them too large for some dogs' mouths. Also, being made of a hard rubber, when they become covered in saliva they are difficult for the dog to carry.

The Dummy Launcher and Other 'Mechanisms'

In the majority of cases I have found that it is quite adequate for dummies to be thrown by myself and my 'assistants'. For the occasion when you may wish to project a dummy over a considerable distance, or over an obstacle such as a river or a tall belt of trees, then a hand-held dummy launcher may be your ideal tool. The dummy is placed over a steel spigot, which contains a central borehole through which a .22 blank cartridge is fired. The blast from the blank propels the special dummy up to 100 yards (90m), simultaneously providing a sharp bang.

It is wise to have accustomed your dog to one of these, particularly if you have your sights set on working tests or scurries, where they may be used. To accustom your dog to this implement, go through the training-to-shot routine, and then gradually introduce the bang from the launcher; the noise can be frightening as it is very sharp. It actually consists of two bangs very close together: one is the explosion of the blank cartridge, the second is when the dummy leaves the end of the launcher and the air is released. So take care in its introduction.

Once your dog has become used to the launcher, the second danger is that he will become excited at its use, and begin to run in each time it is fired, even though he may be steady to hand-thrown dummies. Whether it is due to the bang, or because you send your dog for every retrieve from a launcher as it is too far for you to want to fetch it yourself, I don't know. Probably it is a combination of the two. The fact is that the dummy launcher has to be used with care, and your dog must be carefully watched to see how he is reacting. One of my dogs in particular walked quite well at heel until either myself, or someone else in the walking line, produced a dummy launcher. The sight of the launcher caused him to drop back, and he had to be encouraged along. Once the retrieve had been fired he loved fetching it, but the anticipation of the shot created nervousness.

In addition to the hand-held dummy launcher, there are now available mechanisms that use

Winger for throwing dummies and birds.

blanks, elastic cords or gas to propel dummies and even dead birds remotely from a distance. These are invaluable for the professional or keen amateur who wants to set up situations at distances up to 300 yards (280m) or more. Using multiple launchers you can simulate many happenings that you will encounter on a shoot day. The big advantage is that you can fire these remotely while standing next to and controlling your dog. In addition to the shot, many of these remote mechanisms also can make noises similar to a duck, pheasant or a person simply shouting to catch their attention.

Other training aids you can make yourself include the bolting rabbit. To simulate a bolting rabbit, get about 11yd (10m) of strong catapult elastic and fasten a rabbit-skin dummy firmly to the end of it. Fasten the end without the dummy to a stout pole or tree, and stretch the elastic tightly by pulling the dummy outwards. Released by you or an assistant, or even by a hand-controlled release mechanism as the dog approaches, the dummy can create an exciting diversion and temptation as it shoots across the

Automated multiple dummy launcher. (Jeff Beals)

dog, bouncing up and down and from side to side. The 'rabbit' must be released at the right time to create the desired effect – release it too early and the dog may miss the show, too late and he can receive a nasty 'rabbit punch' at the side of the head. This doesn't do a lot of good to a young dog and certainly wouldn't please an old one either. Like every training tool, your dog will get to know it too well if it is used often enough; one of my spaniels would drop and wait the moment he saw a piece of elastic stretched out in his path. So use it sparingly, and think through the situations to make it effective.

Leads and Check Cords

The most popular form of training lead for gundogs has been the rope slip leash, and with the majority of dogs this will give you the control you require. A normal leather or canvas collar allows the dog to get his shoulders into pulling and limits the control we can exert. The slip leash, if popped with a wrist action, closes on the dog's neck with a snap that gains its attention.

Easily carried and set up in locations up to 400m distant to enable long, marked retrieves. (Jeff Beals)

In my years of training I have known a number of dogs that have been a little difficult on the leash. A pulling dog is not uncommon. They will fight or simply pull against any form of restraint, and in doing so can get out of traditional collars that have not been fitted well. The slip chain or leash does not come off easily, dogs cannot slip their heads out of it, and a good quality chain or rope does not break. The other positive factor with a slip collar is that when a dog is struggling against the leash the pressure is evenly applied all the way round the neck, whereas with a plain collar the pressure is applied on the opposite side from the pull of the leash. Thus if the dog is pulling forwards, the pressure is on the larynx, and if a flat collar is pulled from above, the entire pressure is focused on the windpipe, which causes a strangulating sensation for the dog. The slip collar evens out the pull around the neck mechanically, and therefore has to be the better alternative, being more comfortable and less painful for a pulling dog.

The secret of using the slip leash is to apply a quick snapping sensation, and then release immediately. To do this the leash must be flicked quickly to the side and released immediately, just as you might crack a whip sideways. It is mainly a wrist action, snap and release; it does not have to be hard. We are using it to gain the dog's attention and have him focus on us, as the trainer; it allows us to communicate quickly and clearly with our dog, and the aim is to guide, direct, correct and communicate, and not to punish. Very quickly a dog learns to feel the movement of the leash and its weight on his neck; this communicates when he is too far ahead, or when he is going to be guided into another action, such as a 'sit'. The weight, the balance and, in the case of the chain collar, the sound of the chain moving, communicates what is going to be asked of him, and as a result becomes part of the command.

A more recent development has been the 'Halti' type of collar, so called because it is similar to a horse's halter. If you train your puppy correctly from the very beginning this should not be necessary, but for some difficult dogs this particular piece of equipment has proved invaluable, and small ladies have been able to lead large dogs quite literally 'by the nose'.

In all these cases the end justifies the means, and therefore you must judge which is the best for your dog. Your lead will be more than just an accessory to hold your dog by: it will be a very useful aid to training, guiding, controlling, steadying, and gradually releasing direct contact. As such, it has to be right for the job.

The Check Cord
Occasionally in your training you may require a much longer leash, and this is where you can employ the check cord, a long lead used to help control a dog at a distance. Sometimes useful for keeping a spaniel within the correct hunting distance, or guiding a dog back to you with a retrieve, it can cause problems when it gets caught up on thistles or other obstacles. There are retractable check cords on the market now, which help to overcome some of these problems; but really the answer is to do the basic training on your dog correctly, and avoid having to use a check cord at all.

If you have to use it, make sure that you use it correctly, and quickly overcome the problem, because your dog will learn in a very short time when it is on or off the check cord, and act accordingly. If you are having problems and think a check cord may help, go back to some of the basic exercises as well, so as to reinforce what you are doing.

Blank Pistol and Shotgun Adaptors

At some time you will have to introduce your dog to gunfire, and it is advisable to do this gradually, increasing the magnitude and closeness of the shot in stages. The blank starting pistol is a very useful addition to the trainer's equipment to help carry this out. The .22 short and long blanks are much cheaper than 12-bore cartridges, and it is easy to simulate shots regularly. Together with dummies, quite realistic situations can be created, which can then be added to as the dog gains confidence, by using a shotgun with a blank adaptor fitted. This adaptor fits inside the barrel of the shotgun in place of a cartridge, and is loaded with a long .22 blank. It is fired by the trigger of the shotgun, and therefore creates a realistic sight and sound for the dog. But don't forget to introduce these new experiences gradually!

Chapter 6

Early Training

HOW OFTEN, HOW LONG, WHEN AND WHERE

A young dog soon becomes tired mentally, and when this happens the last thing you should do is try to train him. Training should be carried out only when your dog is attentive and alert. First thing in the morning is a good time because the dog has rested well, and is keen to be out and with you. Your own timetable of work and home life may dictate the times for training. Your dog will quickly adapt to them, so if you are a nine-to-five worker, then one session in the morning and one in the evening will be ideal. It is more important that you do not overdo the training, which should be little and often. You should also avoid certain times that may be uncomfortable or distracting for the dog; therefore don't train immediately after he has eaten his main meal, nor in the heat of a summer's day, nor on a very wet day, and especially not on a very windy one – windy days can make your dog unresponsive, he can be rather silly and rush about almost mindlessly.

The saying 'You cannot get enough of a good thing' is somewhat misleading when training a dog. If your training is going well, then you may be tempted to do more than you should, with the result that your dog in the end will probably do something wrong. Putting the dog back into the kennel or taking it home on a bad note is not a good idea, as he will probably think about what has happened, and a problem is created. Finish on a good note. If you have set yourself a target of training for the day and the dog does the training session well, then call it a day while he is happy and successful. You will be surprised how well your dog will remember that high point the next time. If you create a

failure during the training session, even though you may then do something simple to finish on a good note, it does not have the same positive mental stimulus that would come from having had no failure at all. But certainly, if things are going wrong and your dog is having problems, do go back a few steps and make sure that you end on a successful exercise.

Before every training session, I allow the dog a little free run so that he can relieve himself. If he needs to answer the calls of nature during a training session you can bet that he is not totally concentrating on you. This initial 'freedom' will become a routine, and many of my dogs will relieve themselves to the words 'Look sharp' – quite a useful piece of training, particularly if you are away from home territory and you want them to do it in a specific place. This pre-training run also allows you to relax and be friends with your dog, so that you can start training in the right frame of mind. This session should not degenerate to a 'letting off steam' period in the hope that it will make the dog more tractable; it should only last for a minute or two, and the dog should be under control and be with you.

With a young dog, five- to ten-minute training sessions are usually enough. If these training sessions are part of a walk, then make sure that your dog is not too tired before you carry them out. I like not only a pre-training relaxation session, but also a post-training one, just to show the dog I am pleased and to let us reaffirm our friendship. This does not mean that we have not been friends during the training sessions, but we have both been (or should have been) concentrating, which can create pressure and stress. So a short walk with a half-time training session can provide the ideal mix of 'freedom', fun and training.

Training should never be carried out where or when there are distractions. As obedience develops and the bond between you strengthens, then distractions should create fewer problems – but avoid them initially. Game scent for a young, well bred working gundog can be too much of a temptation. During these training times, watch your dog for behaviour or signs of boredom which are not normal. Dogs have off days like us, so be sympathetic, and stop the training for that session.

I have also found that dogs' senses, which are more highly tuned than ours, pick up 'atmospheres', and this can make them sensitive, even 'jumpy'. Noises we do not hear, smells alien to their noses, vibrations we do not feel – there are many different stimuli that dogs notice and react to. Again, don't train where this is happening; move to a different training area, or leave off training for the day. I don't think it is my imagination that some dogs have a sensitivity dictated by the moon. Some trainers may say this is mumbo-jumbo, but I have had dogs in particular that behave differently when there is a full moon.

Bitches coming into season or in season may react adversely to training, and, apart from the problem of taking them out, it is sometimes better to restrict their training during this time. You may be surprised at how much of a difference your bitch's first season makes: in some it can bring about a growth in maturity and a keenness to learn, in others the complete opposite. Watch your bitch for changes, and be ready to change your training approach if necessary.

You will need to vary the ground where you carry out your training, so as to accustom your dog to the different types of country and obstacle he will encounter. But when you first start, your back garden and other easily accessible places, such as a quiet park or playing field, will be ideal. Even indoors, a lot of basic training can be done and good habits can be created. Once you progress to the more advanced lessons, then woodlands, water, bramble, bracken and other cover will be necessary. You will need to vary the training place to some extent because otherwise your dog will perform well in only the one place.

As soon as the training environment is changed, your dog will react differently. Many people who attend training classes have been heard to comment that their dog never does that at home! Initially you will progress more quickly if you are alone with the dog, free from any distractions, but as the dog develops and learns the basics, he will gain from being amongst other dogs, such as at a training class. Also, after the basic exercises have been learnt, you and your dog will benefit more, eventually, from having a knowledgeable or well trained friend who will throw dummies and help you set up other exercises.

When out training your dog, try very hard always to put him in a position where he is doing right: the right place, the right time, the right mood (for both of you), and the right amount of training done with a positive approach. Err on the side of your dog when things are not going right, and think what the reason could be for problems occurring. Many times the fault could be yours.

THE BASIC COMMANDS

The secret of giving commands well is to keep them short, clear and consistent, in a tone appropriate to the command and situation. You have been using particular words all your life that have a meaning and come naturally, so why not continue using those words? I have listed the words that I use, but if you wish to use 'hup' instead of 'sit', then do so. Just because 'hup' is the word traditionally used for spaniels it does not automatically work. Consistency is important: use the same word for the same command, and don't lose it in a string of words. 'Why don't you sit, damn you!' means very little, other than an angry tone.

Dogs are fairly good at deciphering words that are similar, but it is better if you can use dissimilar words for the various commands; also, it is better if the commands can have two distinct sounds, such as two syllables, with the emphasis on the second one. Some of the commands, such as 'No!', will be learnt during everyday life; others, one at a time in association with a training exercise. In fact I rarely use 'No', and prefer to use a guttural sound such as 'Aah!': this means 'stop doing what you are doing' or 'stop thinking about what you are intending to do next' – it is always better to be ahead of

(1) With a pup, use a white dummy to help him see it more clearly. Here it is covered with a worn white sock to make it smell of you, and also so it is softer to hold.

(2) Make coming back fun and a pleasure. Guide him with your voice and posture.

your dog, and stop an unwanted action before it occurs.

It is also advisable when naming your dog to abide by the two syllable rule, and if you have two dogs, not to name them where the flow of the word and vowel sounds can be confused, for example Moppy, Poppy, Holly. Dogs appear to recognize the vowels and the rhythm of words, but do not hear the consonants.

Some trainers begin by using their dog's name to send them for a retrieve, especially if they are handling more than one dog. I use the dog's name to indicate which I am talking to, and then give the command. Never use the name after a command, as the last word is usually the one they hear; if this word was the dog's name every time, it would mean nothing.

The aim of the command is to communicate and direct, and it should therefore be given with the correct tone. Give your commands quietly; you can always raise the volume or increase the severity later, but if you start at full blast

(3) Don't grab at the dummy, but let him enjoy it. Open your body and tap your thighs, using them to channel him into your body. (Pat Trichter)

you can never increase it. I also feel that your dog hears a lot more than you give it credit for, and by keeping the volume down the dog will be concentrating on *you* that much more, so he doesn't miss what you are asking him to do. The whistle should be used in the same way as the voice, 'playing' it just enough to communicate your wishes. The tone of your whistle will communicate as much as the tone in your voice.

BASIC EXERCISES

The Sit

Sitting is the mainstay of any training that we are going to do. If you can get your dog to sit at any time to the different commands or actions that demand it, you can maintain the control that is essential to good gundog handling.

Basic Commands		
Meaning	**Command**	**Whistle/Action**
Sitting the dog	'Sit'	One long whistle blast. Initially, raised open hand (like a policeman). Hand signal then phased out
Stay where you are	'Stay'	Raised open hand
Calling the dog up to you	'Here'	Multiple pips on whistle. Arms outstretched (welcoming)
Sending for a seen retrieve	'Fetch'	Indicate direction with arm
Sending away from you, from your side	'Get out'	Indicate direction with arm
To get dog hunting	'Hi lost'	
To start a spaniel hunting	'Seek on'	Click fingers and cast across body
To turn a hunting spaniel		Two pips on whistle and show new direction with hand
To forget flushed game or game shot at and missed	'Leave it' or 'Gone away'	
To push backwards with the dog at a distance from you	'Back'	Arm raises from praying position in centre of chest upwards as far as you can reach
To walk alongside you	'Heel'	Slap the side of your thigh
To jump or cross any obstacle such as a fence, ditch, river, wall	'Over'	
To get into cover or car	'Get in'	Point with hand
To stop what the dog is doing	'Aah', 'No'	Look as though you mean it

Sitting by showing the dummy and waiting for the action before throwing. The reward for sitting – the retrieve that follows. (Jeff Beals)

Sitting using pressure on the rear. (Pat Trichter)

During training you need to obtain the 'sit' to verbal command, whistle command, hand signal, thrown dummy, shot and, later, flushing game. The 'sit' command must be thoroughly taught to your dog if it is to be an immediate action when the situation demands it. It should become an instant reaction that the dog does not really think about; with this particular aim in mind, you cannot start soon enough with the 'sit' command. Once this has been mastered, the 'stay' command, and concentration on you for other exercises, both come more easily.

Once you can stop your dog, you can prevent him getting into trouble, calm him down, get his attention and prepare him for the next action. So spend time on obtaining the 'sit' as a prompt response. The word 'stay' should then be superfluous, as 'sit' means 'sit until told to do something else'. However, being human, the word 'stay' has a meaning in our minds and therefore we tend to use it without thinking; but provided you are consistent in the way you use these words, no problems should arise.

When you get your puppy, the two activities it will enjoy most are eating and playing.

You can start to introduce the word 'sit' in order to gain the reaction required in association with these enjoyable times. When you take the puppy its food, hold the dish up high so that the puppy looks up, and push its backside gently on to the floor, saying 'Sit'. Once it has sat, even for the shortest of times, put the food down. Very quickly your puppy will learn that when the food bowl comes in, if it sits, it will get the food more quickly. You are developing more than one habit in this way: first, you are getting the puppy to sit; second, it is beginning to watch your hand and learning the raised hand 'sit' signal; and perhaps more important, it is getting to know you as a provider and leader. Initially you can expect it to wriggle about and try to escape from your hand pushing it into the 'sit' position, but don't worry and don't get aggressive, it will quickly learn.

I have been surprised at how quickly pups learn to sit without even being shown by pushing them down. I remember once taking on two puppies from a litter: with both hands full of dinner and two puppies to make sit, it was somewhat difficult to carry out the initial sitting

Sitting by lifting the leash… (Pat Trichter)

…and releasing the moment his rear hits the ground. (Pat Trichter)

operation. So I just held the bowls up high and said 'Sit', and after a while the pups, unsure about what was happening, actually sat to puzzle out the situation. As soon as that happened the food went down. It did not take long before two small puppies sat waiting as I went in with their food.

To extend the sitting time, hold the puppy's backside down that little bit longer each time, not releasing it to eat until you have given the signal that it can: I usually say 'Dinner!'; you may use something else, but remember to be consistent. You should soon be able to gently release your hold on the pup, which will not move until you give the appropriate signal. Not only are you now getting the 'sit', but also the 'stay' is being developed. Your pup is waiting for your command, controlling its strongest desires and looking to you increasingly as a leader.

The chain of learning can now be brought into play. Once the pup has mastered the art of sitting and waiting to the spoken word, you can combine it with the raised hand (policeman style). This is an extension of the raised dinner bowl, and if you transfer the bowl to the hand

that is not raised, you will probably find that the pup will still continue to watch your raised hand because that habit has been imparted. In a short space of time you should notice your pup sitting to the raised hand signal given with no verbal command. You now have a firm foundation on which to build all the 'sit' stimuli.

You can now extend the 'sit' command to places away from the dinner area and where food is not present. When out in the garden or around you in the house, make sure the puppy is close to you and give the command 'Sit'. If it does not respond, push its backside gently but firmly to the floor, and praise immediately it happens. Reinforce it with 'Stay!', and gradually increase the time the pup is expected to sit in one position. Just because your puppy sits for its dinner to the command, do not expect it to sit at any other time. If it does, consider it a bonus. But the habit will be 'rooted' and will grow from the dinner bowl exercise.

Try not to expect too much of your pup to start with by commanding it to sit when it is a distance away from you. And if you shout and stamp your foot you are more likely to end up

Sit and slowly step back: 'Stay'. (Pat Trichter)

with a cowering pup. Build up the sitting distance gradually.

Introducing the 'sit' whistle is again an extension of the previous exercises. Before you say 'Sit', blow one long whistle – not too loudly – and raise your hand. The raised hand command may get the desired response, the whistle having caught the puppy's attention. If it does not sit, then the verbal 'sit' command should bring about the desired result. This chain of learning will result in your puppy sitting to the whistle as it looks to you for reinforcement of the command that will come from a hand signal. Remember it is whistle first, followed by the command he understands, 'Sit'.

When you do encounter difficulties, such as the pup staying away from you, use a leash to control it. Use it gently, and with the word 'sit', raise your hand and the leash in it calmly and slowly to exert a slight upward lift to the neck. Usually this will result in your dog raising its neck and lowering its backside. Occasionally if there is confusion or resistance, put your free hand on the top of his backside and push gently down. Show your dog what is expected, and then gradually use less and less pressure as he learns and responds.

If at any time you find that your puppy is resisting you or seems confused, don't panic or get angry, but go back to the exercises that were successful and build up to this one again, but in slower stages. This exercise can be a little dull, so try to keep it interesting and enjoyable by the tone of your voice, and praise the pup when it is done well.

The Stay

To some extent you will have developed the 'stay' command in the 'sit' exercise. You may feel comfortable saying 'Sit – stay' or just 'Sit', not expecting the dog to move until commanded. It doesn't really matter; what is important is that you should be able to get your dog to remain in one place for quite a long time even though you may be out of sight. I have never found the need to develop the dog's 'stay' command for longer than fifteen minutes, but I have friends who leave their dog in one place while they go fishing for hours. The dog's trust and belief in its owner, and that he will turn up again, is amazing to me in these situations. But it proves that a dog can be trained to wait for a considerable period of time.

Once you have trained your dog to sit and to stay sitting, stand in front of him with your arm raised, say 'Sit', and take a step backwards. With many dogs this is the cue they require to follow. If this happens, attach a leash if you do not already have one on him, and guide him back to the place where he was sat. Lift the leash lightly to gently hold him there, and then take a very small step back. Do not try to back away too far to begin with; start with a small amount at a time, gradually building up to longer distances. At first you may only be able to take one very small step backwards before returning to reassure and praise the dog.

Always return to your dog at this stage, never call him up to you, or he will begin to anticipate the call up and move when you do not wish him to. Returning to the dog is the secret of steadiness. Little by little, over a period of time, build up the distance, always going back to praise the dog. If your dog moves forwards even the slightest amount, then calmly walk back to him and take him back to the original spot, emphasizing 'Sit and stay' before moving away again.

It is only when you have a reliable 'sit and stay' that you can occasionally call him up to you – and the first time you do it, don't be surprised if he doesn't move: after all, that is what you have taught him to do until this moment. So encourage him to you – but for each 'recall on a stay' exercise, be sure to walk back to him at least four times. If you are using a leash, initially you can drop it to the floor as you increase the distance; then as you and your dog gain confidence, remove it altogether.

Some dogs, cocker spaniels in particular, have the habit of crawling after you as you back away. This can be quite frustrating, and the only solution is to persevere and not allow the dog to get away with disobeying. Some do it in such an amusing fashion that you have to smile, which unfortunately is tantamount to encouraging this behaviour; so try not to be amused, and put on an act of firmness. With this lesson, as with all others, concentration and quick reactions can pay dividends. The moment the dog even thinks about moving, say 'Sit', reinforcing the command you have already given, even moving towards the dog, pushing your hand signal towards him firmly and lifting the leash. As the dog learns and matures you should not have to repeat yourself, but with a young dog it will help.

When you are able to walk a considerable distance from the dog and are confident that he will not move, you can then set up situations where you disappear from sight. Trees, walls, buildings and hedges are good objects to move behind. Walk around a large tree at first so that you are only out of sight for a short period of time; after a while, take a little longer before reappearing from behind the tree. Walk behind a hedge, because it is an advantage that you can still keep the dog in view even though as far as he is concerned, you have disappeared. At the slightest movement on the part of the dog you can then say 'No – sit!'

A good exercise is to leave the dog in the garden and go indoors where you can view him from a window. An upstairs window is an advantage because very rarely will the dog look up, and if he moves, your command comes as quite a surprise – how can you know what he is doing if he cannot see you? It reinforces this invisible link between yourself and your dog, who thinks that wherever he is, you are still watching and in command. So look for walls and fences with holes, hedges with gaps and other vantage points where you can use your ingenuity to develop this particular skill in your dog.

When you first start this exercise, a minute seems a long, long time and the exercise a tedious one, but it is worthwhile and will pay dividends in the long run. To make it less boring for yourself, stop on a walk where the view is a good one, sit your dog away from you and then have a smoke, a drink or just watch the world go by and enjoy being outdoors. The relaxation will be good for both of you.

Stopping / Sitting on the Whistle at a Distance

You already have the dog sitting on command and on the single blast of a whistle at close distances, and it is important to teach him to sit (or as he gets older, maybe just to stop) at a distance. Only by stopping him and getting his attention will you be able to give him direction commands.

Build up by degrees the distance at which the dog will sit on the whistle. Some dogs will sit quite readily at distances, others will have a distance at which they will sit, but anything over that they do their own thing. Get your dog running around and relaxing, then when he is close enough for you to exert your influence, blow your stop whistle and raise your hand. When he responds, go up and praise him. If he does not respond, reinforce the command with a harsh 'Sit!' and move towards him. If you are still unsuccessful, then you have not built the foundations strongly enough.

Sitting and stopping is such a negative action for a dog that you have to try to make it into a positive one by praise, maybe following it with something pleasurable. Once your dog is steady to the dummy being thrown, a useful positive exercise is to throw a dummy immediately he is sitting. If the dog enjoys retrieving, then the quicker he sits, the sooner he will have the pleasure of a retrieve. You will find that the dog does not have to be sent for every thrown dummy to view it as a pleasure, and therefore the positive sitting reaction will be imparted.

In fact it is important not to send the dog for every thrown dummy, but on most occasions to fetch them yourself, commanding the dog to stay while you do so. If you send your dog too often you will quickly develop in him the habit of running in and an anticipation of future actions, which will be difficult to eradicate.

Coming When Called

Your dog must come when called, no matter what the situation or other temptations. To achieve this, he must realize that at the end of the return to yourself, there will be praise and pleasure; if ever he associates a return with punishment, you will never get the response you want every time. The first rule of getting a dog to come to you is never to punish him when he returns, no matter what he has been doing before.

With very young puppies that have been used to following 'mum' or sheltering in her protection when there is a hint of danger, there is very little problem in getting them to respond. Generally, the problem is that you will be falling over them as you walk along because they are keeping so close.

Take the opportunity of calling your pup up to you regularly and then praising and playing with it, and don't be afraid to pick it up and show it affection. You are becoming the 'mum' and then the leader, providing the security expected from the head of the family.

Call your pup with a high-pitched voice, catching its attention by clapping your hands. Crouch or kneel down on the ground, and make your expression a soft one by smiling or half closing your eyes. Very young pups I am sure do not notice the expression, but as they get older they will certainly read messages from your face – so make them the right messages. If your pup is eager to join you and runs into you, this is a benefit: you can always steady down a good excited return, but it is difficult to overcome a casual or nervous one. So encourage the return right into your body. Tap the inside of your thighs encouraging this closeness, and show pleasure, praising the pup for wanting to be with you.

Don't be in too much of a hurry to get the puppy to sit as it gets to you. A firm 'Sit' as it approaches you can be off-putting, and many will stand off or run around their owner expecting the command. Get the returning habit really embedded before moving on to the 'sit' as it reaches you. With some pups you will also find that they wet themselves with excitement at greeting you. This is nothing to worry about, providing you keep your shoes and trousers out

of the way! I had one little spaniel that was so keen on returning he would jump up and then run around my shoulders – and he was another one that wet himself with excitement, which was rather unfortunate for me.

One of your dog's natural instincts is to chase, therefore if you find that the pup is not returning to you, walk or run in the opposite direction. Never run after it unless you know you can quickly overtake it, or if you can stop it with your voice – when you run after it, then the 'chase' is both of you running together and great fun it can appear to be! By running in the opposite direction not only will your dog want to chase after you, but he will feel a sense of insecurity and want to be with you. If, on the other hand, your dog is quite happy to be by himself and not follow, then you have a real problem, and will have difficulty becoming the centre of attention.

With dogs that are independent and do not respond to the above tactic, I sometimes find that a titbit will work, or the use of a long lead where I call the dog to me and gently reel it in. I try to use titbits sparingly because I want the dog to come because he wants my company, and not the food. If it does work, gradually reduce the number of times you give the titbit and give it only occasionally, until you don't give it at all.

Another method to which you may get a quick response is to hide behind a tree, or if you are out in the country, take an alternative path to the one the dog is walking freely down. Call him, and he will notice that you have disappeared, and this will make him want to be with you.

With young puppies I introduce the recall whistle by whistling a 'pip-pip'-type morse code pattern through my teeth; this can easily be transferred to the dog whistle in a multiple-pip recall pattern. The whistle catches the dog's attention much better than a voice, and the high frequency seems to elicit an improved response. You can then add this to the 'sit' and 'stay' commands he has learnt. Sit your dog down, tell him to stay, then walk a distance away and when he is steady, give the multiple-pip recall whistle.

The first time you do this you may find that he doesn't move, particularly if the 'sit and stay' command has been well learnt. But with a little encouragement you will succeed. It is important at this stage not to build a natural reaction in the dog to return to you each time he is told to sit and stay; this leads to anticipation, which is a backward step. Therefore, with a high percentage of the sit and stay exercises, continue to return to your dog, only calling him up occasionally on the whistle.

To encourage your dog to come in quickly to you, stretch your arms out wide when you whistle, and as he comes near, tap the inside of your thighs as you did when he was a pup, encouraging him to snuggle up to you and place his head up towards you.

Once he is coming in reliably and speedily, you can then develop the sit. On returning, gently push his backside to the ground saying 'Sit', rubbing his chest in a circular motion with the other hand. This chest rubbing will tend to lift his head – a forerunner of the good delivery. With the sit and stay well drilled, it should be now quite a simple progression to say 'Stay', upon which the dog will calmly wait for the next command.

As with every command, there should be an immediate response. 'Here' should mean now, not when he has finished sniffing around or when it suits him; if you allow a second, it will soon become a minute and more. So if a young pup ignores you, attract its attention with even greater effort. If an older dog ignores you, move towards him growling a warning ('What do you think you are doing?' will do – it's the way you say it that matters), and as soon as you get his attention, call him to you, praising him as soon as he reaches you.

The 'sit' and 'stay' and the 'come to you' commands are the foundation of your training. If you can stop your dog and get him back to you, control is already there, and you have a solid base upon which you can build.

Walking to Heel on and off the Lead

One of the most common things that any dog must do is to walk on the lead, yet it always seems to cause problems, mainly because the dog will get its shoulders behind the lead and pull. The lead is an essential tool to start your dog walking to heel before progressing to no-slip (no lead) retrieving, where your dog walks to heel or sits at heel without a lead. I also find attaching a lead to be a useful way of putting the dog into neutral: he should quickly learn that when he is on the lead he will not be expected to carry out normal gundog work, and can therefore relax.

I don't teach my spaniels to walk to heel until after I have developed a good, keen hunting pattern. You may even decide not to train your spaniel to walk at heel because it isn't necessary, providing he will walk comfortably on the lead. Some Guns, however, prefer spaniels, and use them as 'no-slip' retrievers, and therefore heel training becomes essential.

Before serious heel training can commence you must accustom your puppy to the lead. Some pups show little reaction to the restriction of a lead, while others exhibit fear, annoyance and even anger at being constrained in this way. The first experience of a lead can change some pups into bucking broncos.

I personally prefer to use a soft rope slip-lead on a dog. To introduce it, I sit with the puppy, keeping it calm, then slip the lead over its head. Make sure the lead is put on in such a manner that the noose slackens when the pressure is released. If it is happy being with you, the puppy will view this as some kind of game and may even want to chew the lead. Don't worry about this; let the pup become used to the feel of the lead and understand that there is no danger from it. Your young puppy should come when called, so move away holding the lead and call the pup – it should follow with the lead still on its neck. When it realizes it has this restriction it may start to resist; stand still, let the pup calm down, and call it up to you. After a while it will understand that when it is on the lead there is no pressure as long as it is close by your side.

If you are right-handed you should now attempt to get your puppy walking on your left-hand side. The handle on your lead should be in your right hand, and your left hand should act as a guide for the lead down to the pup. If you are left-handed do this the opposite way round: handle in the left hand, guide with the right hand and keep the puppy on your right-hand side. Walk slowly forwards, encouraging it to follow. If your pup enjoys being around you and following you without the lead, this should be relatively easy, but be ready for a few 'battles'

Putting the leash on – dog on handler's left.

if he decides that the lead is constraining. If he runs ahead, stop and encourage him back alongside you before walking on again. I also find that doing a number of 180-degree turns has the puppy looking to you to see what you are going to do. In this instance as he walks ahead, turn, and with the leash held at the level of his shoulder, use a wrist-action 'pop' – a light sideways snap of the hand – to catch his attention; and when he looks, be walking in the opposite direction. In this way you are always leading.

The aim in heel training is not to walk somewhere, but to train your dog to walk alongside you; therefore it doesn't matter if you never go more than a few yards. After a while your pup will realize that you are going nowhere together unless he walks on a loose leash with you. If he stops or pulls back, gently put a little pressure on the lead, encouraging him to walk along with you. If you persevere at this, the pup will realize very quickly that the most comfortable position, and the position that gets him to a destination on a lead, is by the side of the 'boss'.

As soon as your dog begins to walk comfortably on the lead, you can concentrate on getting the positioning right. You can use many

different aids to achieve a close 'heel'. Narrow country paths will keep the dog close to you, as will walking along the side of a wall or a fence. With the dog between yourself and the fence, you can concentrate on keeping him from going forwards or dragging backwards.

A little 'square bashing', at first for short periods of time and then gradually increasing, will develop your dog's ability and also concentration. Walk along with him by your side; if he pulls forwards, tap your thigh and turn sharply to the right, or do a complete about turn so that he is behind you again. Lower your hand holding the leash so that it is at his shoulder level, and even give a slight 'pop' with that hand to catch your dog's attention and turn him round to be alongside you once more. If he drags behind, tap your thigh and encourage him up to you.

Increase the patterns that you make with your dog at your side by turning left and right, and doing complete about-turns. If he is not concentrating, turn without warning and then tap your thigh – it will encourage him to keep an eye on you. It may help to have two trees or posts, or any objects that you can negotiate round, and to walk in a figure-of-eight so that you are turning right and then left round these obstacles.

Vary your walking speed also during these exercises, sometimes walking normally, at other times fast, even trotting, followed by slow walking. I have found the latter particularly beneficial, as the dog appears to pay more attention and concentrate on what you are doing. When you stop, get him to sit. If the lead is held in your right hand, you can slide your left hand downwards and push his backside to the floor as you stop, and say 'Sit'. It does take a bit of practice to do this well, and sometimes you will find that your dog anticipates and moves forwards more quickly than your hand can push.

A useful method of training your dog to walk correctly at heel is to have the lead in your right hand, but behind your body rather than in front. Again, your left hand can guide the lead, but if your dog tends to move forwards, the lead comes up against the back of your legs and their movement actually gives the dog a small pull backwards. I have also found it easier using this position to achieve the sit when you stop; the dog cannot move forwards, and your left hand is relatively free so you can push his backside to the ground. I suppose it goes without saying that if you have a strong-pulling dog, this particular position can be difficult and uncomfortable! It is a very useful exercise, however, for 'fine tuning'.

Your dog should now be walking comfortably at heel on the lead, and paying attention to what you are doing and where you are going. You can now start to release the physical contact you have through the lead. As the dog is walking by your side, drop the lead gently along his back so that you are no longer holding the lead but your dog is carrying it. You can let the lead hang loose, though some dogs are disturbed by a lead dragging between their legs. Wrap it around the neck of your dog, tucking the end under the wrapped coils, and continue with the exercises; thus you will be maintaining a contact with the dog even though you are not holding the lead: you are creating a 'mental lead', which will remain when the real lead is removed.

If you are successful with the half-way loose-lead exercise, take the lead off the dog completely. Your full concentration will be required

(1) Placing the leash over the dog's head.

(2) Leash in the right hand, the left hand can guide. (Continues over)

*(3) Correct by pulling low and across. It is a
pop-like action rather than a pull or jerk.*

*(4) The right hand alone can be used to snap the leash.
Note the hands are at the level of the dog's shoulder.*

*(5) Leash behind the legs, the left hand can
still be used to control or push the dog's
rear to the floor on the 'sit' command.*

*(6) The leash behind the legs, the thighs
do the controlling, popping action.*

(7) The leash dropped across the back of the dog.

(8) The leash wrapped round the dog's neck.

(9) The leash held, but not in contact with the dog.

(10) No leash, and the thigh tapped to hold the attention to position. (Pat Trichter)

for this because the dog will realize that he is loose, and may revert to sloppiness or running ahead.

Go through the exercises, reacting quickly to his every move. If successful for just a short time, stop, sit the dog and praise him. Let him play and be free for a short period, then bring him in and do the heel exercises again for a short period, followed by another period of praise, freedom and play. The dog will then look on heelwork as a pleasure: it is part of the routine which precedes play and other pleasurable occurrences, therefore it becomes a pleasure itself.

If at any time your dog does become sloppy and lacking in concentration at heel, go back to the lead and reinforce the good habits. Never be afraid of going over previous stages of training. Your dog is not a robot, but a living, breathing animal with animal behaviour, so now and again you have to remind him what is required.

The walking at heel is to prepare the dog not only for walking to the peg, but also for walking up game. If you are right-handed your gun will be in the crook of your right arm. Your dog is on your left away from the gun and next to your free arm. When a bird is flushed and you stop to shoot, the dog should also stop and sit, awaiting your instructions. Comfortable, reliable heelwork with a prompt sit when you go into action is not only something to be proud of, and envied by others, but also is a very safe practice for you and the dog. I have seen Guns who walk along with their dog fastened to their belt, and in one case it was fastened to the Gun's leg! You can imagine the situations and dangers that arise when the dog is not steady and this practice is adopted. Perhaps the worst case of this involved a certain earl and his pair of Irish setters that were attached to his braces. When he shot, they both pulled, breaking off the backsideons on his trousers, and rushed off together with his braces trailing behind!

INTRODUCTION TO THE GUN

With most working gundogs, the introduction to gunfire should present few problems if done correctly. Some dogs may be gun nervous, but few are gun shy. Gun or 'bang' nervousness can be created in dogs quite easily. I have a little black Labrador bitch that I was training in my own grounds one day. She was only young, and had not been introduced to gunfire. We were working on the boundary of my woods when a gun was fired from the other side of the fence by a pigeon shooter I did not know was there. This frightened not only me (and the words I shouted did not hide this fact), but also my bitch. From that moment on, the slightest bang, even in the distance, had her tail dropping and a 'spooky' look in her eye. I overcame the problem by gradually introducing sharp noises at times when she was enjoying herself, but this is only one example of how a difficult situation can arise.

Introduce your puppy to noises gradually; sharp noises in particular can be disturbing. I clap my hands when I call the pup to me, which not only attracts attention but ends in pleasure as it gets praise and a fuss from me. You will be developing your pup's sitting before it receives dinner, so add to this a handclap. The pup will now be associating sitting with a clap or sharp noise – you are preparing it for the sitting to shot. I have often read that you should bang bowls and make a lot of noise before you feed your dog. This may be worked up to, but if you do it with a young pup you may very easily frighten it. The other problem is that on hearing these noises 'off stage' the pup knows that dinner is coming and can become very excited, yipping and barking, and this is the last thing you want your dog to do on hearing gunfire.

Once your puppy is used to the handclap, you can introduce the clap while it is running around, saying 'Sit' or blowing the 'sit' whistle when you clap your hands. Go one stage further if your pup is steady to the thrown dummy: throw a dummy and 'salute' it with a handclap, making your pup sit. Very quickly, because it is thinking of the pleasure of retrieving a dummy, it should begin to sit promptly to the handclap and the dummy flying through the air.

The next stage is to introduce a gunshot, and for this I prefer a starting pistol loaded with short blanks. Ideally, it is better if initially someone else fires the gun. Sit your dog alongside you and, from a distance of about fifty yards (45m), get a friend to fire the gun. Watch your dog's reaction; if he is unconcerned, get your friend to move closer and fire again. Again, watch your dog's reaction, and if at any time he shows concern, praise and reassure him, and stop there for the day. Gradually get the gun closer until you are shooting over the dog.

Building up to this position may take a few days or weeks, but don't rush it. You can always associate the gun with something pleasurable, which will help overcome any problems; I have mentioned making noises before food, and firing the gun before taking the food out to the dog is one possible method of introduction. I do find, though, that if you have introduced the handclap as a preliminary to a thrown dummy and the retrieve, if you substitute the gun for the handclap, the pleasure of seeing the dummy and fetching it usually overcomes any nervousness. If I do this when I am by myself, I put the gun inside the dummy bag that I always carry, before firing it, because the bag muffles the shot and is therefore not as startling. I then move on to firing the gun behind my back, before bringing it out in the open and holding it over my head prior to firing.

If your dog is happy with the starting pistol, you can now start using the 12-bore shotgun. Go back to having a friend fire it at a distance, and watch the dog's reactions, slowly moving forwards until again you can fire over him. There are, however, two fears with a shotgun: first, there is the noise; but secondly there is this object which will be sweeping the sky and coming up and down over the dog's head – not only will you have to introduce gunfire, but also the gun. If you walk around with a stick, you may have few problems; if you have used that stick to give the dog a 'tap, you may have a big problem.

If a dog is nervous of the gun, take him out with you using a walking stick, sit the dog, take a few steps backwards, and purposefully but slowly move the stick about in the air. If he sits there quietly watching you, go back and praise him. If he looks nervous, move further away, wave your stick and throw a dummy. Send your dog, and, while he is going out, put your stick on the ground behind you so that you can take the retrieve without worrying him. Again, gradually move closer, until one day you will be able to wave your stick vigorously over the dog without him showing any concern.

Once your dog shows no concern for the stick or the gunshot, you can then put the two together and fire the gun while it is moving in the air over his head.

I have known some dogs that are not nervous about the gun – in fact they are completely the opposite, and become very excited when they hear or see it. In my experience this is usually because the dog has been overexposed to the gun and the pleasures it provides. Introduction to the real thing and the power of the gun at a very young age can lead to an excitable and noisy dog.

Even though your dog accepts the gun and you shooting it, there will be situations when he may experience stress and concern. During training you may have only fired one or two shots over your dog, and then on the first day of the shooting season you expose the dog to a 'baptism by fire' – and a lot of it. This may be too much for him. The volume of noise and the echo from pigeon shooting in a hide and grouse shooting in a backside, together with the number of shots fired, may cause your dog to become very nervous indeed. Be aware of the situation – even an experienced dog can become concerned.

I often hear owners of young dogs say that they are going to take their pup along to a shoot or a clay shoot, to let it hear and see what happens. My advice is – don't, unless you have gone through the introduction and development exercises mentioned previously.

More Gun Work

In familiarization with the gun we talked about introducing our dog to the gun – but there is far more to gun work than just this. Once we have introduced the gun, and our dog is familiar with its sound and movement, we can then use it to teach him other aspects of work in the shooting field, work that will help us put game into the bag and be proud of our dog's ability.

Early on in training when your dog is steady and you are teaching him to mark the fall, begin pointing your arm above his head in the direction of the fall. In this way your dog begins to look along your arms for the fall, and becomes familiar with your arms moving above his head and indicating the direction of a fall. Some trainers use a walking or plain stick and point it in the right direction. The aim, as always, is to help your dog look in the direction and mark a shot bird. I have to add here, never use this stick to hit your dog, as this can easily make him shy of a gun being raised. In my training I use my arm, and accompany the movement with the command 'mark', often clapping my hands together to make a 'crack' before pointing in the direction I want him to take.

As I progress and my dogs become aware not only of this but my body angle and movement, I phase it out so they become accustomed to moving their body with mine, and face in the direction a bird will fall. However, in the competitions I run in America we have to fire a shotgun using blanks in the direction of marked and unseen retrieves. When training with a gun, a dog very quickly begins to learn that if it has been fired and it runs out in the direction the gun was pointed it will find a retrieve, even if it has not seen a fall. This is a real scenario for hunters who go out and shoot over their dogs, and therefore of great benefit to teach. Even those dogs that hunt the ground out in front of you and have not seen the flight of a bird or run of a rabbit, learn to look at the gun to see where it is pointing.

When teaching your dog to work with the gun, take your time pointing and firing, and afterwards hold your gun pointing for a few seconds in the direction of the fall. Give your dog every opportunity to see it, and to see where it is pointing. Earlier on I mentioned the use of live shot, and this can be of benefit here: live shot along the ground leaves a trail that your dog will learn to follow, once more helping him to learn how to work with the gun in the field. Again as before, I cannot emphasize enough that safety has to be of paramount importance at these times.

Training a dog with a shotgun in your arms is good training, not only for the dog, but also for yourself. All too often we train without the gun, and then when we do use it in the field we are not practised at handling both dog and gun together. Fumbling and uncertainty leads to actions that are different to the ones you have used in training, causing your dog to misinterpret what you want, and in doing so easily damaging earlier training.

The sound of a shot should not mean 'fetch', but 'sit and concentrate until I send you', and it is important to teach your dog to sit to shot and to stay until sent. This is quite easy to do by firing a gun and then commanding 'sit', or blowing the 'sit' whistle, but this control is all too easy to lose. As a hunter we often want to get the bird or rabbit back to hand as speedily as possible, and therefore in our urgency send our dogs too quickly. This is especially true if the bird or rabbit is wounded and looks as though it may be lost. However, 'running in' is very unsafe. Some wildfowlers have told me they want their dog to run in to ensure they do not lose a bird on the tide or downriver, but if your dog sits to the gun and is steady you can always send him quickly or slowly with the word 'fetch'. So teach your dog to sit to the shot, and also to remain steady for increasing lengths of time.

For wildfowlers and dove/pigeon shooters, steadiness to shot and falling birds is essential, as the sight of a dog dashing out on a retrieve can easily scare incoming birds. It may be many minutes before there is a lull in the shooting and you can safely send your dog, so train him to wait. On a formal shoot, it may be as much as an hour before the keeper wants your dog picking up dead birds, and a dog running into a drive can quite easily spoil the whole day, reducing both his and your own popularity to an all-time low. Even when rough shooting, the sound of the gun or its movement should never mean 'fetch'; if your shooting is anything like my own you will occasionally miss – well, maybe more than 'occasionally' – and when this happens, the last thing you want is your dog rushing out and looking for a non-existent retrieve, and disturbing other game you could have had a shot at.

Often in training, when we have introduced the gun, we ask an assistant thrower to fire it to catch the dog's attention and indicate the direction of a fall or where a dummy could be lying for an unseen retrieve. This is good training, but for the shooting man in the field it is usually himself that is firing the gun. All too often I have seen dogs out for the first time, and although familiar with the sound of the gun, they do not realize it has been fired by their owner and are looking in all directions simply because it has always been fired by someone else. Some places echo when a gun is fired, and some magnify the sound of the shot. In these instances your dog can look completely confused, and even rush off in the wrong direction when sent. Our reaction is to think he is being stupid or wilful, when really he is doing what his brain tells him is right to find a retrieve. Be aware of these situations, and if possible train using the gun in a variety of environments.

If you hunt your dog like a spaniel, teach him to sit to the shot at a distance and to be sent in the direction the gun has pointed; and where your dog is sat by your side, teach him to look along the barrels and see where they are pointing, because that is the direction to take. To put game into the bag there is nothing better than a dog that works to and for the gun. I have had a number of spaniels that learned to work game out of cover to where I was stood waiting with gun in hand. I often thought that this was a sign of intelligence, and a natural thing for a dog to do where a true hunting partnership has been established. However, I think we can help this to happen more often by teaching our hunting dogs to go into certain pieces of heavier cover, such as a round bramble thicket a little ahead, and work it back in our direction.

When training a hunting dog, I will often let him go into the cover and then encourage him back towards me where I have hidden a dummy or ball. Initially I did this because it was easy to put a dummy down, without him seeing me, just in front of where I was stood and inside the edge of the cover. Now I do it to get him to work towards me, and realize that if there is game, it is more likely to be in front of where I am stood. Of course, the advantages of training this are that a dog is generally closer, therefore easier to control, and we have a better chance of shooting whatever bursts from the cover. He will also then see the gun and the direction of

the shot, and learn quickly how he can get his 'reward' of a retrieve.

When rough shooting put your dog into a tangle of cover where it will be advantageous for scent or there is an opening, and then move round to the side where your dog is pushing any potential game. If the game flushes before your dog emerges and he sits in the cover where he cannot see, it can help him to call him out to a place where he can see you pointing your gun and command 'sit'. The clever dogs quickly learn to move out and wait at a vantage point on the edge of the cover when there is a flush, and where, if they cannot see the direction the game has taken, they at least can see the direction your gun is pointing.

On occasions where possible I use live cartridges in the gun. By using the gun with live cartridges in training, where it is safe and acceptable to do so, a dog will learn to take the scent trail left by the shot stream. This he will do especially if it is shot along the ground as though at a rabbit. For blind retrieves I have found that shooting along the floor towards the hidden dummy trains the dog to recognize this scent and to follow it to the dummy. In the field not only does this help with a rabbit, but also I am sure that the scent of the shot on occasions actually falls through the air, leaving a trail the dog can follow. So gun sense and shot trail sense is enhanced and assists your dog in finding and retrieving the game.

In the field, shooting over our dogs with the gun is an important part of the scenario, and can create many problems for your dog, or help make it a memorable day. Dogs do learn so much if you train them with the gun, so use it sensibly in your training programme, firing it yourself and getting others to fire it for you. In this way you will both be prepared.

Chapter 7

Retrieving

If you have gone to the trouble of selecting a puppy from good working stock with natural retrieving ability, you can expect it to be a natural retriever as well. Retrieving may start before you even begin to throw objects for the pup; many puppies I have had will naturally pick up items such as sticks, slippers, leaves and sometimes very unsavoury items. If your pup does this, then be pleased, and don't tell it to drop the item, or snatch it from its mouth. Call the pup up to you, praise it, and leave the object in its mouth for a period of time before saying 'Dead', or whatever your release command is, and then gently taking it.

If it is carrying an acceptable object I will often give it back to the pup; we are then sharing the retrieve, and a partnership is being formed. If you take the object from the pup's mouth and it then promptly disappears into your pocket or the rubbish bin, the pup may quickly get the idea that if it wants to keep something, it should not take it to you.

TEACHING THE RETRIEVE

The first retrieves I give the pup consist of something small and soft, such as a rolled-up sock or piece of cloth. An old leather glove is also a useful first retrieve: it smells of you, is easy to pick up and carry, and won't hurt the puppy's mouth. If your pup has been happily picking up objects, carrying them about and bringing them to you, it is better not to let it chase a thrown object right from the start: if it doesn't learn to chase, then you won't have to cure it.

If your puppy shows no enthusiasm for picking anything up and carrying it, you may need to tease it a little with a retrieve before throwing

the object and encouraging the pup to run immediately to pick it up. As soon as it begins to pick up and carry with a degree of interest, hold it and do not allow it to run in again. It should only retrieve when you give the command and allow it to do so.

It can be beneficial to have taught the pup to sit and stay before you begin teaching the retrieve; once told to sit and stay, it will then wait until it is given the command to retrieve – 'Fetch'. It is more important, however, that it returns to you willingly. The pup can be easily restrained by holding it, from running in to the thrown dummy, but once it has the dummy in its mouth, if it does not wish to return, you may have difficulties encouraging it up to you. If it does not return to you, then the way you handle that situation will either resolve the problem, or it can make a rod for your back for months, if not years, to come.

I like to create a real interest in retrieving with my dogs, and therefore do not wait until they are fully steady to the sit and stay. Start the retrieving habit at a very young age when often, through insecurity and a need to be with you, a pup will return as soon as you call. Find an area where it is a little restricted and cannot run away from you: a narrow pathway, a fenced-in corner of the garden, the hallway of your house, all these are ideal. It should be an area where the pick-up surface is soft, such as short grass or carpet. Hold the pup gently with one of your arms while you kneel on the floor, and, after showing it the retrieve and tempting it a little, throw the dummy a short distance with the other hand. The pup will probably wriggle to be free and chase the retrieve.

Hold it for a few seconds, and then release it with the words 'Fetch'. The moment it puts its head down and its mouth goes round the dummy, call it back with the high-pitched 'come to you' command. The call may be 'Pup, pup, pup', or a shrill staccato whistle through the teeth, or the artificial whistle, but it must be one the puppy responds to. At an early age the pup will usually return as soon as you attract its attention, and if you restrict it to an area such as a narrow passageway, it cannot get past you even if it tries, and you can guide it to your body. Stroke its chest, praising it, but do not take the retrieve immediately; let the pup hold on to it. Then, saying 'Dead', ease the dummy from its mouth.

Resolving Early Problems

If everything goes well, you now have a good basis on which to build your retrieving training. Some pups, though, will prove difficult. The point to remember is never to lose your patience, and not to worry if the pup does not do things right first time. By restricting the area, you are overcoming the problem of the pup running away with the retrieve. Always try to avoid situations that can cause difficulties. Your pup will feel secure in its bed or kennel, and many dogs, once they have picked up a retrieve, will head for that area of security. If this is the case with yours, why not take it well away from these attractions to where the only recognizable piece of security is the area close to you? When this is not possible, why fight it? Sit in its bed or in its kennel, and when it retrieves to those places, you are waiting there to share in the pleasure, and praise it.

I remember once visiting a friend who had a Weimaraner. When you threw any retrieve for the dog he would pick it and then return to sit in one particular area of a flowerbed under the sitting-room window. If you went towards the dog he would drop the retrieve there, and then wait for you to pick it up and throw it once more. No amount of calling would convince the dog that you were the person to whom the retrieve should be brought. I asked my friend if I could try, and how much he would give me if I could get the dog to retrieve to hand. He was not so silly as to put money on it, but felt it would be worth a drink.

I picked up the retrieve, sat the dog, threw the retrieve and told him to fetch. As he was

going out, I moved over and crouched in the flowerbed just back from where he would always sit or stand with the ball. Of course, he returned to the flowerbed as usual where I was, I praised and patted him, and then took the ball from his mouth. It sounds easy, and it was! I was accused of cheating, but it got the desired result. The next time I stood just in front of the flowerbed, blocking the dog's path, and it worked again.

At this we stopped, while I was winning, but I am sure that with a little perseverance, and a gradual move away from the flowerbed, a good, natural, 'to hand' retrieve could be achieved. What was wrong was that the owner was attempting to overcome a weakness instead of using it as a strength: he saw the return to the flowerbed as a problem, when really by standing in front of it, the dog made a perfect retrieve every time and was developing a good 'up to hand' retrieving habit. In time, the owner would be substituted for the flowerbed.

It doesn't always work that easily though, and sometimes you have to think creatively of ways to overcome the various problems. A young pup might find it intimidating if you stand tall above it, whereas if you crouch down, or sit on the floor, or even lie down and let it run all over you with the retrieve in its mouth, this is much less imposing, and encourages it to come back. Pups are always inquisitive and far more confident of approaching low objects, so by making yourself lower to the ground you are much more interesting and fun to return to.

As I mentioned previously, it is an advantage if the pup will return willingly, but some can be possessive, and when you do trust them with a little more space they can run off with a retrieve. The last thing you should do is chase after them; rather, catch their attention and run in the opposite direction, or disappear behind a wall or a tree, or maybe even lie down in the long grass so they have to come looking for you. If you have a puppy that does not want to return with the retrieve, it may be better at that stage to forget retrieving until the pup returns reliably each time, without the dummy.

Luckily it is rare that well bred gundogs, at least, will not retrieve. I have had one or two that have been reluctant, but generally it is a case of finding what they will carry, and working from there. I have had pups that will only carry a piece of rag that they had been given at a very early age; dummies they will not touch. So we started retrieving with the rolled-up rag, which was then tied to a small dummy or put inside a sock so that the smell of the rag was still present, and progressed to the proper dummies by a simple sequence of building on the dummy and removing the rag.

One little springer came in for training who resisted all attempts to get him retrieving. I had managed through very gentle handling to get him to hold objects and carry them alongside me; but if thrown, the dummies, rags, gloves, rabbit skins and cold game all received the same cursory sniff and were then left.

I had had the dog for a month and was almost ready to give up, when into the next-door kennel came a golden retriever, who brought with him a yellow plastic bear toy. It was one of those toys that had once held a squeaker, but now, as the squeaker had been removed for safety, contained only puffed air. One day I was around the kennels and noticed this young springer lying on his side reaching under the bars and scraping the yellow bear towards him. I went and picked the toy up and took the spaniel out of the kennel on to the pathway that led to the garden. I squeezed the toy a couple of times in front of his face, and then threw it into the garden away from the kennel, and immediately told him to fetch.

You can imagine my delight when he went straight out, picked it up and then came back along the path to the kennel where I was waiting. I took the toy from him and repeated the process, and again we got the desired result. With lots of praise and fuss we returned to the kennel. We did this little exercise for two days, and then attached a small dummy to the toy, which again proved successful. Then we took out the dummy and the toy as two separate items. I threw the toy first, and with that success under our belt, I threw the dummy by itself, which was also retrieved.

Very quickly the spaniel learned to retrieve the dummies I threw, and then moved on to rabbit skins and cold game. What had seemed an impossibility for me had by pure chance been solved. I don't know what had caused the initial mental barrier, but it took that yellow toy to

overcome it, and once that had been achieved we were soon retrieving the real thing.

There are techniques of force retrieving a dog, and in America many trainers believe that this is the only way to obtain a perfect, reliable retriever. If your dog is not a natural retriever, then it may be better to let a trainer experienced at forced retrieving train your dog, because it can so easily go wrong. I personally prefer to bring out the natural abilities of the dog, rather than make him do something against his will. However, there is no doubt that the forced retrieve taught correctly has many benefits in the training and control of your dog.

I have told the above stories of how two dogs were encouraged to retrieve, not to show how clever these techniques were, but to make you think about ways to overcome some of the problems you might encounter. Don't fight your dog if he has a weakness, but think of ways to overcome or avoid it – and don't give it time to become a dominant weakness. If the dog has a strength, then build on that strength and the particular aspect of retrieving that he enjoys and does well.

RETRIEVING TRAINING

Developing Steadiness and Delivery

Once your dog returns to you willingly with the retrieve, you can then begin to develop steadiness and the delivery. You have been holding the dog with one arm in front of him, making him stay until he is sent. If you say 'Fetch' the moment you release your arm, the dog will anticipate your command as soon as your arm moves or loosens. Instead, as you gradually release your grip, say 'Sit', and make the dog wait for longer periods of time before you send him.

If your dog will sit and stay, throw dummies and pick them yourself to emphasize to him that not only do *you* fetch them now and again, but also that he should not expect to fetch a dummy every time it is thrown. He should not be anticipating what is to happen next, or he will be acting before you give the command. If he moves towards any retrieve before you have sent him, make him sit and stay while you fetch that dummy, no matter what the distance.

(1) If your dog will carry and hold a dummy with enthusiasm, don't let him run in. Hold him firmly but gently, then give him the command to fetch.

(2) Don't throw the dummy too far.

To reinforce the sit and stay and to ensure that the dog does not go wrong, stand in front of him with your arm raised saying 'Sit', and then throw the dummy behind you. If your dog moves towards the dummy, you are in a position to block his path and then pick the dummy yourself. If the dog does not move, you can move to one side, and, with a clear direction with your arm, send him for the retrieve. Immediately the dog's head goes down to pick the dummy, blow your recall whistle, which will encourage him to pick it quickly without playing with it, and to hurry back to you. With a young dog, encouragement may be necessary all the time, but there is no need to keep calling and whistling if he is coming back directly to you at a good pace.

(3) A good, clear command to 'fetch'.

(4) Enthusiasm is wonderful, even though lack of coordination makes it look funny. Laugh and encourage.

(5) Give him time to pick the dummy up.

(6) And encourage him back. Remember not to grab either pup or dummy. Touch the pup as he comes close, praise and guide him, and then take the dummy after allowing him to hold it next to your body. (Pat Trichter)

To get a good front delivery, take both sides of the dummy and gradually guide your dog's head upwards. (Jeff Beals)

The American style of delivery is at your side. (Jeff Beals)

Again, don't worry about having the perfect delivery: it is more important that the dog comes back to you speedily and wants to give the dummy up to you. Trying to get him to sit and put his head up in the perfect pose can create hesitancy and make him stand off. If the dog manages to dodge around you and fetch the dummy without being sent, say nothing, take the dummy, and create a situation where he cannot get past you — use a narrow alley-way. Whatever happens, never punish the dog if he has a dummy in his mouth. Once he has got the retrieve he will associate punishment with carrying that, not the running in. If you punish a dog that is carrying a retrieve it can easily create a hard mouth, because the dog grits his teeth in anticipation of punishment each time he returns with a dummy or game.

Watch the way in which your dog picks up the dummy and returns with it. If he readily picks the dummy and immediately comes back to you, it is not necessary to blow the recall whistle. In fact, watch out for a bad pick-up and

sloppy carrying which can happen if you try to get a dog to return more quickly than his abilities will allow.

When your dog waits until you send him, and returns willingly to you, let him keep the retrieve in his mouth, and encourage him to stand still and lift his head by rubbing the chest in a circular motion or scratching under his chin. When you take the dummy, take it gently, rolling it towards you out of the dog's mouth.

If your dog holds the dummy firmly and will not release it, place the fingers of one hand behind the dummy in the dog's mouth, and, pressing downwards on the lips against the teeth, roll the dummy out of the mouth with the other hand, giving the release command 'Dead' or 'Drop'. Don't let this releasing of the dummy generate into a tug of war.

To develop steadiness, sit the dog and throw dummies and balls around and across the front of him to simulate falling birds and bolting rabbits. Leave the dog sitting and walk around picking up the dummies and balls yourself.

Some dogs are less likely to drop the dummy, and will deliver right up to you if you crouch down and allow them to jump up. (Jeff Beals)

Guide your dog using hands, knees and body into the right delivery position. Make him wait before taking the dummy. (Jeff Beals)

With a dog that is not interested in dummies, try using a rolled-up sock. It smells of you and is therefore more attractive. (Pat Trichter)

Occasionally leave a dummy on the ground and send the dog for it. Sometimes leave the dummy and call your dog up to you, walk away from the dummy for a short distance and then send the dog for it. This will help to develop your dog's memory as well as steadiness. If he has not remembered where the dummy is, help him by taking him back and guiding him on to the retrieve.

Gradually increase the distance and the complexity of the seen retrieve. Get another person to throw the dummy, after first catching the dog's attention. You should also get the dog to watch what is happening and pay attention – use the command 'Mark' to tell him to watch and mark where the dummy has fallen before sending him.

Remember to walk out and pick up a dummy yourself occasionally to minimize the chances of your dog anticipating the retrieve and running in.

The Unseen Retrieve

An extension of throwing a dummy a short distance and then walking the dog away from it before sending him, is the unseen retrieve. To develop this, use a path or a track where you can drop a dummy which the dog sees, and then walk on with him. After a short distance stop, turn the dog round, and send him back for the retrieve. When he is doing this efficiently at a longer distance, drop the dummy behind you when he is not looking. Walk only a short distance forwards and then, crouching alongside the dog and clearly pointing the way with your arm, say 'Get out', followed by 'Fetch', encouraging him to go back along the track. If it is only a short distance the dog will quickly find the dummy and return.

Slowly build up this distance on retrieves where the dog has not seen the dummy dropped, and then move into a wider area where he will have to take a direction indicated by your pointing arm to find the dummy. With patience your dog will learn to look along your arm and set off in that direction. All too often he may veer to the left or the right, in which case you have placed the dummy too far back for that stage in his development; bring it a little closer, and you will find he will succeed. Use the line of a fence or a hedge and send your dog back along it so he is guided to the dummy.

I prefer to be developing the dog's ability to search for hidden dummies at the same time as his marking and seen retrieving ability. In this way he will begin to believe you, and if he has seen a dummy thrown, but you send him in the opposite direction for a hidden one, he should trust your guidance and look for the hidden one. This can be a difficult exercise to carry out, but if the seen retrieve is thrown a good distance away and you can stop your dog if he tries to go in that direction, and if the unseen retrieve is only a short distance away so the dog will succeed quickly, then once he has the confidence in himself and you, he will learn what is required with ease.

Bring out your dog's natural abilities by encouraging him to hunt, but do be understanding with regard to the state of the scent, and if you can see the dummy but your dog cannot find it, be patient and help. Let the dog develop his initiative and drive.

Increase by degrees the amount of time your dog waits before he is sent for a retrieve. In the shooting field or in competition a considerable time may elapse before your dog is sent, and therefore it is wise to prepare him for this. Some dogs will develop their memory to such an extent that they can remember not only one bird, but a number of birds that have fallen, even though they have waited throughout a drive.

The Multiple Retrieve

You should also develop the dog's ability to work on multiple retrieves. Initially, start with two thrown retrieves, wide apart. Position yourself alongside the dog and clearly point to the one you want before sending him. Whistle as soon as the head goes down for the dummy, and be prepared for the dog possibly going to the second dummy before running back to you. So call and encourage him the first few times that you do this exercise.

Build up the number of dummies in a multiple retrieve exercise. Very rarely will you get a dog that will remember more than about six dummies, so don't expect too much. It is better to get the dog following your arm direction and trusting your command, rather than

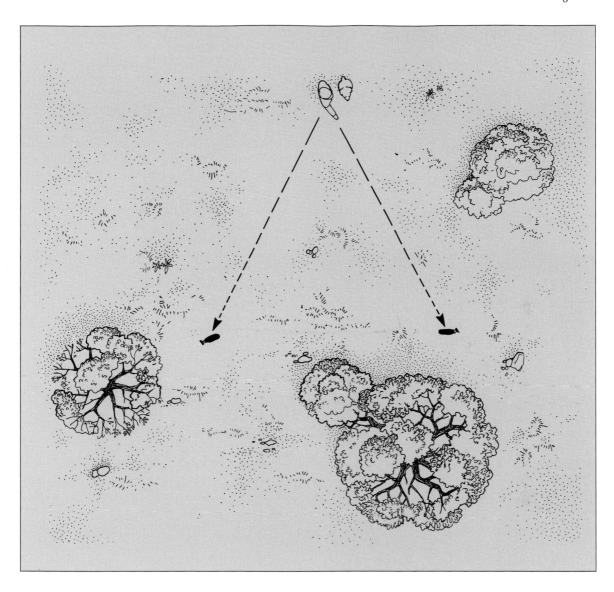

The two-dummy retrieve.

remembering. With this exercise, fetch one or two of the dummies yourself.

When the dog returns with a dummy, don't take it from his mouth too quickly, and make him wait before you send him for the next. The knowledge that there are other dummies waiting to be retrieved, together with you eagerly taking the dummy and sending him for the next, can quickly develop bad habits in him. Your dog could start to drop the dummy or throw it at you and begin the next retrieve without being told. So be warned, multiple retrieves are not a race, but another exercise to develop your dog positively for the field.

Perfecting the Delivery

The ideal delivery you should develop is where the dog comes up quickly, sits in front of you, and then raises his head so that you can take the retrieve with one hand (when you have a gun under one arm, you will have only one hand free).

To perfect the delivery once your dog is bringing the retrieve right up to your legs, say 'Sit' in a gentle tone and push his backside to the floor. Rub the front of his chest and under the chin; when he lifts his head in pleasure, take the dummy gently from him. When he is coming up and sitting willingly, I will often click my

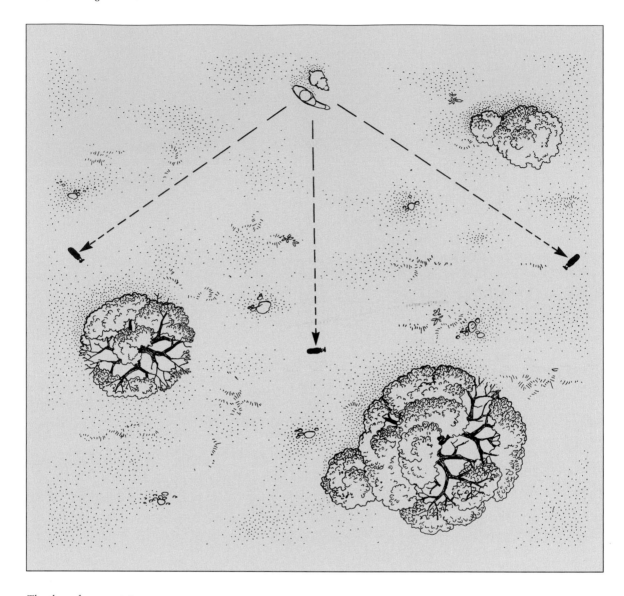

The three-dummy retrieve.

fingers, slap my chest or catch his attention by calling his name to make him lift his head before removing the dummy. Some dogs will put their head to one side, or lower it as though guarding the dummy; gently direct the head to where you want it to be, rub the chest and praise him before taking the retrieve. It is important that this habit is firmly implanted.

Some dogs tend to lie down; with these, lift the dog to the sitting position, and again praise. I have often found that if you crouch down and lift the head so that it is resting on your knees, the dog is happy with this; and then you can progress to a half crouch, followed by the standing position. By this time, the dog should be coming in, and if you have progressed gradually and firmly with him, he will press the retrieve into your legs, lifting his head so that his chin lies up the line of your legs.

If your dog is the 'run around the back' type, or runs back to you so quickly that he overshoots where you are waiting, stand with your back to a wall or a fence, and at his approach call him coaxingly up to you. Read your dog though, and if the coaxing method does not work, try something a bit firmer with the voice, watching his reaction all the time and adjusting your approach accordingly.

Avoiding Problems

Always look for the potential problem, and work to avoid it. If there are no fences and your dog runs around you, think of ways that may stop him doing this – back yourself in amongst nettles, brambles or any cover that could restrict his running around, and guide him to you. If you have taught him to heel first, if you walk away from him and tap your thigh saying 'Heel', he may come alongside and walk along carrying the dummy; a gentle 'Sit', and you have him in a position where you are in control. I have known this 'walking alongside you' ploy work very well where a dog is prone to dropping the dummy. Let him carry the dummy alongside you, and then as you walk, gently take the dummy from him, and praise him. After a while you will be able to walk very slowly – even stop – and then take the dummy. It is a gradual development from then onwards to the perfect retrieve.

A word of warning: if you give your dog treats, be careful not to give one immediately he delivers the retrieve; if you do, it will not be long before he is dropping the dummy to get the treat quickly.

As your retrieving training progresses, vary the terrain where you carry it out. Long grass will hide the dummy and the dog will have to work harder with his nose; introduce light bramble and bracken to encourage him to enter cover. Always be on the lookout for areas that will enlarge the experience of your dog in new handling situations.

GOOD MARKING

Whatever form of shooting we do, when we send a dog out on a retrieve we not only want him to pick the bird, but to do so quickly, cleanly and with the minimum of disturbance to other game that could be on the ground. To do this effectively it is an advantage to have a dog that marks the fall of a bird accurately, that has the ability to take a straight line to the bird, and can estimate the distance. Some dogs have a natural ability to mark the fall, to pinpoint exactly where that bird hit the ground, and I am always amazed watching dogs on the grouse moors that go directly to the fall, when all we can see is a mass of heather and nothing to help us fix the spot. There are dogs that are born with a natural marking ability, but there is also no doubt that all dogs can have their marking improved through training and experience.

One of the prime indicators of a good marker is a dog that focuses on a bird, and fixes it not only with his eyes but also in his mind. Even if he glances away, this dog has a mental picture, which when he looks back to the fall, he compares with the present view until they match once more. We have discussed retrieving and the way to develop a good retrieve, but for a dog to be a good marker there must also be a real enthusiasm for the retrieve: he has to really want it, be determined to succeed, and not be half hearted in his approach.

By this stage you should have been 'reading' your pup and getting to know the type of dog you have: does he sometimes give up on a retrieve before he gets to the fall area? If he cannot find the dummy immediately, does he give up and return? On a memory retrieve, does he forget where the dummy was dropped? Is he distracted by other scent when out on a retrieve? You should be asking yourself these and many other questions, and deciding what needs to be done to create the focus of attention that you require. Often the reason is a lack of effective basic training and a weak relationship with the trainer. So get to know your pup, and if the enthusiasm and keenness for the retrieve is not there, go back to some of the basics and make the training session the highlight of the day.

To build up experience and confidence in retrieving from a distance, throw the dummy to the same place and increase the distance by moving further and further away from that place. In this way your dog is always going back to a 'confident' area, one where he knows he has found dummies before. Throw the dummy near a natural marker, such as a bush, a tree, a tall clump of grass – something your dog can focus on – and if there are no natural markers, use a traffic cone or pole stuck into the ground to mark the 'drop zone'. Initially send your dog for retrieves downwind to encourage him to use his eyes to get to the area; most dogs will also run further with a following wind than one that is blowing into their face, which many dogs do not like and often will turn away from.

These retrieves should be done in light cover to enable your dog to find quickly, because nothing succeeds like success. With some dogs I will even use white dummies or a white sock on the dummy to give them an added advantage and succeed quickly.

Once your dog is going back to this confidence place successfully, create a different picture by moving around the field but again throwing the dummy back to the same place. In this way you are sending him from different angles, the view and the wind direction will be slightly different, and he will have to really focus and concentrate on the place where the dummy fell to take a line to it irrespective of wind direction.

As your pup gets the idea of what is required and really begins to pinpoint the fall area, you can then start to move to thicker cover where he has to use his nose. In fact, thicker cover can be used to advantage when a dog has a propensity to overshoot. Find a clump of heavier grass that is surrounded by open ground. Throw the dummy into this grass, and now when the dog overshoots on to open ground he should quickly realize the dummy is not there, and will work his way back to the cover where, using his nose, he will find it. In this way he learns to work back along his own line until he hits the scent, and with practice can overcome the overrunning habit.

For those of us who train alone, it is sometimes difficult to give long, marked retrieves and send the dog within a few seconds of the dummy hitting the ground. But if your dog enjoys retrieving tennis balls, a good way of sending them a considerable distance is with a tennis racket – and not only can tennis balls be hit a long way, but they will bounce and leave a short trail, teaching the dog to use its nose once it gets to the fall area. Tennis balls and dummies can also be launched from a special dummy launcher, should your pocket be deep enough to buy one. But a word of warning: ensure your dog is introduced to shot, and especially the sound of the launcher before using it.

Enlist the help of a friend to throw dummies and increase the distance. Some wounded birds may tower and fall way back, some birds will be shot by a dogless friend, and it will be advantageous to develop the ability to mark down a bird up to 100 yards. When someone else throws dummies for you, start close and be sure the pup recognizes that a thrower or gun means there will be something to retrieve. Do single retrieves from different angles, and help your pup to identify and concentrate on the thrower. The thrower can make a noise (Hey! Hey! Hey! or a trilling sound) to attract the pup's attention before throwing, and as distance builds up, can use a starting pistol. This will also enable you to introduce shot at a distance and associate it with something pleasant – the retrieve.

Although we want the dog to watch the thrower, the dummy should not be so close that he runs to the thrower; he has to learn to switch from focusing on the thrower to focusing on the dummy as it is thrown. To encourage and guide your dog into a long straight run, use a hedge, fence line or even a straight path that he follows to the retrieve.

Once your dog begins to complete these retrieves with ease, you can change things. Have the thrower 'out of the picture' – hidden behind a bush, have him throw at angles, short and long and to either side of where he is stood, as well as throwing square. Be careful in this: the important point is never to stretch your dog beyond its capabilities, and when it does encounter a problem, go in and help. Often the thrower can do this by moving towards the dummy resting on the ground while making the 'throwing noise' to catch the dog's attention. You don't want to do this too often, however, or the dog will begin to stop and look to the thrower for assistance. If the thrower has to help regularly, you have stretched the dog too far.

Once your dog has really begun to focus on the fall and to estimate the distance, you can begin to include obstacles such as thicker and varied cover, and falls out of sight behind bushes, reeds, over the brow of a hill, or even across a stream or forestry ride. When introducing obstacles, again go back to shorter retrieves and increase the distance gradually. Build on success, and never think that you can take big strides based on how your dog is doing at any one particular moment. So many times we are trying to create good marking, and we end up

OPPOSITE: *A dog that watches birds in and marks the fall well puts the bird in the bag quicker. (Paul Pederson Action Snapshot Photography)*

attempting to handle the dog instead. This leads to frustration on our part and confusion on the part of the dog. If you are teaching marking — teach marking. What we are developing is a dog that uses his eyes to pinpoint a fall and to get out to the right area, and then switches from eyesight to nose 'sight' and sticks to the fall until he finds the bird or the track it has left behind.

There is no doubt that marking is a complex skill, and as such needs to be developed carefully and gradually; but once it is achieved, it can produce the memorable retrieves that we talk of for years.

DEVELOPING THE DOG'S MEMORY

I have already mentioned that you should encourage your dog to use his memory by dropping dummies and walking on before sending him for the retrieve, and also by developing multiple retrieves. Build on these exercises by increasing the distances and making the retrieves more complex. For example, when out for a walk, drop a dummy and work up to a situation where you can walk on for a considerable distance. This will strengthen your dog's memory and give him excellent controlled exercise at the same time, keeping him fit and speeding up the return, as over a long distance he will want to be back with you quickly.

Once your dog is going back for retrieves readily, don't just drop the dummy on the path but throw it to the side, first into some short cover, and gradually into longer cover, so that not only does he have to remember, but now he has to work for it as well. With the multiple retrieve, send your dog for the dummies in a different order from the one you routinely use; in this way, he will be developing memory and trust in your directions.

I believe that the dog's memory needs to be developed from a very early age. It is surprising how much they do remember, if they want to — like all of us! I have had one or two dogs that couldn't seem to remember any dropped dummy, no matter how short the distance, or the ways that were used to make sure they noticed what I had done. Others you think have forgotten, because of their relaxed manner, but one little command sends them rocketing back to the dummy.

The 'half unseen' retrieve takes the memory retrieve a little further, and can build the expectations of the dog so that he will begin to go back for hidden retrieves. To do this I sit the dog and then walk away for a distance with the dummy in my hand. Usually, a keen dog will watch this action intently. I don't throw the dummy but place it purposefully on the ground, then return to my dog which I send from the place he has been waiting. Next, I increase the complexity by walking the dog away from where he has been waiting, and then sending him from a new position.

By carrying out these exercises, the dog will begin to go out for retrieves whether he has seen them down or not. With those dogs which may give up hunting if they do not find a dummy fairly quickly, it is sometimes wiser to put down two dummies unseen, not too close together, so that once the dog finds one dummy he does not come across the second. Putting two dummies down will increase his chances of finding something quickly.

I am often asked how to put down dummies unseen when the dog is watching every move. If your dog is that attentive, please don't complain: he is a gem. One way to do this is to leave him in the car or kennel, making sure he cannot see you. Another is to give him a good seen or memory retrieve as you walk along, and while he is running away to fetch this dummy, throw and hide a second one. You will be surprised how quickly he grasps this trick, and then always expects there to be a hidden dummy behind, or one to be fetched immediately a seen dummy has been retrieved. So out-think the rascal: hide a dummy, remembering where you have put it, and then send him for it later. If you are out for a walk and training, hide the dummies on your way out and retrieve them on your return journey.

Think through all your exercises so that you develop initiative, drive, hunting ability, memory, enthusiasm and willingness to please. And most of all, think through what you are doing to avoid problems, particularly your dog's capacity to anticipate, where he becomes altogether too clever.

STICKING TO THE FALL

In the shooting field we need a dog that will stick to the fall and have the determination to succeed. Some dogs will give up when they do not find quickly; others will stick to the hunt no matter what you do to call them off. The latter is a different problem, one of control and obedience. So let's have a look at ways in which we can encourage a dog to stick to the fall and find the bird or rabbit no matter what the difficulties.

I can remember two seven-month-old Labrador puppies that I worked and trained, brother and sister. When they was younger they were quite different: when the dog saw a dummy fall, if he got to the area and could not find it where he thought it had dropped, he would immediately begin to hunt the vicinity. The little bitch, on the other hand, would go flying out to the fall area and if she could not find it where she thought it was, would come flying back; this started to happen the moment I began to steady her to the throw of a dummy and to give her memory retrieves. It was as though her drive to retrieve was a little lower through the steadying process, and she had not got the motivation to hunt if she was not successful at the first try.

With her, all I did was allow her to run in and chase once more, to build up her enthusiasm. I also used a tennis ball, which will, of course, bounce and roll, and is not where she first saw it hit the ground; this encouraged her not only to keep trying but, where the grass was a little thicker, to use her nose. I then began to use a tennis racket to knock the ball further, to give longer retrieves and stronger bounces. When I steadied her again, this lack of interest in finding the dummy had gone and was replaced with a desire to hunt and find.

In a previous chapter I mentioned the idea of 'seeding' the ground with more than one dummy so that your dog finds quickly. If you have a problem with your dog sticking to an area you can again 'seed' the ground with dummies and begin removing them one by one as your dog succeeds on each retrieve. In the end there is only the one thrown dummy for him to fetch, but in the course of the exercise he has learnt slowly and in increments to stick to the ground for longer and longer periods. Teach your dog a verbal command that means he is in the right area and to hunt it; many handlers use the words 'Hi lost!', which sounds like 'Hi low-sss'. Teach your dog that when he hears these words he is in the area of the fall, and to start working with his nose.

To do this is quite easy. When your dog is within about five to ten yards of a retrieve, just call gently 'Hi lost', and if he doesn't find it, encourage him again with these words when he is in the circle of contact. Only call the command when he is within a close distance of the fall – this can vary according to the terrain and scenting conditions, but is usually within five to ten yards of the fall.

Another way of teaching this and encouraging hunting is to roll a ball into long grass up close, and then instead of sending him to fetch, encourage him and move forwards with the words 'Hi lost!' to send him to find it. Very quickly you will be able to roll a ball, unseen by your dog, into the long grass as you walk along, then call him across and with the command 'Hi lost', set him off hunting for it. If he is obedient to the recall whistle, by using it carefully to call him into the area and giving the command 'Hi lost', you can control and hold him within the 'strike' zone until he finds it. Initially it should not take long for him to find the ball, though you should never hesitate to go in and give a little help if he is struggling. As he gains more determination and skill at this hunting you can hold him there longer and longer.

Another variation of this, which builds up the hunting time and determination, is to throw a ball about ten yards away into grass or cover where it will not be seen. Then throw a second ball as far as you can where it is easy to find, and send the dog for this second ball. When he is on his way, quickly go and pick up the first ball and put it in your pocket. When your dog returns with his tennis ball and delivers it, send him for the first you threw and have now picked up. Using 'Hi lost' and a gentle recall whistle when necessary, hold your dog in the area and then, when he cannot see you do it, throw the ball back into the area and let him find it. Gradually increase the amount of time your dog has to hunt the area before you throw the ball back into the hunt zone; in this way he will learn to stick to that area because he does find

in the end. The important thing is to watch your dog and not wait until he is discouraged by not finding; if you read him right you will be able to return the ball just before that critical point occurs.

Once your dog understands the command 'Hi lost', you can teach him to obey it at a distance. Some dogs find distance a little insecure and return straightaway if they do not find the dummy immediately; others seem to lose orientation and run everywhere and anywhere – I have even seen them run across to another place where a dummy may have been thrown previously, even though it is fifty or more yards from where the dummy you require actually fell. Where a dog appears to want to run wide and deep and not stick to a smaller 'strike' area, I look for ways to restrict his hunting perimeters, for example by having the retrieve just out from the corner of a field where fences or hedges will limit his hunting area. Walls, paths, streams and other natural features can be used to this effect, and encourage him to stick to a certain area.

I also play a variation of a previous technique I mentioned. In this case I use an assistant to throw a dummy about fifty yards away while I make the dog wait; I then throw a second one in the opposite direction and send the dog for this one first. While he is going for it, my assistant dashes out and picks the dummy he threw. Upon returning with the first dummy my dog is then sent for the second dummy that has now been removed. Again using a combination of the whistle and 'Hi lost', I hold my dog in the area, and when he is looking in the opposite direction the assistant rolls the dummy in, where I encourage the dog to find it successfully.

Another variation of this is to use something that is not retrievable, such as an earth clod that breaks up as it hits the ground. The dog sees an object thrown, goes out to the fall, but finds nothing to retrieve immediately. The clod will have scent on it, and many times a dog will keep returning to that scent, which teaches it to start its search from where the scent is greatest. Once more after the dog has worked the area for a period of time (a short period at first, but increasing as the dog gains in experience), unseen to the dog, your assistant again rolls in a dummy past the clod fall for the dog to successfully find. A further enhancement to this technique is to use live gunshot fired at the ground around the dummy or the clod when it is thrown, to lay a stronger scent.

In the shooting field we need a dog that not only gets out to a fall, but also sticks to that fall until it is successful at finding the game or finding the trail it has left. A dog that runs deep and wide with seemingly no real purpose or 'canine common sense' can disturb unshot game, and will also take far more time to locate a bird, than one taught to stick to the fall area. Good, clean, sharp retrieves not only look slick but are also far more efficient in putting more game in the bag. So this form of training is worth working at if you want a dog that will really stick to the fall area and find game promptly.

Distractions

When training your dog, moving from distractions that are created using tennis balls and dummies to distractions created by live game is a big jump, and in the field wherever we are shooting this is bound to occur on a regular basis. For example, you have sent your dog for a diving wounded duck, and he has made a great job of getting it and is returning. Suddenly another flight of duck comes over his head, and you take a shot and bring one down dead to splash in the water. Even though you left your shot until the duck was bound to fall away from him, he cannot resist the temptation to retrieve it, and drops the wounded one and heads off for the dead one. This is surely a scenario that many of us have seen on more than one occasion, especially when picking up on a shoot, whether pheasant or duck, where wounded birds are collected the moment they hit the ground.

The faster your dog returns to you with the first bird, the quicker you can get him on to the second one: therefore it is essential that you develop as fast and reliable a return as possible. The dog will soon get to know that in the event of two shots, the moment he gets the first bird back to you, he will be turned round and sent for the second one. Control and the basic foundations of training are essential, and it is at about this stage that you will find out whether you have established and practised the basics enough; the relationship between you and your dog should be such that he not only knows, but

wants to bring the retrieve in his mouth back to you and share it.

To return to our distraction scenario: when another bird falls from the sky as he is returning, reinforce the return with the recall whistle if he is seen to hesitate at all. Do this especially in training so that he knows he is expected to come back with the one in his mouth. Some dogs learn to stop and watch the falling bird, others will continue returning but will be watching the bird that has just been shot as it falls. This can be good, as he may be expected to go for that one afterwards and it will help if he has marked the fall. As long as he does not drop the retrieve in his mouth, there is no problem with this. If he does drop the retrieve, move closer, stop him going towards the second bird, and insist that he first brings back the one he had in his mouth; in this way he will realize that he does not get the second until he returns with the first.

A moving bird or rabbit is always more interesting and motivating to your dog than a dead or captured one in his mouth, and this is where the problem arises: his motivation to chase and retrieve one falling from the sky is stronger than bringing back to you the one he already has in his mouth. Hence the need to have good control: he has to know that he must bring the one he has already retrieved back to you before going for another.

Training in a Rabbit Pen

One of the best ways to train your dog to do this is by using a rabbit pen, if you have access to one. For the dog, active rabbits are always far more interesting than going for a retrieve in the pen; therefore once you have steadied him and he is happy to hunt around and watch them scuttle away, or walk around with rabbits running everywhere, begin to do short, simple retrieves in the pen, so he learns to focus on the retrieve and ignore the distraction of the rabbits. With some dogs I find that the retrieve object has to be one they really enjoy, such as a dead bird or a dummy covered with rabbit skin. Where the dog is only really interested in cold game I gradually wean them off this in the pen until I can have them retrieving anything I throw, whilst ignoring the running rabbits. Usually, however, I find that a tennis ball creates enough interest.

(1) Taking straight lines with the help of a fence.

(2) Use a white marker to identify the fall area, something your dog can focus on. Here there are a number of dummies, and the dog picks one after the other, running the same straight line.

(3)With a quick recall he learns to pick just one and bring that back, ignoring the others.

(4) A nice delivery to the side; his body is already lined up to go for the next. (Jeff Beals)

Once you can do this with your dog, start giving him memory retrieves in the rabbit pen. Drop a dummy or tennis ball, and then either hunt him or walk him away from it, flushing rabbits as you go; then turn him round and send him for the dummy. Initially do this at short distances, and after only a short hunt or walk so that he doesn't forget the dummy. Remember, watching and working the live rabbits will initially clear his memory easily and quickly. I have demonstrated this with both retrievers and spaniels: in one exercise, I encourage the rabbits to congregate in the centre of the pen by putting a pile of food there, and then I bring in the dog and give him retrieves where he has to run through the feeding rabbits: they scatter in all directions, but his focus is on the retrieve – and that is what we are looking for.

It is more difficult to do this without such a pen, but if you know a gamekeeper who trusts you and understands what you are attempting to achieve, he may allow you to do similar exercises in a pheasant pen. I was lucky in that one of my gamekeeper friends would invite me into and around the pens at feed times. We would first either hunt or walk the birds back to the pen, and then feed them around the dogs, which would sit there and watch as feed was sprinkled around their feet and sometimes even on their backs for the birds to peck off. I would then give them a retrieve of a dummy in the pen. Occasionally if the keeper found a dead bird he would put it on one side for me to use as a retrieve; we would bare a little of the flesh, and use this for the dog to fetch from among the healthy pheasants. Very quickly the dogs learned what was to be retrieved, and what was not to be touched, and on shoot days this gave me the privilege of being the one who picked up in the pheasant pen after a drive. The dogs scented and knew which birds were damaged, and which were healthy, and left the healthy ones alone.

Training Without a Pen

If working in a pen is not an option for you, then you could try this exercise: think about the type of retrieve that motivates your dog the most – a canvas dummy is usually the lowest on the list, a tennis ball is more interesting, a rabbit-skin dummy even more, a cold dead bird slightly better, a warm dead bird even better than that, and the *most* exciting is a live bird or rabbit. If we use a dummy for the retrieve and then throw a tennis ball as a distraction, the tennis ball will usually be more tempting; if we throw cold game it will be even more of a distraction; and if your dog associates a gunshot with a retrieve, firing a shot when you throw the second dummy will be an even greater temptation. Therefore gradually introduce and use distractions that tempt your dog to drop what he is carrying and go after that one. Each time use something that he will find more tempting than the last, and be increasingly on your toes: encourage your dog to come back with what he is carrying, and then while he waits, go and pick the distraction yourself. Only when you are certain that he is coming back straight and true and not being strongly tempted should you send him for the distraction, and then not every time.

Training in Water

The biggest problems can arise when duck shooting, as once the dog is in the water it is difficult to get to him to insist he brings back the retrieve he has in his mouth – and he will quickly learn how you are handicapped in this way. It is important therefore to get it right – really right – on land first, before you move on to water. One method I have used to stop the dog swapping birds, and to reduce the chances of him doing so, is to ensure that he never gets the 'distraction' bird. On land you may have an assistant who quickly picks the distraction should the dog go for it; when working on water, attach a long piece of light cord to the distraction and quickly reel it in if the dog is at all tempted and heads towards it. If the distraction is close enough to the shore, the look of amazement as the distraction 'bird' flies out of the water, sometimes even over the dog's head, is quite something to behold!

It also helps to go out occasionally with a fellow trainer and let his dog have the second retrieve. You can then do the same for him. By picking the distraction birds yourself, and having an assistant and also a fellow trainer's dog pick them, as well as allowing your dog to have the occasional turn, your dog will never be sure when it is his bird to pick. Only *you* will determine that, and he will learn to bring back the best 'prize' he has at that moment, which is the one in his mouth.

TAKING A STRAIGHT LINE

One of the principles of good gundog work is that the dog should take as direct a line as possible to the fall. This is to avoid disturbing ground, thereby minimizing the chances of flushing further game that we would wish to find after the retrieve. Some trainers feel that 'lining' a dog is unnecessary; however, I have found that teaching the dog to go in the line I want minimizes the amount I have to handle him. It also helps him to succeed more quickly, which gives him more confidence, and it is a skill that does put game in the bag much quicker. Some trainers insist that a dog must never run round anything, even a pond when a bird has fallen on the opposite side – though the size of the pond would be a determining factor; however, common sense should dictate how to handle such a situation – for instance, a wounded running bird needs to be picked in the quickest possible time.

There are a number of exercises that can be used to train your dog to run straight lines and not veer off course. One of the easiest is to use hedges and fences, or straight narrow paths as a guide; using these you can gradually increase the distance and, using memory and then blind retrieves, teach your dog to keep going until he finds the retrieve or you whistle to give him a direction. When you send a dog for a blind retrieve he should be thinking that he is going in the right direction, and keep on that line until you whistle him. When marking a fall, he should be able to use his own abilities, after your training, to judge where the retrieve is. Training a line can however also help in marking. A dog that knows to take a straight line will often keep on that line, checking at times to the side when he thinks he is the fall area, and then moving forwards again on the same line.

Teaching Your Dog to Take a Line

The important part of teaching a dog to take a line is the positioning of his body by your side. As your dog learns, through various exercises, about the placing of his body in relation to yours, you can begin to move him small amounts. Imagine you are the centre of a wheel, and you get him looking down any one of its multitude of spokes. With him sat on your left-hand side you can 'push' him to the left by manoeuvring your body to the left – do not actually physically push, but move small amounts so that he learns to move with you. You can also 'pull' him around to the right by, again, moving your body to the right and encouraging him to move with you, positioning himself by your side. When sat alongside you, his rear, shoulders and head should all be facing in the direction you wish him to go. The head is essential in its placing and especially his eyes, which should be looking intently in the right direction.

One tip that will help you to 'aim' him is to look at the fall area, then draw an imaginary line to where your dog is sat at your side. Now look slightly ahead of his body and identify a mark on the ground – it could be a stone, a weed, a flower, anything – and when his body is in line with this and his eyes are looking directly over it, then is the time to send him. You use this mark like the sighting of a rifle. With everything in line, your hand can then also confirm the direction, and you can give the 'fetch' command.

In my experience, if you teach your dog this positioning and he becomes confident about going in the direction he is looking, even the hand signal becomes unnecessary. He will go on the blind retrieve command, which in my case is 'Get out'.

Exercises to Develop Lining Skill

To help develop this lining skill, use white markers to show where you would place the dummy, or throw it to; these markers might be white posts, or posts with a white bag or T-shirt on them. On a short grass field do the exercise called **sending to a pile**. In this case it is helpful to use dummies that are white, or white and black, and can be seen easily. You put a number of these dummies in one specific place that is marked or easy to see, and send the dog to this same place on more than one occasion to pick each dummy one by one. Some may be concerned that he will learn to swap dummies; however, I have found the opposite. If you use

When lining, have body, head and eyes looking where you want him to go. Teach him to know when he is looking exactly where he is to go to. (Jeff Beals)

the whistle to teach him to pick up and return promptly, this is exactly what he does, and although he may attempt to change or 'shop' the first few times, he soon realizes that if he brings back the first he picks, he will still be sent back for the remaining ones.

In addition to marking the pick-up area, teach your dog the **wagon wheel or star exercise**, where a number of dummies have been put out at the end of the spokes on the imaginary wheel. Initially put out only four, so you have one every 90 degrees, but increase this as your dog learns until you can have as many as sixteen out; you can also increase the lengths of the spokes as you go. Line him up for each retrieve at the end of each spoke, and when his body and eyes are exactly on the one you want, you can send him. In this way he learns, and so do you, how to move through small angles simply by little steps and turns with your feet.

Finally teach him **pictures**. In other words, show him that dummies lie at the base of trees, or telegraph poles or fence posts or in the gaps between them. Get him to focus on each and teach him a gentle 'No' when he is wrong and encourage him to move slightly to the next picture, until he is looking exactly where you want

Dummies in line like distant rungs of a ladder. He picks the closest, then the next, and so on. (Jeff Beals)

him. When focused on the right place, say 'Good' and send him. If his eyes will not move, take a step or two forwards towards where you want him to go, tapping your side. Tell him 'Dead' for an unseen retrieve, or 'mark' for one he has seen fall, and again line him up. Sometimes, to teach him to look where you want him to go, you may have to walk forwards a few times before sending him. But eventually he will begin to learn this, and do it without you moving forwards.

Many of my dogs, when their body is positioned as near as possible to the line I want them to take, will simply move their eyes. At a distance over one hundred yards it is difficult to get the body exact. However, watch their eyes, and when they are not looking exactly where you want them to go, tell them 'No' in a calm voice, and then encourage them to look somewhere slightly different – thus they begin to learn to do this, and to do it with very small eye movements.

This lining technique can be invaluable – though of course there may be other scent of live, or even of dead birds that have been picked on the line out to a fall. You should therefore teach your dog the **'ladder' exercise**, where you place dummies in a line as rungs on a ladder, but not as close together. Thus, on a one hundred yard training ladder retrieve exercise you might have the first dummy at thirty yards, the next at forty yards, the next at sixty yards, and so on – or they may be even further apart and a longer distance to the last one. The aim is for the dog to go out and collect the first, followed by the second, and then the third. After picking the first, in each case the dog is running through old scent and learning to ignore this and keep on the line.

With handler and dog skill gained through training and experience, there are times when dogs will pick a blind retrieve perfectly by taking a straight line to the dummy or bird, and times when only a small direction may be needed. Therefore it is important after teaching lining to remind the dog to still trust you, and show him that although the line is good, he still has to stop on command and take minor adjustment directions; also to hunt for the bird, when asked, and when he is in the area of the fall. Remember, we do not always know exactly where that is.

Lining is well practised in America, and can be very beneficial; however, it should not be carried out to the extent that we no longer trust our dog to hunt and to use his nose. A dog is there to find birds we cannot. At times, the place where we thought the bird fell is not quite where it did fall – or in the case of a wounded bird, where it has walked to before tucking in. Use lining to get the dog quickly to the fall, and then let him do the work he has the skills to do – to find that bird and get it back in the bag.

INTRODUCTION TO WATER

A gundog has to undertake his work in a variety of environments and terrain, one of these being water. For the wildfowler and ardent duck shooter, water work is essential. For the normal shooting man, water work may not happen often, but when it does a dog is needed far more than on land if that bird is to be brought to hand. A bird floating downriver, dropped in the middle of a lake or being carried away on the tide, demands the resourcefulness and fortitude of a good dog. Although serious water training is better started after you have developed a lot of the skills on land, the introduction of your dog to water should be done as early as possible.

Dogs generally like water, some more than others; in fact some dogs are fanatical about it, and make for any muddy pool or ditch to have a splash and wallow. A river or pond is a luxury to such dogs. However, don't presume that your dog is a natural water lover even if he is a Labrador, whose ancestors made their living jumping off boats into the water to fetch all kinds of objects that were cast or fell overboard. The introduction to deep water and swimming should be a gentle one, and is better done in summer when the water is warmer, and from a gently sloping bank. Walk into the water a little way with your dog, encourage him, and show him that there is nothing to worry about.

If he is happily retrieving dummies, throw a dummy a little way out, but not so far that he will be out of his depth. In other words, the dog should be able to walk out in the water and pick up the dummy. By degrees, increase the distance and depth until your dog has to take his feet off

The moment he is out of the water is the time to really encourage him up to you: a fast return with no shaking.

the bottom and swim. This will take some bravery on the part of the dog, and may need a little verbal encouragement from yourself. You can then gradually increase the distance your dog has to swim to fetch the dummy.

If your dog is reluctant to enter water, there are a number of ways of overcoming this. While out on walks, cross streams and splash through puddles, encouraging the dog to do the same, possibly even keeping him on the lead to do so. Walk along the shallows of a lake or river with the dog alongside you; if you have another dog that likes water, let them play together in a stream or pond. The final resort is to put on a swimming costume yourself and go in with the dog.

In most cases, gundogs take to water very quickly, but the occasional frightening experience can create problems. One of my young Labradors had such an experience. We were playing in 'real' water for the first time; we had splashed through streams, but here we were on the edge of a pond. She was a keen retriever so I took her to the edge of the pond where, although it was shallow, it did slope away very quickly. I threw the dummy only about one yard out into the water. She put her foot into the edge of the pond and then thought better of her actions and stepped backwards. She now thought about how she could reach the dummy without getting her feet wet. All this time an

offshore breeze was carrying the dummy further away from us, so now it was two yards away from the bank. I was encouraging her, and she so desperately wanted the dummy that instead of walking or running, she leapt in and of course went under. That was enough for her, and I had created a problem. We had to go right back to the first stage of water training and build confidence. She loves water now, and the very presence of it makes her want to go and have a quick swim around just for fun, but it took a lot longer to achieve than it should have done because of that one mistake.

Never be tempted, however frustrating it may be, to throw your dog into the water. A really problematical dog may be lowered very gently into the water, the emphasis being on 'gently', so that you do not frighten him, and let him swim just a short distance to the bank.

The first time your dog swims, it may look like the rear view of a Mississippi paddle boat as the paws thrash the water. Similar to myself when I first started swimming, my aim was to keep my head out of the water as far as possible. Initially this splashing dog paddle is used to get the dog very inefficiently to a dummy and then, the dummy being a little heavier in the mouth, the head is held nearer the water, the back end rises and a good swimming position results. The dog soon learns that this improved swimming position will get him to the dummy

Get your pup splashing and having fun retrieving from the shallows first.

more quickly, and he will gain confidence in his ability to breathe, even though his chin rests on the surface of the water.

With confidence, your dog will enter water more purposefully. Some dogs are so purposeful that they leap as far as possible out into the water before starting their swim. This looks spectacular and shows a dog with determination and drive. It can, however, make the dog lose his mark on a bird, and, more important, if there are any obstacles he can hurt himself quite badly if he lands on one. How you stop a dog which enters water this way is a problem, and it may be a better course of action to make sure that there are no obstacles or dangers before sending him.

Whichever way your dog enters water, he should do it with a purpose and determination to reach the fallen bird. Most retrievers, probably because of their ancestry, have an inbuilt judgement of water flow. If you throw a dummy into a moving river and then send a Labrador, he will often not go straight to the flow but will aim slightly downstream, calculating his speed of swimming, the flow of the water and therefore the path taken by the dummy, so that he intercepts it exactly right.

Increase your dog's confidence in handling a wide variety of water types, and do not make the exercise too difficult. There are two problems that you may encounter: the first is when the dog drops the dummy after leaving the water, and the second is shaking. Some dogs do both together. With a dummy, no difficulties arise from dropping it, but can you imagine your dog coming back with a wounded bird which he then puts down while he has a shake? Off goes the bird, and another chase ensues. If your dog does not put the bird down while shaking himself vigorously, he can quite easily damage the bird. A retrieve from water should therefore be brought immediately back to you and placed in your hand before the dog is allowed to shake.

If your dog has been encouraged to return to you as fast as he possibly can on land, this problem may never occur. But if you have a sloppy return on land, be ready for a problematical one from water. The way to overcome or avoid these problems is to meet your dog, on the way back from the water retrieve, standing in the water. By standing in the shallows your dog will not have left the water, and will not be considering shaking. You will then be able to work gradually away from the water's edge. If at any time your dog looks as though he is considering putting the dummy down and/or shaking, say 'No!' very promptly and call him up with a very encouraging tone.

You must never appear to be concerned that you are going to be made wet from the dog shaking after he has presented the dummy. Put

A bold entry is exciting, but ensure there are no dangers at the water's edge. (Paul Pederson Action Snapshot Photography)

A powerful entry with all his attention focused on the bird he wants to retrieve. (Paul Pederson Action Snapshot Photography)

your leggings on or just ignore the fact that you have been showered, otherwise your dog may see this concern as something which he has to be wary of, and will stand away from you or put the dummy down just before reaching you. It will help if, when your dog delivers the dummy, you can get him to sit for a few seconds before stepping back a pace, saying 'Good boy' and then letting him shake. Everyone is successful and happy – and you are dry!

Directional training can be extremely valuable for retrieving from or across water. Often you will have to send a dog across a river and then direct the dog for a bird it has not seen down. It is important that you get the land training right first and that your dog is steady before you progress to directional training, but this should not stop you from introducing the dog to water and giving him simple retrieves. If your dog is not steady, and runs in when a dummy is thrown into the water, getting after him and stopping him before he gets the dummy in his mouth can be rather difficult!

More Waterwork

The very basics of waterwork are getting your dog into water and having him come back to you with a retrieve. But as anyone that goes hunting realizes, it is not always that simple. A fast-flowing river or tide can easily wash a bird very quickly from the fall area; even a strong wind can move a floating duck some distance from the fall. Also there can be obstructions in the water, such as rushes, reeds, fallen branches, and for tidal waters, waves obstructing the dog's view of the fall as he swims out – plus, of course, mud: a big obstacle for many dogs unless they have experienced it. So often, although our dog is good at what we give him to do in training, he struggles on the real thing because we never really prepare him for what we will encounter in the shooting field. For example, a simple thing, how many train their dog to sit in a hide and catch only a glimpse of a falling bird, plus hear the shot from inside the hide? We expect them to be able to handle this even if we have never prepared them for it before.

To be really sure of your dog and its ability to deal with many differing situations, it is only fair to prepare him as much as is feasibly possible. In summer the conditions are not the

Teach your dog to go over to a far bank, and return promptly… (Arno Brosky)

same as winter, but we can simulate many situations to some degree. Part of the training for duck shooting in winter has to be to get your dog marking the sound of a splash, especially in poor light. Therefore once you have him confidently retrieving from water, take him out in the early morning or late evening when light is poor, and start with short retrieves, building up

…the same as on land. Your dog should ignore other distractions and bring back the retrieve he has been sent for. (Arno Brosky)

to more difficult ones over rushes and behind bushes along the bank. Teach him to mark with his ears.

A word of warning, however, when you cannot see very well either: always pre-check the areas you are asking him to enter the water when at dusk you cannot see what is there yourself. The last thing you want is your dog injuring himself on hidden stakes or other obstacles.

However you progress in water, the most important preparation is to get your training right on land first. If your dog is obedient and willing

Underwater obstructions such as water lilies can create problems. Teach your dog to handle these. (Paul Pederson Action Snapshot Photography)

Looking for the handler, intent on getting it back to hand. (Paul Pederson Action Snapshot Photography)

on land, then water is a steady progression; if he is not right on land, then there is no way you can correct him in water, and he will learn that all too quickly. Once I have my dog entering water confidently I start to angle the retrieves so that he works and enters the water at varying angles and distances from the bank. I give retrieves among rushes, reeds, water lilies and other water plants as his ability and confidence grows, and in this way he becomes skilled at swimming or marking over or in them. Reeds and rushes can be a big problem for some dogs, as they will stick in them and hunt, rather than go through to get to the fallen duck on the other side. If you lower your head to your dog's eye level you will realize why this is. He sees it fall and it looks to him as though it is in the reeds. From our height we can see, and we know from experience it has fallen beyond. In addition, reeds and rushes hold scent that is like a magnet to a dog; it only needs one hiding moorhen or coot to create a strong distraction.

So now we have to get him 'punching' through reeds and recognizing that a retrieve lies on the other side. Teaching your dog to go back on hand signals is a great help, but repeated practice at retrieving over rushes or through a riverside bush quickly develops a dog's natural ability to recognize the situation. With some it takes time, yet others seem to get the idea very quickly, and they keep going in a straight line through everything until they hit scent or see the bird. These dogs have a confidence in their ability to mark the line of a fall, and if it isn't where they thought it had fallen, then they realize it must be further out on the same line.

When your dog has become confident at retrieving from water, begin to give him retrieves across to the far bank. Initially make the distance across the water short, but then build it up, and also of course increase the obstacles along the way to the retrieve. The reason for this is that once you have your dog finding dummies in the water, he can easily begin to assume that everything shot falls in the water. Therefore, for the situations when a bird falls on the far bank, he needs to be taught to get over and not stick to swimming around in the water. Even when you have got a dog that will swim over to the far bank, you then have to teach him to go through the reeds on that side also. Again, these can hold

Happy tail, not stopping to drop the bird or shake. (Paul Pederson Action Snapshot Photography)

No shaking even if your coat is full of water. (Arno Brosky)

a lot of scent, so your dog needs to be taught to go right over and hunt the far bank when required. Repetition to give experience helps tremendously, but once you have taught him to handle on land an unseen retrieve (dummies that he has not seen down), this ability will provide you with a first class way of picking those elusive birds over water.

Depending on your dog's age and ability, plus the length of retrieve, give him three or four retrieves across water, and then possibly one in the water. Often I will throw the last one in water as a 'diversion' to simulate me shooting another duck while he is retrieving a previous one. Again, this must have been done on land first to obtain the control and obedience. Once he is good at working on this distraction, you can begin to do double retrieves, and even throw another dummy as the dog is swimming out to one and tell him to leave it and get the original. On shooting days all types of situation can occur, and your dog has to handle them, so build up his abilities gradually and then set up realistic scenarios.

The most important bird to get when shooting is the one that is wounded or is floating away. Easy birds we can pick at leisure, therefore your hunting companion needs to be taught to take commands and pick the ones that will prove difficult to collect if not done promptly.

Dummy launchers are quite useful for wide rivers and lakes when you are working alone or there is no bridge close by, but don't use a launcher ball as this can cause the dog to gag as he swims back. Use a launcher and thrown dummies, and begin to build up working situations to simulate runners, unseens and dead birds on and over water. A wildfowler's dog may also have to face decoys, and these can be very distracting so it is wise to familiarize your dog with them. Some dogs will spook at them, others will go across to investigate and forget what they were sent for, and on occasions a dog can become quite afraid of them if it gets tied up in the anchoring strings and panics. Initially lay them out in a field and let your dog walk around to sniff and check them out; then follow up with some simple retrieves through them. Once he is totally ignoring them on land, set them up on water and again do some simple retrieves among them and then through them, until the distance the dummy falls behind is long or on a distant bank.

Go to different stretches of water with more difficult entries and exits; not everything is easy, and your dog has to learn to negotiate difficult banks. Usually a dog will attempt to exit water the way he has gone in, but sometimes he will attempt to take a short cut to the nearest shoreline, or he may be washed downstream by the current where that point of exit could prove to be difficult. Therefore you have to teach him to keep his head and find ways out that he can manage. When working him, if there is any doubt and he is struggling, never be slow to go forwards to help and guide him.

For anyone who shoots where there is water, it is worth spending time training your dog in water. For the enthusiastic wildfowler it is essential, and will minimize the loss of birds. Nothing brings a thrill to the heart like a dog that is seen coming back, duck in mouth, after a difficult retrieve in water – it feels better than any shot you can make. Therefore use the warm summer months to build the experience and training, and have fun doing it – your dog will.

Chapter 8

Developing the Hunting Instinct

Hunting is one of the basic natural instincts of a dog. In the working gundog this instinct has been maintained, even enhanced, through selective breeding and training. It is an important feature of gundog work, in my mind the most important. The retrieve cannot be carried out unless a dog has found the dummy or shot game, and in the case of spaniels and pointers the game cannot be shot until the dog has found and flushed it. Without hunting ability, the amount of game brought to hand will be reduced dramatically.

A working gundog should be a natural hunter, but some owners without thinking actually repress this natural skill. The busy little spaniel that is always 'buzzing' about and gets under the feet is taught to walk on the lead and at heel, or constantly nagged to be still because of the fear of losing him in the countryside. I have experienced Labradors that have become so reliant on their owners, they are constantly looking to them for help, and not achieving the balance between hunting, using their own initiative, and obtaining owner guidance when the real need arises or the owner demands it.

Puppies love to explore and experience scent: encourage them to do so while you are close by. If they are keen on retrieving, let them find the occasional ball or dummy in the cover, and then encourage them back to you with it. Some puppies can get bored with hunting unless they find something of interest, others will hunt a 'billiard table' with eternal optimism. Judge the type of dog that you have, and adapt your hunting training accordingly. Hunting, like all aspects of training, becomes interesting when your dog is successful and gets enjoyment from being successful. Success will breed success.

Begin to use the hunting commands. For the dog that has been sent for a retrieve and is in the area where a dummy has fallen, the command 'Hi lost' is used to encourage the dog to hunt that area out thoroughly. If you are lucky, you will have a dog that is a natural, and sticks to his ground once he is given the command or touches recognizable scent. Other dogs have to be taught to stick to their ground by controlling them within the required hunting area. If they begin to move away from the area where a dummy is down, encourage them to return to the 'drop zone'.

DEVELOPING SCENT SENSE

Much of this hunting ability will develop from the dog's skill at picking up and reading scent. You will be able to help the dog in this development by watching his actions and noticing when he is hot on scent, when he is not, and when he is moving away from the hot zone, and by acting accordingly. Experience is essential for the dog to develop scent sense, but you must try not to give him the experience by having too many retrieves, or letting him hunt where there is a lot of live game: build it up a bit at a time.

Begin by hunting your dog into the wind so that the scent is being brought to him. This will give him a greater chance of success, and will minimize the risk of him running too far forwards, because he can work up to the scent. If the wind is behind you and the scent is being carried away from the dog, young dogs tend to hunt further and further ahead. This is called 'pulling', and causes problems in that if a spaniel 'pulls' too far ahead, he can flush game out of gunshot.

A useful aid to develop hunting is the tennis ball. Smaller than a dummy, it can tuck down amongst cover and therefore needs more perseverance on the part of the dog to find it. As he gets more experience, push the ball under cover – tuck it under a grass sod so that the dog only receives a small whiff of scent, and really has to work body and mind to locate the ball. Why make it difficult? The reason is, of course, that birds and rabbits are not always shot in the open; most fall into cover, and some wounded ones will tuck in under roots, down rabbit holes and into other little nooks and crannies.

As your dog gains experience on the real thing you may also find that he not only learns to hunt the ground, but also above his head, because game can get caught up in the branches of bushes and trees. One flatcoat, in particular, that picked up on a shoot where I worked my dogs, did this very well: he would find hung-up birds, and if he could not reach them, he would sit under the bird and bark until the owner came and gave a hand. I also knew another 'flattie' that did the same thing, except that he did not bark and therefore the owner had to play 'hunt the dog'. The sight of this handler peering into bushes and hedges looking for his dog and cursing its very being, in not too quiet a tone, always caused amusement.

THE HUNTING SPANIEL

The main task of the spaniel in the shooting field is hunting. There is nothing more exciting to me than working behind a good, stylish hunting spaniel, one that works every piece of potential game-holding cover, and drives through that cover in such a way that any game residing there is left in no doubt that it should move very promptly indeed. To see a keen spaniel enter cover, work it out fully, change up a gear at the touch of live scent, drive that game out to the waiting gun, and then sit and wait on the flush watching the game away, is pure poetry.

As the rough shooter's dog and a beating dog, the spaniel needs to cover its ground thoroughly. A good hunting pattern will ensure that game is not missed. If you have a rough shoot where there is only a small amount of game, the thoroughness and efficiency of the pattern can determine whether you have a shot that day.

Developing the Hunting Pattern

As I mentioned previously, if you have bought from good stock, and encouraged your dog to hunt, the act of hunting should not be a problem. You will, however, have to work at developing and maintaining hunting pattern and hunting distance. If you consider that the maximum normal killing range of a shotgun is 40yd (36m), then in order that you have a chance, your spaniel should be working no more than about 20 to 25yd (18 to 23m) away from you. At this distance, if a bird is flushed and flies directly away from you, it should still be within killing distance by the time you have got your gun to the shoulder. In practice, the good handlers keep their dogs closer most of the time, taking all the ground in small 'bites'. In this way, if a bird is flushed it will be seen, and will be flying for longer within the range of shooting; the gun has a less rushed shot and more chance of success.

From the moment you get your spaniel puppy, encourage it to hunt about and explore new ground – but don't encourage it to explore the ground away from where you are. Keep your pup close; in fact with a young pup, I like them on the end of my toes. When they get older and more aware of game scent, they will 'pull' away from you, so the risk of you falling over them then will be most definitely minimized. Too many people think that they have to encourage their spaniel to get away from them, but in fact the problem then is, as they get older, to get them back close enough. It is easier to push a dog out later when he has the habit of keeping close, than trying to bring him in close when he has the habit of being away from you.

A ground with game scent will help to create interest in hunting, but make sure that the ground is free of live game. This may mean that you have to walk the ground or hunt an older dog over it first. It may be a chore, but it is good training for the older dog if you have one, and will avoid problems with your younger inexperienced one. Take your young dog to the ground on a lead, sit him down, remove the lead and make him wait before casting him off to the side, with the command 'Seek on', and clicking the fingers (a habit of mine!). I usually sit my dog on the left of my body and cast him

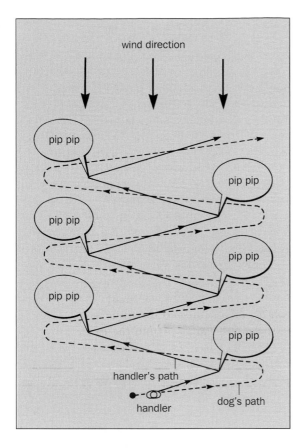

wind direction

pip pip

pip pip

pip pip

pip pip

pip pip

pip pip

handler's path

handler

dog's path

The path of the handler and spaniel, when first developing a hunting pattern.

off with the right hand across to the right. This routine will be the normal one on a shoot day, so it is advisable to accustom the dog to it from the beginning.

First of all, work into the wind in light cover. To develop the pattern of hunting, walk a zig-zag path with your dog. After casting him off to the right, walk with him a short distance to the right (about 10yd/9m); then with two short pips of the whistle to catch his attention, do an almost about-turn, and walk slowly to the left, encouraging him in that direction. Again, after walking a short distance, catch his attention with two short pips of the whistle, and turn back to the right.

The aim of this exercise is not to move forwards, but to get the dog to cover his ground from side to side. As you walk along, encourage him to investigate each little piece of cover by rattling it with your hand, and encouraging him

with your voice. Be consistent in the timing of blowing your whistle, and the distances walked from side to side; this will create a habit pattern in your dog, and he will quickly learn when to expect the two pips and will know what they mean.

You may not feel at first that you are covering sufficient ground, but don't be tempted to walk too far to the left or right, or to walk forwards too fast. Walk at a pace that will allow the dog to cover the ground and investigate it thoroughly. More important, don't walk fast to keep up with your dog if he is not covering the ground correctly.

After a while you will find that the dog will begin to turn naturally at the distance you were going to blow your two pips, and also that you will not have to walk to the left or right. The half-way stage is where you turn only your body to the right or left and indicate with your hands where you want the dog to go. The polished product is where you walk in a straight line, gun in hand or hands in pockets, and the dog does it all with only the occasional guidance and check.

Hunting in Cover

Gradually increase the density of cover that your dog has to hunt. Introduce him to reeds, heavy tussocky grass, bracken, bramble, and, unfortunately, nettles, though I tend to leave nettles until the underbody of the dog has toughened and the nettles are not young and freshly full of sting. As you increase the density and complexity of cover, your dog will grow in confidence.

Be careful that this confidence does not lead him to hunt further away from you than you wish. Bushes such as rhododendron often hold birds and scent, creating a hunting desire that pulls the dog away from you. As you may lose sight of him, this can create a problem, and hunting a dog in such cover requires as much skill from the handler as it does from the dog. By the time you put your dog in such cover, the stop whistle, the turn (two pips) and the recall should have been ingrained into his consciousness: using all these, the control of your dog is in your hands, and you must learn to judge the situations as they arise.

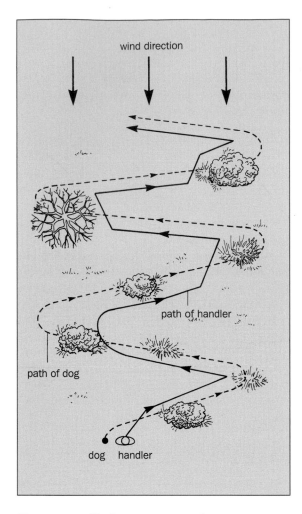

Using cover and bushes to encourage a hunting pattern.

Hunting in Kale

The one piece of cover I dread for a young spaniel is a field of high kale, where your dog is out of sight the moment he enters the field. As he gains experience and you feel that you can trust him, you may risk allowing him to hunt out kale. The birds running under the kale and the trapped scent can, however, create too much excitement. My advice, particularly with a young dog, is to put him on the lead and walk through the kale together. Some older dogs learn to hunt and then stand on their back legs to see where their owners are, before disappearing and continuing the hunt. I have been beating on estates where the keeper actually asked the dog handlers to put their dogs on leads while they walk through the kale, as the resultant flush could be less than controlled otherwise.

One of my experiences in kale was at a trial, where the field we were asked to hunt had been sown with the crop. The dog and handler in the line with me on my left were lucky, they had the short kale on the edge of the field. I had the long stuff! From the moment I cast off my dog neither myself nor the judge could see him work, only the movement in the kale tops indicated where my dog was hunting, plus the quick bob of a brown head above the sea of green as he checked where I was. He flushed a bird from the kale, which was shot and dropped into the crop. I sent the dog by voice as he couldn't see me, and when he returned with the bird I put my hands below the level of the kale tops and took it. How the judge could mark all the work of my dog I do not know. I do know I was pleased to be out of it, though, when he said, 'That will do you'.

A lovely story I was told, which was reputed to be true, concerns a very well-known trialler and trainer who was running a Labrador in a trial. Again, the crop they were walking through with dogs at heel was high kale. The handlers could only keep a passing eye on their dogs by pushing the kale to one side with their hands and looking down to see if their dogs were still where they should be. As they walked along, a bird took flight and was shot. The trialler was asked to send his dog, at which he parted the kale to give the dog the instruction. The dog was not there. Being very quick in mind and not without a little cunning, the trialler pushed his hand forwards in the direction of the retrieve and said 'Fetch', then stood back to watch his imaginary dog take off after the retrieve. Unfortunately his luck did not hold, and the dog did not get into contact quickly enough to get the bird, but it does highlight the problem of kale.

Dealing with Wind

Once you have your dog hunting well into the wind, you can begin to help him deal with wind coming from different angles. Always be aware that a dog will prefer to hunt into the wind if he can, and should turn at the end of each cast into the wind so as not to miss any potential scent. You should therefore be aware of where the wind is coming from, and work your dog accordingly. The windscreen-wiper action left to right in front of you may look good, but if the wind is blowing from left to right across the front of you, your dog should be working into that. If the wind is behind you, then your dog should be going out away from you and working the ground back to you.

With good training and consistent working, taking into account the wind and therefore the direction of scent, your dog too should become scent and wind conscious.

GAME AND GUN SENSE

One other ability that comes with experience is game and gun sense, where the dog, realizing the position of the gun, actually works the game out so that he flushes to the gun. It is very difficult to teach, but dogs that are shot over regularly realize that, by working the game in such a way that you can shoot it, this results in them receiving the final pleasure – a retrieve.

During the hunt you will expect your dog to sit when a shot is fired, a bird is flushed, or when you just want him to stop. So while hunting up a young dog, as he crosses in front of you and is so near that you know he will respond, blow the stop whistle and raise your hand to signal the sit. Don't do this too often or you will end up with a 'sticky' dog which is constantly expecting to be stopped.

Advanced hunting of a spaniel – a following wind.

Advanced hunting of a spaniel – a cross wind.

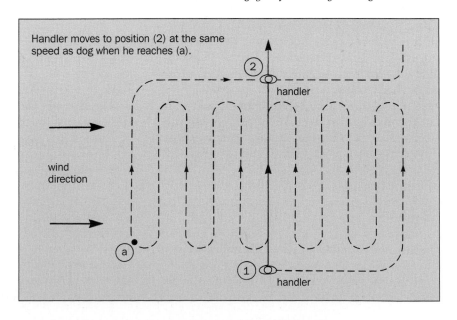

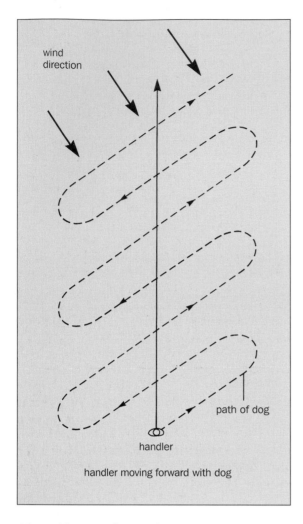

Advanced hunting of a spaniel —
wind from the left quarter.

If he doesn't stop quickly enough to the stop whistle, go back to the basics and put him on the lead. Walk him along, blow the stop whistle and make him sit promptly by jerking him into the sitting position. Remember, however, that while the dog is hunting, he is satisfying a natural animal instinct which can make him oblivious to everything around him. So initially when you blow the stop whistle, do it with a very positive hand signal and with a determined blow, even moving sharply towards the dog to catch his attention.

Once the sit is an instant reaction to your whistle, you can increase the distances at which you should be able to stop and sit your hunting dog. It is also advantageous to introduce the handclap as a sit signal while he is hunting. After

you have introduced him to gunshot, you will be able to use the starting pistol or the shotgun itself.

TEACHING THE HUNTING PATTERN

Not every gundog hunts naturally; some have to be encouraged and shown that there is pleasure in the work. It can be done by hiding a dummy or ball, which the dog can find. To develop the quartering action in a dog which is reluctant to hunt, hide a number of balls or dummies in a zigzag pattern and then encourage the dog to find each one by working from side to side. Some people have had success by hiding toys and other objects in their living room – under cushions, rugs and newspapers – and then encouraging the dog to find them. This game is then extended outdoors.

Where a dog wants to hunt too far away, I will throw a ball or dummy just in front of me and wait for him to come back, and place myself so he finds it in his path. Then I begin to use the recall whistle, which I gradually reduce to become the turn whistle to do this, and quickly he begins to believe that all the nice things happen just in front of me.

Where I have a dog that only stays close to me, I will hide dummies and tennis balls out to the side, and guide him out sideways where again he will find. As the dog progresses you can do this with dead birds or even a pigeon, which he can flush and it will then fly home. In America pigeons are used extensively to train hunting pattern in a spaniel in this way.

The really nervous dog or reluctant hunter may need more adventurous methods, and you may have to go to the extreme of allowing him to work on live game, even to the extent of letting him chase a few times, to develop interest and enthusiasm. I often feel that for the ordinary shooting man, a dog that stays calm and does not hunt like a demon initially, because you have imparted a high degree of obedience and control, becomes the ideal dog. Over-control in the early stages is better than too little control. You can always relax your dog and yourself, letting him hunt more freely, but if you let him get away from you in the early stages and lose control, you may have a very hard job getting the desired control back.

Spend time developing your dog's hunting pattern, encouraging him to quarter the ground thoroughly. You may find that at first the pattern is quite haphazard, the dog even going behind you from time to time. Don't make a big thing out of this, but encourage him to work in front, and put yourself in a position where you can guide and help. If your dog enters cover willingly, let him use his initiative, providing that you do not lose contact. Too much whistling can bring about 'whistle deafness', the whistle just becoming a background accompaniment. The other extreme is where you whistle and over-control so much that the dog loses his drive and becomes uncertain.

While your spaniel is hunting, you will need to simulate the flush of a rabbit or bird by throwing a dummy or ball across his path, and sitting him with the stop whistle and hand signal as soon as the dummy is released. Pick many of the dummies yourself, leaving the dog on the 'drop' (sitting). Occasionally, send your dog for a retrieve, but make sure that you do not throw dummies too often for your dog while he is hunting; if you do, he will begin to anticipate the throw and watch you, rather than hunting. The dog can then become very 'sticky', not wanting to hunt but waiting for you to throw. It is quite amazing how some dogs, even though they appear to be hunting, notice the slightest movement of your hand to the dummy bag or pocket, and sit waiting for the throw.

If this begins to happen, hunt the dog for a few weeks without any retrieves at all; maybe even take him to very scenty ground so that there is more interest in the scent than in the dummy. If you ever go to gundog tests for spaniels, you will see the type of spaniel that has been over-dummied while hunting or has become test conditioned. He appears to be quartering his ground but he is not really hunting: the head is up and he is bouncing over the tops of the cover waiting for the slightest movement from a dummy thrower or gun to herald the retrieve. Usually, once a dog is doing this consistently, it is time to stop the thrown dummy and introduce him to the real thing.

The pace of your dog will alter with scenting conditions and type of cover, so do not expect him to hunt in the same way each time. Sometimes scent will be high, other times low, and it will also vary in intensity. With experience, your dog should learn how to pick up the scent and use it. So many people expect a spaniel to have his nose always firmly glued to the ground. Although this may be the best position for it to pick up the type of scent that is of interest most of the time, occasionally the scent may be higher and 'floating' above ground level. Watch your dog; the clever one uses all levels and works out the best trail of scent to lead to the eventual goal – live game.

By reading your dog as he is hunting, you will receive many signals: the change of pace, stepping up a little as it hits scent, the tail becomes more lively, even the steps become shorter and the action more perky and purposeful. The head will lift as the dog begins to bring into play ears and eyes as well as nose. There is a sense of excitement and anticipation as your dog tells you that there is game here for the gun.

With young dogs, there is sometimes a tendency to dwell on old scent. If you think this is the case and the bird or rabbit has already gone, say 'Gone away' and direct him in the opposite direction, away from the place of interest. When your dog becomes more experienced he will very rarely mislead you. Many is the time that after flushing one bird my dog has gone back into the same clump of cover and flushed a second, when I had been thinking he was dwelling on the interesting scent of the first. If you can see that there is no game present, and your dog is dawdling on one spot, then encourage him to hunt on. Once he begins to potter, he isn't really doing the job of finding game.

Good Hunting Habits

Good hunting habits are developed from natural instincts, with you and the dog working together to ensure that you read each other, and leave no blade of grass undisturbed in the search for game. After developing a good pattern in woodland and field areas, it is worthwhile developing the hunting ability in hedgerows and ditches, up steep slopes and down sharp banks. If you are a rough shooter you have to try every possible hiding place, so look for the difficult type of terrain the dog will have to hunt, and build the experience of yourself and your dog in handling these awkward landscapes.

Although a lot of retriever work is at a distance, there are times when the dog will have to work close and 'sweep' the ground in search of fallen game. It can be quite beneficial to have a Labrador that will work close and hunt in a similar fashion to a spaniel, particularly if your sport is picking up after a shoot. To do this, work your Labrador as you would a spaniel on hidden dummies that are a short distance away, encouraging him to hunt the ground thoroughly and not dash off to the usual distance a dummy may have been thrown or hidden. Once more, make sure that the dog succeeds quickly to start with, as nothing develops enthusiasm as much as success.

WORKING A CLOSE PATTERN

Hunting a good pattern so your dog does not miss game is important, otherwise missed game means no shot. One of the traps that many handlers fall into is allowing their dogs to pull steadily away from them until at times they are working out of gunshot range. The solution many handlers seem to adopt is to walk as fast as possible to keep up with the dog. But this leaves you with another problem, which is that in walking at a speed necessary to keep within gunshot, you are probably missing a lot of ground, and cover which could hold that elusive rabbit or bird.

Your dog needs to be trained to work an effective pattern of ground which takes into account wind direction, scenting conditions and type of cover. This pattern should be such that nothing is left unchecked, every tussock, bush, bramble scrub, whatever has to be gone through and worked well. Some of the early trials this year have been run in awful weather, with heavy rain, wet ground, tucked in rabbits and poor scenting conditions, which meant that dogs had to cover nearly every inch of ground; even hunting a foot one side of a rabbit usually meant that it was missed, as scent was just not carrying. These extreme conditions are rare, but they do occur.

There are some grounds where scent is notoriously poor, and what causes it we can only guess at; and not only are there these grounds

that produce little scent, but even odd corners of usually good scenting ground can be poor. Therefore the essential training in your hunting is to get your pattern right.

When hunting a young dog I like to have ground where I can see it at all times; reeds and rushy grass is ideal, but light woodland bottom and stubble turnip can also be perfect – in other words, somewhere where you can keep in touch. Generally when you first cast off a dog to hunt after it has been waiting, its pent-up energy causes it to go off in a rush, and if you are not ready it will have gone too far ahead of you before you can touch the whistle. So be prepared the moment you cast your dog off: have the whistle in your mouth and your concentration on full alert.

Where possible I always prefer to hunt a dog into the wind. It is difficult to teach a dog to take the wind direction into account when quartering – some dogs do it naturally, others never seem to get the idea – but if you work into the wind the dog tends to keep closer and develops a more even pattern.

When you do cast it off, cast it to the side and don't move forwards; give it the turn whistle, and bring it back across the front of your body, making sure that in those first steps you don't walk over ground that hasn't been worked. Get your dog going in the flowing 'windscreen wiper' pattern from the very beginning. Even if your dog ignores the first 'turn' whistle, get out and remind it to turn with a tug of the ear or a pull of the fur under its chin, pulling it towards you with a pip-pip of the whistle.

Some dogs turn on the whistle, look at you, see you are walking forwards, and come across in front much too far ahead. If this happens, try standing still as you blow the turn whistle, and watch whether your dog turns more towards you, coming into your body as it quarters. If it doesn't, give a recall whistle as it turns, bringing it in close before casting it off using a flowing hand movement in the opposite direction. Do this regularly, so the dog goes out, turns, and works back towards your body before hunting out in the opposite direction. After a while it will realize that it is expected to cross close to you, and a much 'flatter' pattern will result.

A 'flatter' pattern, where the dog is only moving a few yards forwards as it completes each beat, means that it has more opportunity of finding game simply because the pattern it is hunting must put it very close to the scent of anything that is tucked in.

During any training, or even shooting sessions, I keep my dogs working very close, especially a young dog. I can keep in total control this way, and they also begin to think that all the pleasures in life come from being close to me. If I allow them to range too far and find game, they will soon believe that all the fun lies out there, and that is where they will want to be. A young dog will tend to bore forwards as well as going out to the side, and you should stop this happening by turning it and not allowing it to go too far ahead.

Keep the patterning tight, no more than 15yd (13m) on either side and 5yd (4m) ahead. If you find there are large bushes that need working, direct the dog into the bush and within seconds use the recall whistle to bring it out again before putting it back in once more. This is essential with a young, inexperienced dog, to make sure it realizes you are still in control, even though you may be out of sight. Under these bushes lurk the dangers of running pheasants and rabbits. Your dog will quickly learn bad habits if it gets away with misdemeanours, because you cannot see what is happening. Can you imagine if, out of sight, your dog flushes a rabbit, and has a short chase before the rabbit goes down a bury. You, not knowing what has happened, recall the dog on the whistle, and then praise it for returning. Your dog, however, is still remembering the chase, which the praise reinforces – and that is not quite what you meant.

In the early days with a young dog experiencing game for the first time, don't be afraid to use the whistle regularly to turn him, bring him back in, and stop him on the flush. Learn to play the whistle like a 'controller', and make sure that he obeys every time: obeying only at the second blow is one blow too late. You may feel that you are blowing the whistle too much, but providing you are doing it correctly and at the right time, after a while you will need to blow it less and less. However, always be ready for the reminder in case there is ever a distraction that just pulls your dog that little bit further than is safe or good for the hunting pattern.

When you get into more haphazard cover such as scrub and woodland you cannot expect your dog to keep working the perfect left, right pattern, and he can miss ground – so this is where your skills come in, helping him to maintain his flow, but at the same time making sure that the bush he has overlooked is checked by directing him to it. If you miss it, you can bet there is a bird hiding in it.

Hunting a dog well needs practice; many handlers seem to spend considerable time on retrieving and handling their dogs on to retrieves, but unless we get the hunting right, we will probably have little to retrieve anyway.

SCENT AND SCENTING

Scent and scenting can have us talking and debating for hours on end. I have already mentioned a little on this, but want to expand further on the subject, and for that I make no excuse in repeating myself a little.

The main reason we have dogs when we go shooting is to find game that we could not find ourselves: first, hunting up unshot game hiding in cover, and second, retrieving it from places we would find difficult to get to, or tracking wounded game that has moved. Watching a dog 'use its nose' is, for me, the most exhilarating part of working him. To see a dog that can really identify the scent he is looking for, stick with it, work out where the bird is or has gone, and then home in on it before bringing it back to hand, is fascinating, mesmerizing and exciting.

Some dogs are born with what appears to be a good nose and are natural hunting dogs, sticking to a scent and determined to find the retrieve; others appear to have little 'nose' and may rely more on their eyes. In training our dogs, the development of 'nose' and scenting ability is essential if we are going to put game in the bag. The first step is therefore to watch and read a puppy, and determine what type of dog he is. Does he give up when he cannot find a retrieve, or does he stick at it? Does he seem able to follow the line of a rolling ball, or does he stay in one place and can't work it out? Watching our dogs, we can build a training programme that will develop the strengths we need in the field – and an essential one has to be scenting ability.

If a dog has difficulty in finding his retrieve and has to be right on top of it before finding, then naturally we may think scent is bad. But how much of it is bad scenting conditions, and how much is poor nose, lack of experience, or the intelligence that gives the dog the ability to interpret scent? In our training we should give our dog every opportunity to build on his experience and also to develop his ability to understand, analyse and work scent. Too often I have struggled on a retrieve with one dog, only to have a second one come in and find it as though there were a white flag marking the place. Nothing gives more satisfaction and pride than completing an 'eye-wipe', where your dog comes in and finds a bird that another dog or dogs could not find previously.

We have to ask ourselves, therefore, what gives the successful dog the 'edge', the ability to find where others have failed? Were the first dogs carrying their heads at an incorrect level to touch the scent? Were they working too fast or too excitedly to even catch or recognize the scent? Were their brain and nose switched on to scenting, or were they using just their eyes? There can be a number of reasons. The successful dog is one that can mark the fall and then, when in the right area, knows how to find and recognize scent and will follow it to the retrieve.

The Dog's Unique Characteristics

The average dog has 220 million scent receptors in its nose, we have five million. It has 7sq m (75sq ft) of nasal membrane that catches the scent and directs it to the scent receptors; we have ½sq m (5sq ft). If we add to this the fact that the dog has a larger proportion of his brain devoted to scent interpretation, then we can begin to realize how important a feature of the dog's natural abilities his nose and scenting is. When breathing in, the speed of airflow increases through the dog's nose because of its structure, and this 'turbo charging' enables more scent particles to make contact with and stick to the mucus on the nasal membranes.

To help a dog determine the direction of scent it has 'mobile' nostrils, moving from side to side, and although breathing will bring scent to the dog, the sniff is completely different from our own. It is separate to breathing, does not disrupt it and places the odours on a separate bony structure known as the Subethmoidal shelf, which humans do not have. From here the scent transfers to the nasal membranes and the scent receptors.

The other unique ability the dog has is to retain the scent above this shelf. Breathing out does not clean the shelf of odour, and scent molecules can accumulate. With this natural feature the dog has the ability to compare progressive sniffs more accurately than we can and therefore detect even the smallest increase in concentration of scent.

In addition to all these nasal abilities the dog also has a pouch lined with receptor cells above the roof of its mouth behind the incisor teeth, known as the vomeronasal organ. Although there are theories regarding what this organ does, no one really knows, but with all this sensitive 'apparatus' installed it must be doing something. This pouch opens both into the mouth and the nose, and it may be that as the dog begins to breathe heavily through its mouth, this organ again detects scent and tells the dog to switch on to the nose where it can concentrate the odours and locate the source.

Nose Sensitivity and Brainpower

The other main factor that affects the efficiency of your dog's scenting is, of course, its 'nose' and brainpower. It is thought that nose sensitivity is inherited, with the physical structure and brainpower being passed on from parents. Certainly scenting ability can be damaged by nasal infection, but physical damage will usually rectify itself. It therefore falls to us to build up our dog's experience, and its ability to read its nose. The trialling world has become very competitive in recent years, with the standard of the top dogs increasing, in my opinion, quite noticeably. Whether it is the hunting or retrieving breeds, there is more emphasis now on the dog's game-finding ability, and the top trainers spend a lot of time preparing their dogs by giving them real experience in the field on live game. Only in this way can the dog build up a wealth of experience not only regarding the behaviour of game, but also to do with the scents that it has to read to do its job.

When a dog works on scent he takes it from various sources: air scent, body scent left on vegetation, or foot scent left on the ground. There are also theories that dogs recognize the crushed grass or broken vegetation where a bird or rabbit has passed. The dog's nose is so complex and such a wonder of natural science, who are we to say they do not? With experience, a dog will learn to relate all forms of scent to the find or retrieve that he wants to make. He will learn the difference between a wounded bird and an unshot one, he will learn to recognize the smallest amount of scent as being a bird or rabbit that has tucked in tight, even though it does not move.

He will learn to recognize the direction a bird has run by comparing the slightest difference in scent along the track it has taken. Scent direct from the body in the air or on vegetation is probably the easiest to understand, but foot scent can be more complex, and your dog may be not just trying to locate the scent of the animal, but also reading the scent path from broken grass and other vegetation. There is also the thought that once an animal has been shot there will be a strong smell given off by the shot. The shot cutting through the air and leaving a trail is certainly of benefit to the many dogs which learn to read it. Good dogs will be seen working to the gun, not only watching, but also going over to the shooter and then taking a line out from him along the path of the shot.

To build the dog's experience at reading this scent I will often use live cartridges to shoot towards a hidden dummy, or have a thrower fire at a marked retrieve as it is thrown. I will also put empty cartridge cases in my dummy bag so the dummies get a touch of the powder scent. When shooting rabbits, taking a line is a valuable skill. However, your dog will have to learn to move away from where the shot hit the ground, and change from sticking on the strong shot scent to following a weaker one mixed with rabbit scent if the rabbit is wounded and moves. I have watched dogs learn this, and have come to the conclusion that a dog that has been given experience learns to use his brain to determine which scent he should be following. He learns to set priorities of scent to follow, and to learn, even reason, which is the best action to take to find the bird or rabbit we want.

Building Experience and Scent Intelligence

To achieve all this we train to build experience and scent intelligence. Some of this training is done in controlled exercises where we help and show the dog, but a lot of the training is done where we allow the dog to teach himself and gain knowledge from experiencing different situations.

As I have said on numerous occasions, we take a dog hunting to find and retrieve game that we would otherwise not be able to put in the bag, and in handling him there has to be a balance between allowing him to use his own natural abilities and experience, and controlling him to ensure that he gets the game we are looking for as quickly as possible. We need to work in partnership. In training we can, however, provide some of the learning experiences that will enable him to work more effectively and understand the scent he is looking for, while still maintaining and reinforcing the necessary control.

Where there is a lot of game, such as when you are picking up on a large estate, it is most important that your dog can differentiate between shot and unshot game. If ever you have attended a trial where dogs are sent for shot birds through fields of unshot game, and on occasions must even take the line on a wounded bird among unshot game, you could be, like me, amazed at their ability to determine the difference and stay on track. This comes from experience, and training. Firstly, a dog has to have the control, confidence and experience to get out to the fall of a shot bird, ignoring all other game and scent. Secondly, when he hits the fall area, he has to be able to differentiate between the scents, and identify that of the wounded bird. Blood scent is one factor that provides the difference, and the other is the scent of gunshot on the bird from the pellets it carries.

To see a dog take the track of a wounded bird through a field containing a lot of game that is either running or flying out is one of the most exciting sights in the gundog world. Even when there is not game, for a dog to take the track of a wounded bird, only seconds old, among the scent of birds that have now left the scene, is really amazing.

The best teacher is experience on the real thing; however, failing this, you can improvise in a number of ways, the most obvious being to lay a blood scent for your dog. This is done by dragging a dead bird or rabbit, with blood on it; it is tied in the middle of a long rope, which is held at the ends by two people, who will then of course be walking a path a small distance away from the dragged game. Initially make the drag a short one, then increase the distance. Take your dog to the beginning of the trail, and encourage him to hunt it until he finds the bird at the end of the drag – and very quickly he will learn to follow the line of the drag on his own. When that happens, put a few curves in it, and some right-angle turns.

Initially I prefer to have any wind movement coming towards my dog but as he progresses, by changing the line of the drag, he will gain experience at dealing with differing angles of scent created by the effects of air movement. Another way that is similar, but now includes a marked fall, is to have an assistant throw out a bird attached to a long piece of string. Once it hits the ground, pull the bird back to where a second bird is lying, not attached to the string. Send your dog only when the assistant has picked up the dragged bird.

A rabbit pen can be a very useful training ground to teach your dog to ignore unshot game and retrieve what you have asked him to. Teach your dog to retrieve dummies where he has to run through a group of rabbits (as described earlier): I throw feed down to encourage the rabbits to congregate in the middle of the pen, and then send my dogs for retrieves right through them. If you have the opportunity to do this, initially throw marked retrieves, then move on to memory retrieves, and finally do blind retrieves in the rabbit pen among the rabbits. During the shooting season, you can build on the experience by bringing home shot birds or rabbits and sending your dog for these in the rabbit pen.

If you know a gamekeeper who is well disposed to you, ask whether you can go into the pheasant pens and work your dog in this way. At certain times of the day and rearing season the keepers will be pleased for you to work on the outside of the pens, bringing the birds back in, and in doing so you can give your dog the occasional retrieve among them. I counted myself very lucky with one keeper who would allow me in at feed time and feed the pheasants around my dogs, which were then given the occasional retrieve either of a dummy or a dead bird among the feeding birds. This experience was invaluable. If you are able to 'dog in' for an estate, where the birds must be pushed back from the boundaries of the property, again you can give your dog retrieves where he has to collect among running birds, or at least where there is plenty of fresh game scent. This can be a very valuable exercise, especially for spaniels that have to switch between hunting for unshot game, which they should flush and not catch, to retrieving shot game.

In America, a common practice is to use live pigeons to encourage the use of the nose and provide a dog with the experience of tracking game. Clipping the flight feathers of one wing means that the bird cannot fly, and if left on the ground for a few minutes will walk. I generally use this as a memory retrieve, allowing my dog to see the bird being put down, then walking him away, before turning round and sending him for the bird. By increasing the distance, and also the time before sending him, the bird will walk further and further away from the fall area. In this way a dog learns to take longer and longer tracks to find the bird.

The other advantage to this is that I learn to read my dogs and know when they are on a track, because in longish cover I will not know where the bird has walked. On more than one occasion I have had a dog that gets to the fall area and then hunts almost all the way back to me before finding the bird at my feet. We expect the bird to move away from us, but of course that does not always happen.

Occasionally when shooting and more often when picking up after a shoot, your dog will have to work through the scent of birds that have already been picked. It can be quite frustrating when a dog sticks to an old scent and will not get out to where the actual bird you want has fallen. An exercise that can help your dog to recognize and go past 'old' scent is where you give him in-line marked retrieves, one after the other in cover where he cannot see the dummies and has to use his nose. With these marked retrieves your dog starts from the same place. The distance of the fall from your dog is increased by about twenty yards at each retrieve, and the dummies are thrown so that after the first, they fall directly behind the one that had been previously retrieved. In other words, the retrieves are at increasing distances and fall in direct line behind each other.

Once you have him recognizing and running through the old falls, you can now do this exercise using blind retrieves, and then substitute dummies for dead birds or rabbits. With this exercise allow your dog to gain experience, and check out the old areas if he stops at them. Give him time to think out the situation, and make the decision to cast himself further out towards where the dummy actually is. Only if he is dwelling too long on the old scent should you stop him and cast him out.

Some dogs are so quick they run over their nose and are too fast for their scenting ability. These flashy dogs catch the eye and are a delight to watch, but their game-finding ability can be weakened by their enthusiasm for speed. Other dogs appear to be thinkers, and when in the area slow down, lower their heads and really puzzle out what is happening. It is as though they are reading the scent 'book', finding out where the wind is coming from, changing their position to locate where the bird has fallen and slowly moving down the scent trail to their quarry. These can be quite difficult to read, as they are so methodical and not very animated. And of course, there are all variations in between.

What you are training for is a dog that understands and works at the 'speed of scent', in other words knows how to find scent over a wide variety of scenting conditions. A good game-finding dog is a shooting man's dream; add style and pace to such a dog, and you have a competition man's dream. As a trainer you can help develop your dog's ability to use its nose and interpret what it is telling him – dogs may be bred to have good noses, but with the right training you can develop it even further.

TRUST YOUR DOG ON SCENT

When we are watching trials and tests, and certainly when training or shooting, we often comment on scenting conditions, whether they are good, bad, fair. Usually we are judging the scent conditions on how the dogs have performed. If they have difficulty in finding birds and have to be right on top of them before either a flush or retrieve, then naturally we think scent is bad. But how much of it is bad scenting conditions and how much is poor nose, lack of experience, or the intelligence that gives the dog the ability to interpret scent?

If the majority of dogs are not having any problems with scent, then we often presume that the dog that is struggling on a find or a retrieve has a poor 'nose'. This is not necessarily so, it may be the different ground it is working. Some ground is good for scent, some poor, and the difference may be only a few yards apart. I have been to grounds where certain areas are called 'suicide corner' because scent in that area vanishes, and even dogs with proven noses have been known to fail regularly in this area. I can remember one trial at Scone Palace in Scotland that this happened, it was in a ploughed field where fallen birds were easy for handlers to see – but not so the dogs!

Early morning frost can create problems, and as it thaws the frost in the shade can remain bad for scent; but where the sun has begun to touch the ground it is much better. In fact the shade under trees even on fair weather days can create problems. Gateways, hollows in the ground and stubble fields have also been known to defeat even the best dogs as scent becomes fickle.

Our problem as humans is that we do not have the same scenting abilities as dogs. In fact the dog's scenting apparatus is known to be far more sensitive than even the best laboratory scent-testing equipment. Sniffer dogs for drugs, explosives and rescue prove the point. Because of all this we have difficulty understanding scent: we can hypothesize, but in the end we are guessing, intelligently maybe, but still just guessing, based on our experience of watching dogs.

The Scent Trail

Many have likened scent flow in the air to smoke rising from a smouldering fire. To some extent this theory can help. On a still day the plume will go straight up without spreading out, giving off only a small spot of scent. In a slight breeze it will move closer to the ground, dispersing and giving the dog more opportunity of catching scent. More fascinating are the days when smoke 'hangs' – it lifts a little and then forms a pale white sheet above the ground. Below and above that 'sheet', the air is clear. If the smoke were the scent from an animal, the dog would have to lift his head to the right level to catch the scent and be able to home in.

Where an unshot animal has been tucked in for quite a time, it may be only air scent that is detectable until a dog is almost touching it. A dog that works on air scent, such as a pointer or setter, with a high head carriage, would be better able to detect the scent, whereas a dog such as a spaniel working on foot scent, or even air scent at a lower level than the scent 'path', would have problems.

The scent trail must therefore depend on how high the plume of scent rises before it disperses or leaves a 'track' on the wind. All this is related to the heat of the animal's body, the heat of the ground and surrounding vegetation, the movement of air, and barometric pressure. A freshly shot animal should give off far more scent, made up of blood and shot scent, plus its natural body scent, than an unshot one. It is often thought that some animals, such as hares, can even suppress or minimize their scent, making them almost undetectable unless the dog happens to bump into them. A shot animal may also give off a different scent, created by the stress of being shot, that the dog will learn to recognize through experience.

Scenting Conditions

Moist, damp days with a light breeze seem to produce the best scenting conditions, especially if the ground is warming up and the air is cooler. But it is interesting to note that different grounds do vary in providing good scenting, no matter what the weather conditions are. On some grounds scenting is always good, while others have a reputation for poor scent. Whether this is created by the scent of the minerals that are combined in the soil, or the ability to deflect heat and body scent, I really do not know. For example, is scent better on sandy soil than on a clay-based soil? I have no research details to know.

Certainly there are few dogs that do not pick a bird when they know for sure it is there waiting to be picked. Why is it that so often we presume the dog is either refusing to pick, or stupid, simply because he does not pick a bird, even when it is in plain sight to us? The fact is, especially if he is an experienced dog, he has not 'seen it' with his nose. And frustrating as it is to us, although the dog is really trying hard to find the bird, he is just not touching the scent that will home him in on it. Anyone who has been in the field with a dog regularly has seen that pheasant lying in the plough with the dog running over the top, and especially the partridge in the stubble with its wings spread out for all the world to see, but which more than one dog has run over and not even recognized is there.

There is no doubt that some dogs are working purely on nose when they get into what they consider is the fall area: eyes get them to the right area, and nose then locates the bird. If they have switched off their eyes and are concentrating on nose, then there is no doubt that without the scent some dogs are 'blind'. A dog that has the ability to use its eyes and nose at the same time is a jewel.

In working our dogs, it is not just the ability of the dog to find scent, but also our ability to understand and recognize where it is coming from. With this knowledge we can help our dog by sending and directing him to where he can touch scent. We feel the breeze on our faces, we pick up tufts of grass and see where they blow, or as a smoker, we watch the flow of the smoke from a cigarette to determine where the scent is coming from, and where our dog may pick it up. However, the scent flow and conditions can be very different where the bird is. Hills, hollows, bushes, trees, woods and other physical features create swirls and change the air movement, sometimes taking it in a different direction, sometimes slowing it down or even speeding it up. With experience we can make estimations on what may be happening scentwise away from us, but it is not until our dog is in the area that we can really see what is actually occurring, because our dogs tell us.

Regarding good scenting conditions, my experience is that scent is usually very good over water. I have had dogs scent birds from quite a distance on many occasions, and these are birds

Increasing the Complexity

Throughout the preceding sections I have stressed that the training be gradual, and talked about steps in the learning process. It is up to you to determine how quickly your dog is progressing, and whether he is doing the present exercises well enough to progress to the next. You must also decide what constitutes complexity for your dog, and increase the difficulty of an exercise through the way it is done, or the terrain over which it is performed; in this way, the complexity of any future task can be minimized. The dog will be constantly building and storing experience which can be called upon whenever needed. Not only will the experience be there, but both you and your dog will have confidence in handling any situation that is likely to face you.

Introduce other types of dummy as the dog matures and handles the basic exercises with confidence. Rabbit-skin and feathered dummies can be used, as well as the plain canvas types. Always be ready for the potential problem: your dog may not like the new covering, or he may like it too much. So when introducing new dummies, watch carefully what happens. Before using a new dummy with a covering of rabbit skin or feather, rub your hands over it to put your scent on it; this will be more familiar to the dog, and can minimize problems. Use a canvas dummy for an exercise, followed by a covered one, and often the dog will pick up the new one without even realizing the difference. Always make sure, however, that the skins or feathers are not too fresh nor covered with blood, and as soon as the dog's head goes down to pick up the dummy, blow your recall whistle to speed up the action and the return.

High root crops, hedges, hills, ditches, fences and other types of terrain can increase the complexity of the gundog's job. By practising, and using dummies where these obstacles and natural barriers appear as part of the exercise, you and your dog can prepare for the real thing.

Never stop reading your dog at any stage of the learning process. There are times when training will go through the doldrums, and your dog seems to have hit a brick wall. Take your time, do the exercises that you can carry out successfully, and wait until your dog has overcome the barrier and is ready to continue his development. Increasing the complexity of the task too quickly can create problems. So watch, read, and act accordingly.

It is a fine balancing act that you have to make between putting enough difficulty in the task to make your dog think and learn, and asking him too much, creating too great a problem for him to solve. If you take the development of your dog and the further complexity of the task gradually, you should not encounter problems; if you do, then you have only to retrace small steps.

---

that are floating well down in the water and not easy to see. Of course there are few obstacles to deflect the scent, and possibly the dampness on a warm wet bird gives off more scent as it evaporates slightly with the body heat; I can only speculate, of course.

Finally, scent does vary with the type of game being picked – and some dogs do not like the scent of certain species. Woodcock and snipe can sometimes be extremely difficult for a dog to find; it may be the size of bird, and it might be the characteristics of the scent it gives off. There is no doubt that a dog has to be given experience in dealing with all types of game.

I also have no doubt that if a dog has been on rabbits for a long period of time, then its brain may not suddenly switch on to and recognize pheasants or partridge scent, and vice versa. Therefore a dog needs to have scent revisions to keep fresh in its mind what scents are to be sought and game to be picked. If your dog obviously does not recognize scent in an area where there is scent, and does not pick what you know he *can* pick, give him the benefit of the doubt and help him understand what he is looking for, and recharge his scent recognition cells. If he has picked game before, he is not ignoring scent on purpose – that I promise you.

Chapter 9

Further Training

DIRECTIONAL TRAINING

In the shooting field there will be times when your dog has not seen the game shot, so has not had the opportunity of marking a fall, and this is where training him to take directions becomes essential. A bird may have fallen across a river and there isn't a bridge in sight, which means that you cannot get to the opposite bank to help your dog or pick the bird yourself. Sometimes the bird that has fallen is wounded and you need to get your dog into the area quickly, even though he has not marked the fall, and start him hunting if there is to be any hope of picking this runner. One of the great pleasures of handling a gundog is being able to get him into an area, start him hunting, and then see him return successfully with the bird in his mouth.

I have heard some shooting people speak critically of directing a gundog using whistle and hand signals, but they are generally the ones who have not trained their dogs to do this. Usually these people say that the gundog should be able to find the game without being handled and shown exactly where the bird is – and to some extent there is truth in this. A dog that is constantly looking for direction and assistance is not using his own abilities and initiative. However, a dog that is using only his own initiative and is running anywhere and everywhere, can easily disturb unshot game out of gunshot, which means less for the Gun. The ideal situation is where the handler 'handles' the dog into the area of the fall, thereby causing minimum disturbance to unshot ground, and starts him hunting with the words 'Hi lost', when the dog then brings his natural abilities and skill into play to locate the bird.

To direct a dog, you must be able to stop him at a distance with the whistle, and then send him left, right or out, away from you, using hand signals and voice commands. By careful training you can also teach him to go away from you at angles, so if a bird is diagonally back from him you can send him directly there with one clear signal. If the dog always goes in straight lines, you will be moving him about on a chequerboard type of grid until he is in the right area for the hunt. With an 'angle back' you can cut corners and get him into the area with fewer commands and less disturbance of ground.

Always stop your dog on the whistle to catch his attention before giving one of the directional signals – and if you cannot stop him at a distance, you will find giving directions impossible. This is why the early foundation exercises are so necessary.

HANDLER POSITION AND SIGNALS

When we handle a dog at a distance we have to realize that although it has keen eyesight, sometimes the environment – such as background and lighting – can affect its ability to see clearly what we are instructing with our hand signals. For example, if we are wearing dark clothing or camouflage, with a dark background such as woodland or a hedge, the dog may not see us clearly at all – though if we are against a light-coloured background such as the sky, then dark clothing is good and easily seen. In addition we have to realize that on the occasions when the sun is shining, if it is behind our heads, then the dog is looking directly into it. And if we are standing in shadows, the dog again may have

You must be able to stop your dog on a whistle at a distance. (Jeff Beals)

Initially exaggerate your body movements, even stepping to the side for 'over' or moving forwards for 'back'. (Jeff Beals)

difficulty focusing; similarly, if you are standing in a line of people – such as you might be in competition – he may have difficulty in determining which is you, and the hand signal telling him which way to go.

Many handlers will wear light-coloured gloves or roll their sleeves up, and some will wear lighter-coloured jackets or very noticeable hats when running a dog, so they can be seen a little more clearly. In training it is important to be seen, and for the dog to understand exactly the hand signal command you are giving.

It is traditional and often encouraged to train a dog with the sit whistle and a hand signal, the sit signal being a hand up in the air like a policeman stopping traffic. I still do this in the early stages, but I phase out this hand signal, as the sit or stop whistle should be taught to mean stop and sit at any distance. The dog at this time is not looking at you, therefore in addition to gaining its attention, one whistle blast should incorporate the commands stop, sit, face me, look at me and wait for a command. With this taught, we now have our hands free in a neutral position. I place them in front of my chest, palms together as if in prayer (sometimes there is a small prayer 'Please go the way I am going to tell you').

From this position in front of the chest, we can now move the hand either upwards to direct 'go back', or to the side left or right, or at an angle from the centre of the chest upwards to indicate an angled movement back. This can be taught easily to the dog. So now we have a whistle command that asks the dog to stop and look. When he does, he sees a stationary figure. He waits for a command, and the arms make only one movement; they do not have to move from an arm up position meaning 'sit' into another before giving a new signal, and because of this the dog does not anticipate the command, and does not move on a transitional movement from the handler – the only movement he sees is the direction he has to take.

In the early stages when teaching the commands it is important to emphasize the hand signals by taking a step sideways when sending to left or right, and a step or two forwards when pushing back. This exaggeration can also be phased out as the dog learns, but can be used when he is a long way away from you, or the environment makes it difficult for him to see you.

(1) Preparation to give a direction signal: the prayer position.

Practise these movements and steps without your dog until they are clearly ingrained in your direction actions. So often we feel that the dog is going wrong wilfully, when in fact he cannot see you, or we have made a movement that is not part of the direction signal, and he has misinterpreted this. Clear, obvious signals are essential.

Sending the Dog away from You

When developing the memory and unseen retrieves, you may already have introduced the command 'Get out' which means 'move away from me in the direction you are facing'. We now have to introduce the dog to the idea that 'back' means 'when you are away from

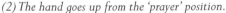

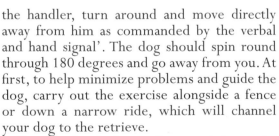

(2) The hand goes up from the 'prayer' position.

(3) 'Back': reach high, pushing the dog back. (Jeff Beals)

the handler, turn around and move directly away from him as commanded by the verbal and hand signal'. The dog should spin round through 180 degrees and go away from you. At first, to help minimize problems and guide the dog, carry out the exercise alongside a fence or down a narrow ride, which will channel your dog to the retrieve.

Sit your dog in front of you and throw the dummy over his head so that he can see it thrown and, by turning his head, see where it has landed. Take a step backwards, and giving the sit signal with the verbal command or as you progress, a whistle, and make the dog wait a second before pushing the signalling hand upwards, saying 'Back', followed immediately by 'Fetch'. Most dogs will come towards you

initially but if you encourage them, repeating the signal, the penny will drop and they will go and retrieve the dummy.

After doing this a few times you can increase the distance and drop the 'Fetch', which was only used as a familiar link in the learning chain, to help them understand 'Back'. You may also be able to drop the 'Back' command, if your dog reacts promptly to the signal with your hand. In fact, with some dogs it is better not to issue two commands simultaneously, even though they mean the same thing, because the dog's mind is so simple that he can only really take in one command effectively. So the movement of the hand alone is often more effective than if it is given with an accompanying verbal command.

Use a hedge to guide your dog ('Back').

To minimize anticipation, have a dummy in front and behind. Which one can he have? (Jeff Beals)

Increasing the Distance

Carry out memory retrieves using the 'Back' command and positioning. Then begin to increase the distance that you walk away from your dog before you send him out and away from you. He will need to become accustomed to being given directional commands from a distance, so build up the distances between yourself and him when you issue the command.

Use a little ingenuity to change the way you do this exercise or the sequence of instructions. The object is not to let your dog begin anticipating and acting before being instructed, so occasionally, call the dog to you before sending him out. Use a dummy in front of him, in other words between you and him to encourage him towards you. Occasionally, send him out a short distance, stop him and then send him out again.

Like so many exercises in training, this is a careful balancing exercise, because you don't want the dog to become sticky, where he only moves a short distance before stopping and asking, 'Are you going to change your mind?' You will find, however, that this stickiness will disappear quickly once you progress to the real thing.

When your dog is confidently going away from you on command, you can start to include unseen retrieves. At this stage some dogs, spaniels in particular, begin to learn that the best way to move off from the handler and have a better chance of finding a dummy is to take a zigzag course. Spaniels have had quartering developed in them anyway by your training, but with experience and practice most dogs will learn to go away in a straight line until stopped and given the 'Hi lost' command to hunt that area.

Once you have found that your dog is going away from you confidently along tracks and

'Back' – the one behind. (Jeff Beals)

'Here' – the one in front. (Jeff Beals)

with the fence to guide him, vary the terrain again and let him experience different situations. Don't be surprised if you have to take a few backward training steps when you do this. The fence and/or track can be a great benefit, but when it is removed, it can leave the dog a little confused. So be understanding, make the exercise simple, and progress only slowly to the more difficult, complex ones.

Although initially with a pup I may use the hand signal to give and reinforce a sit, I find that very quickly the one whistle blast is enough to make him sit, and then as my hands are in a praying attitude in the middle of my chest, the moment I begin to move it is much clearer to him exactly where I want him to go. The 'back' hand signal is raising my arm from my chest upwards, and it is far clearer to do this, than to have my arm raised high already (in the 'sit' position) when he looks back, and I must then attempt to send him back with a pushing motion.

Sending Left and Right

You can begin to develop your dog's ability to go left or right from a very early age – and once more, it is all linked with food. If your dog is steady to food being put down, make him sit to one side of the bowl before giving a clear left or right signal as an indication for him to move that way for dinner. However, because he does this, it does not automatically follow that he has totally understood the signal: in his mind the signal just means food, not go left or right. But it is the start of a sequence of learning.

When your dog is steady to the thrown dummy, sit him down and throw a dummy to the right. Then, with a clear signal, push your hand out to the right, telling him to 'Fetch'. Make sure that these signals are clear. Do not use a pointing finger, but an open hand and an exaggerated movement, your body bending in that direction. Do the same with a left-hand dummy

Directional training use of corner of field ('go right').

Use of hedge to guide when starting directions ('go left').

A good, clear signal – right. (Jeff Beals)

A good, clear signal – left. (Jeff Beals)

and signal. A hedge or the crossroads of country paths can again help with this exercise; with his back to a hedge the dog can only go left or right. Slowly increase the distance away from your dog to give the signal, and obtain the desired response anywhere.

You can now introduce two dummies, one to the left and one to the right. Make your dog wait, and then clearly send him for one of them. Usually, it is better to send him for the first one you threw, as the inclination of the dog will be to go for the last one he saw thrown. When he has brought back the first dummy, praise him and take him to the exact spot where he was sitting when you threw the dummies; move back to where you were standing and then, with a clear signal, send the dog for the second dummy.

Build the complexity of this exercise by having one of the dummies as an unseen. At first, the unseen should be nearer to the dog than the seen, and the wind should be bringing the scent of the unseen towards him – everything has to be in favour of him succeeding. When you send him for the unseen, his initial reaction will be to go for the seen, or to sit still, uncertain what to do. Move forwards and encourage him to go

towards the unseen and find it for you. Success in this will develop a very close bond, where the dog begins to believe that you know better and can help him find what his heart desires – a retrieve.

In all these exercises I must reiterate that the dog needs to succeed. If at any stage he does the wrong thing, particularly picking the wrong dummy, take it from him, say nothing and go through the exercise again, trying to ensure that it is done correctly. When it is, you can then praise his success. Provided that your stop whistle has been correctly taught and the dog is under your control, you should be able to stop him before he picks the wrong dummy, and then guide him accordingly. If he gets quite close to the seen dummy before you stop him, bring him back to the start position by either walking him back at heel or calling him up to that position, before attempting to send him once again for the unseen dummy.

A further extension of this exercise is to have three dummies out, sometimes called the 'three card trick'. One dummy is thrown to the right, one to the left and one over the dog's head, behind him. You then proceed to pick the dummies in the order you require.

Three-card trick using white dummies and marker poles. (1) Go left.

(2) Go right.

(3) Back. (Jeff Beals)

Angle back right. (Jeff Beals)

Angle back left. (Jeff Beals)

Angle back to white dummies and a pole marker. (Jeff Beals)

Sending Back at an Angle

Once we can send our dog left, right and back, we can then move him around into the right area. However, we can minimize the number of movements necessary to do this if we can send him back at an angle, because using one directional angle back we can cut the corner that would otherwise take him two signals to negotiate. This is easy to teach, and your dog will pick up this signal very quickly once the right and left has been taught. To create this command, throw a dummy at a 45-degree angle behind your dog and send him with your hand angled to this amount in relation to your body. Teach a left angle back and a right angle back, and then you can put them both together, selecting which one you wish your dog to do when there are two dummies down at an angle behind him.

I have found this directional work very advantageous to enable your dog to get to a fall in the quickest possible time, and in fact as he learns, he will be able to understand differing angles to take from where he is positioned, based on the angle of your arm relative to your body.

PRACTICAL TESTS

You should now have reached a stage where you can hunt your dog, send him for seen retrieves, memory retrieves and unseen retrieves; you can also handle him on to unseen retrieves. With these skills under your belt, you and your dog can begin to handle a wide variety of situations. Set practical tests for yourselves, developing exercises and situations that simulate exactly what could happen on a shooting day, as here:

- Distractions – where a bird is seen to fall dead, but a runner was not seen by your dog and has to be picked first.
- Your dog is sent out on a retrieve, and on the return another bird is shot nearby. That second bird has to be ignored until the first is to hand.
- Your dog is sent for a retrieve, but another dog runs in and gets there first; your dog has to be called away and must return without a retrieve.
- Birds fall in difficult places, or tuck themselves into awkward spots. Your dog has to learn how to deal with this.
- A bird is seen to fall at a distance, but another has fallen unseen closer to you. You have to stop the dog going too far and hunt close.
- A dead bird is shot close but a runner falls at a distance. You must get your dog past the dead bird and on to the runner.

All these, and many more situations occur, which make demands on your dog and your own skills. Be creative in thinking of ways to develop these skills, and work hard at building them to make a complete team.

TRAINING CLASSES

In my early 'dog days' I thirsted for knowledge about dogs, and training gundogs in particular. My first sources of information were friends who had dogs, but they generally admitted that they knew very little, only what they had picked up themselves. So then it was the book that became the source of all information, and I quickly accumulated a collection of 'how to do

it' books. I bought books by contemporary authors and I also sought out the older books by Carlton, Hutchinson, Sharpe and others.

Being in training (of people) as an occupation, I did realize that all books of this nature are written from a subjective viewpoint, and that dogs, like people, do not always obey scientific or technical rules. I therefore used the books to gain knowledge and obtain information on what dog-training techniques worked best for the authors. This gave me a pool of knowledge and ideas from which I could work, and which I hoped would inspire inventiveness. But the problem was, who would watch me, listen to me and advise me when I was doing wrong, or encourage me when doing right? This is where the training class came to play an important role in my potential role as trainer. And I found that not only did I gain skills, but also, with the right trainer, I was given the motivation to get out and do something with my dog.

The training class is a good way of getting advice and assistance specific to yourself and your dog. There are many gundog societies and other bodies or individuals that run training classes throughout the country, and it is easy enough to find one in your own locality by asking breeders, shooting organizations, country sports bodies and of course the Kennel Club at Clarges Street in London. However, I am sure I don't really need to say that by attending them, and by telling people that you are doing so, will not result in a trained dog: training classes are for training trainers, not dogs.

Your dog will learn from being at training classes and will gain from the experience, but this is minimal compared to what you, as a trainer, should learn and then put into practice when alone. My own feeling, however, is that although most people would agree to this, they do not in fact benefit as much as they might do from training classes: their will to concentrate and learn is not always 100 per cent. Many times I have looked back to a group of waiting trainees while running through an exercise with part of the group, only to see them chatting, rather than watching – as their instructor, I have certainly not become their 'centre of attention'.

The training class should not be the only time that your dog is being trained. It sounds obvious, but some participants at my classes have said that they are pleased to be able to come along as they don't find time to train the dog otherwise; one 'trainee' even went so far as to request more regular classes, as that was all the training the dog got. There is no doubt that some people are lacking in confidence and need encouraging, motivating and guiding, and this is as much a part of the training class leader's job as imparting the dog-training skills; but work must also be done with the dog at home.

At the beginning, the most successful classes for handlers are often where the dog is left at home and 'teacher' demonstrates what to do, preceded and followed by discussion. After this, the small-group practical workshop with dogs can be more rewarding and fruitful. But whatever the class, watch and learn from what others do. Listen to commands and the voice. Watch other communication signs between handler and dog – eyes, hands, body, face, voice. Notice where things go right or wrong. Why did it happen that way? Talk it through and gain more understanding and experience.

The training class should not degenerate into a series of tests where handlers are 'competing' rather than learning. It is all too easy to set a test that will give experience and skills to both dog and handler, and then not capitalize on it by examining what happened and why.

Whatever happens at the class, try not to take comments and criticism personally. If you and your dog are perfect, then there is no need to be attending classes. Training classes are not for everyone, and certainly some people are particularly averse to them.

The main benefit to your dog, apart from having a more knowledgeable trainer, will come from being amongst other dogs and experiencing 'crowds'. The training environment, however, can create a different dog while you are there. There are many distractions for him, and generally you, too, will behave differently. You may be embarrassed at being watched, or on the other hand you may try to 'show off'. You may not react quickly enough to what the dog is doing because you are waiting for the class trainer

Martin instructing at a workshop in Holland. (Arno Brosky)

To Jump or not to Jump

I am always in two minds whether to teach a non-competition dog to jump. Dogs that enter trials and particularly tests are often required to jump, and therefore they need to be taught. The countryside is full of large expanses of barbed wire as part of fences or topping walls, but this is nasty stuff, and if in doubt about a fence, do not ask your dog to jump it. I have seen bitches with ripped teats and dogs with even more sensitive parts damaged. The tears from barbed wire can be very painful and put your dog out of operation for a long time. But gundogs do have to cross obstacles – walls, fences, streams, rivers – and it is important to have the command 'Get over' understood and acted upon.

Don't start jumping your dog over high obstacles until his bones and muscles have had the chance to form. With most dogs, low jumping (up to 18in/45cm) at six months will be acceptable, but full fences should not be tackled until the dog is nearly a year old.

To start your dog jumping, get a piece of netting and set it low. Old sheep netting is useful, but not set to its full height initially. Lay the netting on the ground to start with, and encourage the dog to cross over using the command 'Get over'. You will probably find that the best way to encourage this is by jumping backwards and forwards over it yourself. Once the dog is jumping happily, raise the netting a little (6–12in/15–30cm) and repeat the procedure. Encourage the dog also by tapping the top of the net and saying 'Get over'.

When he is jumping confidently at each height, throw a dummy to the other side of the net and encourage him to retrieve. Jumping with a weight in his mouth demands extra confidence, so be understanding and supportive. Within a few days your dog will be jumping this netting confidently up to 2ft (60cm) high and more. He will also be enjoying it more than you may realize, because there is something about jumping that dogs revel in.

Use a low fence, here 18in by way of introduction. Straddle the fence and encourage the dog over. (Simon Parsons)

Stand on the opposite side of the fence and encourage the dog to you. (Simon Parsons)

A nice clean jump over a low fence. (Simon Parsons)

'Get over' (often abbreviated to 'Over') is a word that can now be associated with jumping over or crossing an obstacle. You can begin to use it to get your dog over a river or over an expanse of water on to an island, as well as over a wall or fence.

Every obstacle looks different to the dog and its level probably quite daunting, so don't forget to be on hand for encouragement and help until he gains in confidence.

After carrying dummies, introduce a cold bird – a pheasant; first over a low fence… (Simon Parsons)

…then over higher fences. (Simon Parsons)

Whatever the breed, teach them to jump. (Simon Parsons)

to tell you what to do – and concentrating on the 'teacher' often means that you are not concentrating on the dog: the result tends to lead to the statement, 'Well, he's never done that before!' when the dog behaves out of character.

Understand the problems of the training class, as well as its many advantages. A dog which performs perfectly at home, where he has become used to doing an exercise at a particular location, can behave quite differently at the training ground. So the more varied the training area, the better. The dog's performance will need to be completely independent of the place where the work is done.

For the dog at a training class there is the experience of new ground, scent, noise, scenery and particularly other dogs. It can also mean the opportunity to 'get away with being a little naughty' because the boss doesn't punish you when others are watching. There must be

a reason why a dog needs lots of practice and praise to get even the simple things right, but manages to learn the wrong things in one easy lesson. That one easy lesson can sometimes occur at a training class – so watch out!

It is essential to get a 'teacher' who knows how to train the type of dog you own. Although many of the basic principles may be the same for all types of dog, certain aspects are particular to individual breeds. The first training class I attended was run by a retriever man, and I had a spaniel. We learnt all the basics of retrieving well, but never how to hunt a spaniel. I was told it would come naturally for the dog. The spaniel became an excellent retriever, but I had difficulty hunting him close. An even greater problem was that because I gave him a lot of retriever training he became retrieving and dummy-mad, and on the real thing – very excitable! The fault really was mine. I hadn't read the personality of

Training class in progress.

Martin demonstrating training techniques at an International Association of Canine Professionals Conference. (Donna Young)

fall of a bird, and mark where it landed. Birds and rabbits do not leave the handler's hands before being shot, and therefore having human help can make the picture more realistic. The training class can be a good source of human assistance. But I must emphasize that anyone who provides assistance must know what he or she is doing and have particular skills — accurate, effective, dummy throwing being one of them. Throwing a dummy does need practice and a bit of 'knack' to get it right.

The training class is just one more aid to getting your dog up to a standard where he can perform well in the field. If you have understanding trainers and fellow students in a class, you can set up situations which you couldn't do on your own. An obvious one is your dog watching while other dogs retrieve; this will help instil the steadiness required even when other dogs are in action. With a group of people and dogs you can simulate shoot days and competitions to such an extent that when your dog actually takes to the field of action, he has already experienced very similar situations. He is therefore only taking small steps, which will enable you to manage and control him more easily. Use the training classes, and the wealth of experience and knowledge to be learnt there, to bring on yourself and your dog, and make them just one ingredient of your training 'mix'.

the dog correctly or the 'signals' he was giving me during training. I hadn't thought about what I wanted the end result to be, and just continued blindly on with the exercises of the training class.

Do put effort into training classes and practise the lessons you learn when you are alone with your dog. It really is a delight for a training class trainer to watch a dog and his owner growing together and becoming an effective working team.

Training and classes should not become a competition — dogs and trainers learn and grow at different rates. So don't be disappointed if you do not appear to be progressing as well as others: your dog may well be a late developer.

When you first start training your dog it is better to do the training alone, but eventually your dog and yourself will gain from having the occasional intelligent, carefully briefed or knowledgeable human help. Dummies thrown at a distance will help the dog to look for the

Martin explains his approach to the audience. The pup is six months old. (Donna Young)

Chapter 10

Moving Up to the Real Thing

ARE YOU AND YOUR DOG READY?

One popular question that is always asked when I am talking to a group of people interested in training a gundog is, 'When should I introduce the dog to game?' The answer is easy: 'When it is ready.' This is not a flippant answer because there is no standard age at which every dog should be introduced to game. Some dogs need to be introduced early to encourage and interest them, others have to be well disciplined and under control if you are to have any hope of 'holding them' when there is game around.

There is a transition period when your dog will work perfectly on dummies and even cold game, but this does not mean that you should be able to give him a full day's work in the field at a shoot. The excitement of the moment, the sounds of beaters, birds taking off, guns firing not just once but many times, birds falling from the sky, fluttering on the ground and sometimes running past him, can ruin all the hard work you have put into your dog. So the emphasis once more is on a gradual approach, introducing your dog step by step towards the time when he can work a full day and be completely under control.

SIMULATING A SHOOTING DAY

Preparing our dogs is not just about developing control, it is also creating situations where they can learn by experiencing what can happen in the shooting field. Before we introduce our dogs to the real thing we need to set up situations as near to it as possible so they can gain experience at dealing with the difficulties they will encounter in the future. Just because our dog can do a great piece of work on a flat field it does not mean it will be able to do the same in high grass, woodland or cover that is dense and/or changeable. Plus, of course, there are other factors to take into account, as we have discussed earlier, such as wind, temperature, weather, hazards, water and scenting.

Keep It Simple

When teaching your dog to understand the different factors that can affect his ability and how to cope with them, it is important that you attempt to deal with one at a time, and build up the complexity in easy stages. So think out what you want to work on each time you take him out, and concentrate on that. If you want him to deal with brambles or heavy cover, only increase the density and the amount of work you do in each in small stages. Increase the distances of retrieves in small stages, and help him to learn how to handle one factor at a time. If you keep it simple and make it so that he succeeds fairly quickly at each stage, both his confidence and yours will grow at a much faster rate.

As an example, strong side winds and retrieving diagonally up a hill often has a dog fading away from the line of the retrieve; therefore when giving him experience of this, and developing his ability to keep his focus on the fall of a bird, begin with short retrieves where he can mark the bird easily. Dummies that are easily seen, a marker where the dummy has fallen such as a tree or a light-coloured object, even putting a marker down yourself such as a small flag, will help him keep his focus and learn how to keep it on one area. From short retrieves of course

Handling cold game through difficult cover in and out of water. (Paul Pederson Action Snapshot Photography)

you can easily build up to longer ones, and then remove the marker once he has learned to maintain his concentration on the fall. This use of markers can help, especially where your dog has to negotiate hazards such as trees and bushes which turn him away from a direct line to the fall.

You will want your dog to work to the gun, yours and often another Gun you are shooting with. Again, start simple so that your dog recognizes that birds fall within a distance of a Gun, and in the direction his gun is pointing. It is also helpful to fire live shots in the direction of the dummy you have to retrieve to help your dog understand shot scent and what it means. Once he recognizes the relationship between the gun and the retrieve, you will find him going to the area where the Gun is, and working distances from him where he knows he will find the retrieve.

Often birds will fall in woods, and in this case all your dog will be able to mark is the gunshot and the sound of the bird falling through the branches and/or hitting the floor. So once more, make distances short, create recognizable signals such as the gunshot and noises that help your dog to learn and understand this, and build up his confidence and ability to go into woodland and search for a bird within the most probable area of finding it.

Overcoming Problems

The important factor in setting up situations for your dog to experience is identifying what problems he will encounter, and what can affect his work. Some dogs do not initially like certain cover or water entries; some find marking in certain situations difficult. You have to identify these and help your dog overcome them. On long marks, make the beginning of his run to the retrieve simple; he is going to be making decisions on the way out to pick the retrieve, so keep them to a minimum until he gains experience at making multiple decisions on the way out. Gradually introduce close-up hazards such as walls, fences, patches of high cover, hedges and streams, and in this way he learns how to deal with each one on an individual basis before you send him through the multiple hazards he will encounter on a shooting day.

Many times we neglect the need for experience on water. Water can create many problems for our dogs, and there is no doubt that for success on water he should be good on land before we entertain anything difficult here. Difficult entries into water over slopes, thick mud, and through cover are only part of the equation. Entering the water at an angle, staying in the water and swimming over to the far side, multiple entries where your dog has to go over water, land and then into water again, plus retrieves over water and for a distance away from the far bank, are all situations he has to learn, to help him do a good job.

To help your dog, again build up gradually, and even when doing advanced work give him two fairly simple retrieves before adding something slightly more complex. On water it is very important to keep it simple and successful because you cannot go forwards to help, and he can learn that equally, you cannot go forwards to correct. On water even more than on land it is therefore important to keep the rate of success as high as possible.

Increasing the Complexity Even More

In any training session where you are setting up situations and doing multiple retrieves, remember to have a balance between the distances the dog has to work over. Not all retrieves should be long ones: the aim is not to see how far he

will run and mark, but to teach him distance perception. Some dogs if given long marks continually will become poor at short distance ones, and will overrun them; so we need to mix in short marks with the long ones. It is the same with hunting dogs: sometimes because we want them to enter and work tough cover, when they begin to do this we hunt them in tough cover all the time – but they must be able to deal with all densities and types of cover, even very low grass.

Although we build confidence by increasing the complexity in small stages and making success a high priority, once a dog is marking well at a distance, you can begin to put the retrieves in long cover where he has to keep hunting to get the dummy. When working in long cover it is also good practice to send your dog for retrieves across or through the paths he has been before, because in this way he will encounter the scent of the birds he brought back previously: this 'drag back' scent will have been left on

Steep banks and angles can create problems, so practise for experience. (Arno Brosky)

the grass, the ground and in the air, and he must learn to ignore it on his way out to the retrieve he needs.

In my experience one particular set-up really helps dogs to understand and grow when teaching blind retrieves: this is often called the three-peat set-up. In this we look for a piece of countryside where there are three locations we can put a blind retrieve with a similar look to them. In the three-peat we send him from the same place, turning him through angles to see the next location as he returns with each dummy. The 'picture' that we and the dog see of each location has to be similar, look familiar, and make him believe that if he tackles each retrieve in the same way he will be, and in fact is, successful. It may be that he has to run between two bushes or trees for each one; perhaps there is a gateway, a tree, or some other identifiable landmark behind each retrieve. Sometimes it is just three paths or hedges you can direct him down. The secret is having a clear 'picture' with identifiable markers for three different retrieve locations that are very similar. In this way we are gradually changing positions, wind, maybe even slope and other factors, but the dog feels confident because he has just seen a similar 'picture'.

Until you have built up your dog's experience, make each set-up as 'clean' as possible: in other words, have few complexities. When your dog begins to struggle or has a problem with some aspect of the set-up, learn from this, identify the problem, and then work at overcoming just that one problem until you can successfully mix it in amongst a more demanding set-up.

INTRODUCING COLD GAME

As you have been progressing with your dummy training, you will have introduced fur and feather by fastening rabbit skins and duck and pheasant wings to dummies. By fastening these wings and skins imaginatively, you can simulate bobbing tails and flapping wings to give a picture of realism to the dog. These dummies will have accustomed the dog to picking and carrying different textures of animal coverings, and will also have familiarized him with the scent of these animals.

The next stage is to introduce cold game — game that has been shot and has been left to go cold. Make sure that any cold game you use has been cleanly shot, and that there is very little blood sticking to the carcass. If the cold game is bloody or has any part of its insides showing, a dog is more likely to sniff and lick it instead of picking it up and bringing it back to you. Out of season, rabbit and pigeon are available for this purpose.

Be careful with pigeon: not only does it have a strong smell, which may be off-putting to your dog, but the feathers are particularly loose so they stick in his mouth, and he may even play with the bird, putting it down in an attempt to remove the feathers from his mouth. Minimize the chance of this happening by putting the cold pigeon in the leg of a lady's nylon stocking. Using this like a dummy, give the dog some retrieves — though when sending him for a retrieve on this new 'dummy', be prepared for him to hesitate; so the moment he puts his head down to the bird, whistle the recall to hasten the pick-up and return.

Once the bird has been retrieved correctly, cut slots in the nylon to allow parts of it to emerge. First, the wings can be pulled outside and fastened tightly to the body with an elastic band. Again, once the bird has been retrieved successfully, cut a slot and pull the head through; this can be followed by retrieves where the elastic band is removed so the wings are flapping. When this has been retrieved satisfactorily, remove the stocking completely, fasten the wings to the body with an elastic band, and give some retrieves. The final stage with a cold bird is to throw the bird exactly as it would fall after being shot, completely unfettered by elastic bands or nylon stockings.

These stages may be completed successfully over a few days, though with some dogs it may take much longer. So watch how your dog is performing at each stage, and build them up slowly as he accepts the new type of retrieve and does the work properly for you. When he delivers the pigeon, make him wait for a few seconds with the bird in his mouth, and after taking it, clear any loose feathers from his mouth.

Each stage in this cold game training should be a gradual progression, with only one or two retrieves given in each training session. Mix

The handling of rabbits is as important as that of birds.

these cold game retrieves with dummy retrieves, and if at any stage the dog appears reluctant to pick a retrieve, rub your hands over it prior to throwing it, to impart 'confidence scent'.

Rabbits have always been the dog's main quarry, therefore their scent has a particular fascination. Many dogs are keen to lick a rabbit rather than pick it up, so be ready to give that recall whistle, sometimes even running away from the dog and calling him encouragingly to make him pick the rabbit up and bring it back promptly.

Increase your dog's experience by using a variety of cold game. You may have problems with some types of game: for example, duck and woodcock can be particularly off-putting to some dogs. If this happens, again rub your hands all over the dead bird to put some of your scent on it, tease and enthuse to your dog about the bird, and then throw it, sending him very quickly for the retrieve. If this does not work, go back to the nylon stocking trick.

Build on the cold game experience by giving retrieves in water as well as on land. The use of cold game will not only train your dog to pick game, but also teach him how to carry these irregular-shaped objects. Finding the point of balance of a rabbit, or the best place to hold a duck while swimming, will come with practice.

It is a good idea to prepare yourself for cold game training by storing different types of game in your freezer, bringing them out when the

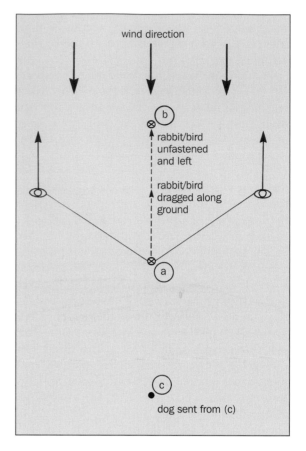

Laying a scent trail – two people.

appropriate stage is reached. Always remember to defrost the game completely first before using it, and ensure that it is dry. Once you have used it, you can re-freeze it again – though do make sure that it is clearly marked as a 'non-edible' item in the freezer. Eating a bird that has been frozen and defrosted a few times, with dog training in between, can lead to a stomach upset, and some disturbing reactions from other members of the family!

TRAINING TO FOLLOW A SCENT TRAIL

I have mentioned the use of hard rubber balls and tennis balls to teach the dog to follow a running line, which will prepare him for handling runners. You can now take this one stage further by using cold game to lay a line for the dog to follow, at the end of which it will find the dead bird. Attach a line to the bird or rabbit, and drag

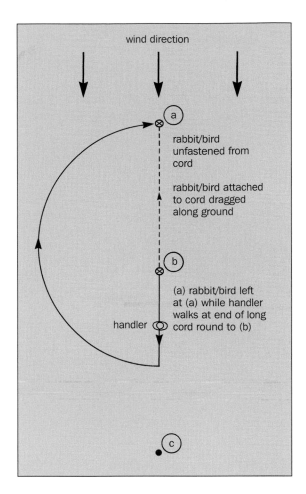

Laying a scent trail – one person.

it along for a distance to lay a line of scent. It is better if you can avoid foot scent fouling the line, as some dogs will learn to follow your foot scent rather than the scent of the dragged bird. As described earlier in Chapter 7 on retrieving, one way of doing this is for a friend to take the other end of the line stretched over a distance between the two of you; the bird is fastened in the middle of this line, and you walk together pulling the bird.

At first, do not drag the bird too far – three or four yards (about 3m) should be enough – and ensure that the dog has a good chance of success by walking and dragging into the wind. Place an unfettered bird at the end of the drag, and then send your dog for this as an unseen retrieve. The dog, upon reaching the beginning of the drag, should switch his nose into gear and work out the line taken, following it to find the cold game 'dummy'. Once your dog has developed the art

of following a line, you will be able to increase the distance of the drag line, and take it into all directions relative to the wind.

If you are by yourself and wish to lay a line, have a long line, throw the bird as far away from you as possible, and walk in a wide arc before pulling the bird towards you.

This exercise is one that will help you and your dog succeed in the future. The prime task of any gundog is to find wounded game; most dead game you could pick yourself. The art of getting the dog to the fall and then working the line of a running wounded bird is one admired by many, and to see a dog work in this way is also one of the most exciting aspects of dog work for both a handler and spectators.

INTRODUCTION TO LIVE GAME

During your training sessions you will have thrown dummies, balls and cold game around the dog while he was sitting, and also across his path as he was walking or hunting. The dog's re-action at seeing anything moving in front of him or flying through the air should now be to sit and mark where it lands, waiting for the command to fetch. Steadiness has been imparted, but don't fall into a false sense of security, be-cause although your dog is steady to the falling dummy, and you know that even with a number of dummies falling about him steadiness is main-tained, when you have the excitement of the shoot in the air and real game falling around, the emotions of the dog step up a rung. So prepare him for this atmosphere and help him to control his natural inclinations by gradually (that word again) introducing him to live game.

The Rabbit Pen

The rabbit pen is a very useful aid to introduc-ing game. If you have a friend who has a pen, and will allow you to use it, then take advantage of this facility. Some pens will contain not only rabbits but also brailed pheasants (pheasants whose wings have been fastened to stop them flying), ducks and chickens.

Walk your dog around the pen and famil-iarize him with the live game. Sit him in the

Hide dummies and cold game in cover for your dog to scent and find.

pen, and drive the birds and rabbits past him; feed them around him as he watches, all the time making sure he remains steady. Moving game, and particularly flapping birds, can be very tempting; if your dog is moving as well, it is even more tempting, so keep him sitting to start with. When you feel he can be trusted, give him a retrieve in the pen amongst the birds and rabbits: he should go out directly to the retrieve, pick it up and return promptly – though be ready to react if at any time he is tempted to do otherwise.

Spaniels should be introduced to the pen using the above methods, but can then be hunted to push up the rabbits. Initially, I walk round the pen with the dog on a lead until he catches the scent of a rabbit; we then work towards it, and as the rabbit flushes, I make him sit by blowing the stop whistle and giving a jerk on the lead. Once your dog begins to sit promptly to the whistle in the presence of a flushing rabbit, you can dispense with the lead and begin to hunt him freely off the lead – but be on your toes and concentrate, promptly reminding the dog to sit the moment he flushes the rabbit; he will quickly learn that the flush means sit. Be aware, however, that if you use the pen too much your dog could become 'sticky' in his hunting as he anticipates sitting and begins to move slowly in on the rabbit.

The other lesson that the dog will learn in the pen is that the flush does not always result in a shot and a retrieve. The command 'Gone away' means that there is nothing for the dog to fetch, and his mind should clear itself for continued hunting. In the pen, therefore, the flush followed by 'Gone away' will prepare the dog for this occurrence.

As mentioned above, the rabbit pen should not be used to excess. Occasional visits for short periods of time will develop your dog for work in the field, and can be used to remind him, if he ever transgresses, of what is required. Dogs can easily become 'pen-wise', knowing when they are in the close confines of the rabbit pen and therefore behaving impeccably. Outside the pen can be a different story. So never lose concentration or stop reading your dog on open ground, even though he behaves perfectly in the pen.

'Dogging In'

Although a rabbit pen is a very useful training ground, it is not essential, and you can 'manufacture' situations that will introduce your dog to game in a similar manner. If you have a friendly gamekeeper, it may be possible to walk your dog around the pheasant pens – though don't ask to hunt your spaniel amongst them! Most keepers will also welcome someone 'dogging in' the boundaries: this is where you walk the boundaries of the shoot hunting your dog, if it is a spaniel, or walk your labrador at heel, tapping the hedges to drive game back into the main shoot coverts, thus stopping them from wandering.

When birds have only just been released there will be few birds on the boundaries, but as the shooting season draws closer, you may encounter considerably more – this is very dependent upon the keeper's ability to hold the birds, and on the attraction of outside influences. 'Dogging in' is particularly good experience for a spaniel, providing him with the occasional flush and the 'gone away'. If you walk a retriever at heel and tap out the hedges, birds will often run ahead of you along the side of a hedge or in the field. This in itself is good temptation training, but by throwing a dummy forwards amongst the birds and then sending your dog, you can develop his ability to concentrate on the retrieve and ignore live running game. Picking the wounded bird from a group of others will come with experience, as he learns to recognize blood scent.

Training is full of contradictions: you want steadiness and control, yet you need a dog that uses his initiative and drive; you demand that he sits to moving game, and yet when the bird is wounded, a runner, he has to pick it even though it is moving. Contradiction is really the wrong word, because what you are striving to achieve is a balance and an understanding, by both of you, of what is required and when.

Introducing Warm Game

It is beneficial if you can introduce your dog to shooting by going out with a friend who will shoot for you. Make sure that this friend knows what is expected and what you are trying to achieve. With your spaniel hunting or retriever at heel and your friend shooting, you have the best of both worlds in that you can both concentrate on your particular job. With the first warm retrieves I give my dog, I prefer that he does not see them shot. To organize this, go to places where you know you will be able to shoot something – a rabbit is ideal.

Leave the dog in the car, and walk up the ground until you manage to shoot one; then leave it lying there, and go and fetch your dog. Hunt up or walk the dog at heel until he is within retrieving distance, and send him for this blind retrieve. If he shows any reluctance to pick, even with encouragement, don't get concerned: rub your hands over the dead game and then walk your dog away and try again. When he retrieves the warm game with confidence and competence, you can move on to shooting over him and sending him for birds or rabbits he has seen fall.

Resist any temptation for your dog to take part in any formal or organized shoot for a long time; nor should you give him a lot of warm retrieves. Pick up some of the shot game yourself, leaving the dog 'on the drop' (sitting). If you want to continue shooting and you can see that the dog is becoming excited, put him back in the car, out of harm's way. You can do so much harm by taking your young 'novice' dog out for a full day's work, particularly if it is a day where a lot of game is shot; the excitement of the moment can cause him to start running in and giving tongue, both of which are extremely undesirable faults.

THE FIRST SHOOT DAY

If you are a Gun at a driven shoot, the first time out with your novice dog don't be embarrassed to keep him on a lead during the drives, nor to pick the birds yourself after the drive is over, and to bring your dog out for only one or two drives in the morning and afternoon. While you are shooting at the peg keep an eye on him, and maintain a calm demeanour. Even though he may be adept at sitting and staying, remind him with the sit command if he begins to fidget or raise his bottom off the ground. He should never be sent during the drive, even if you see a runner; let the picker-up handle this. At the end of the drive, make your dog wait while you unload your gun, and maybe even put it in a slip. Then pick one or two birds yourself before sending the dog for a retrieve.

With a dog that has never been on a shoot day, it is a good idea to pick all the shot game yourself; the dog will therefore not anticipate being sent for any of them. You may then use one of these birds that you picked for a retrieve by dropping it and sending the dog back on a memory exercise. He must not get the idea that he will be sent for every bird shot, and he must not be allowed to become over-excited.

When you have had two or three outings, and the dog has successfully retrieved warm birds, add to his experience by sending him for a bird that is still alive but cannot move. This will give him the experience of a blood scent on a live bird. Once he manages this you will be able to move on to runners.

Handling Runners

Resist the temptation to send your dog for runners that are running in full view over open ground. Remember that one of your dog's natural instincts is to chase, and you have been training to suppress and control this; sending him on such a chase at this stage could quite easily ruin all your hard work. Wait until the bird has entered cover before sending your dog. The dog will have to use his nose rather than his eyes in cover, and it is more likely that the bird will 'tuck in' once it has reached a place of hiding. Hen pheasants 'tuck in' more often than cocks, and if you are lucky enough to get this situation, a hen pheasant is a much easier introduction to running game.

In fact, if the runner is a strong old cock bird, I would ask the experienced picking-up dog to handle it. A strong cock with heavy spurs can give a nasty kick to an inexperienced dog, which may not pick it quickly and correctly. Two things could then happen: your dog could be put off retrieving for a while, or even worse, in retaliation he could squeeze the bird to stop it kicking. When he realizes that a quick squeeze stops the bird fighting, he may do it more often to every runner he catches, which can result in a damaged bird. Crushed or broken ribs caused by a hard mouth are not only undesirable but in

a field trial mean disqualification. I have known some dogs that become so adept at this that they damage only running cocks because these are the fellows that have hurt them.

If ever you find yourself in a situation out by yourself where there is a runner, and your dog is inexperienced, don't be afraid of putting another shot into the runner to finish it off before sending your dog. Do likewise with a wounded duck, which will often dive and confuse a young dog. Provided it is safe to do so — and beware of ricochets — it is best to shoot it again on the water.

Handling runners can be very exciting not only for the dog, but also for the handler who does not want the bird to get away. Try not to create too much excitement or stress, but work calmly with the dog to find and retrieve the bird. If the bird has tucked well into cover, don't hassle the dog to get it out quickly: he has to learn how to extract game from cover without damaging it. Some dogs take great care when they have game in their mouths; others become so excited and want to remove it from the cover so quickly that they can easily damage it. Dogs learn from experience how to handle runners, but these experiences must be few and far between initially, to keep that delicate balance between control and initiative.

Dog Training Comes First

The transition from dummies to cold game and on to warm game should be a steady, step-by-step process. The most difficult stage, if you have not done the preparatory work, is the move to warm game. Even if you have done all your previous homework, there can be a temptation to move too fast at this stage. Read your dog and see how he is reacting to warm scent and freshly shot game, together with the atmosphere of a shoot day. It is better to err on the side of over-caution rather than over-confidence.

So often in the heat of the moment you can make a mistake, which will take you a step backwards in the dog's development. You should not be afraid to say 'No' when you are asked to do difficult things with your dog when he is not ready for them; politely point out that he has not reached that particular stage of training, and ask for a more experienced dog to be used. Your dog will be your partner for many years, so why spoil that partnership because of a few minutes of careless thought?

If you shoot over your dog either at a peg or when rough shooting, always try to be a dog man first and a Gun second, at least until your dog has learnt the good habits required. If you see your dog running in after a flushed bird, do not shoot. If you shoot the bird and the dog gets the retrieve, how can you punish him when he has the retrieve in his mouth? It is better to let the bird escape and deal with the dog. Perhaps some of the fault was your own.

While hunting a spaniel, or indeed a retriever if that is the dog you use, you should be reading the signs from the dog. You will be able to tell when a flush is imminent, so prepare yourself to blow the stop whistle the moment the bird takes to wing or, if it is a rabbit, when it bolts. Blow that stop whistle promptly, watch the dog – make sure he sits – and then take the shot. Yes, you may miss the shot in this way, but at least your dog is on the way to behaving as you would wish. If the dog moves even a small amount, drag him back to the exact spot where you blew the whistle and blow it again, making him sit. Keep him sitting in that position while you go and fetch the bird yourself, if you shot it. On your return keep the dog sitting and thinking about what has happened. Letting your dog get away with even the smallest movement is the beginning of a bigger one, until one day he runs in the full distance.

If your dog sat on the flush or to the whistle and shot, leave him sitting while you reload your gun. Initially, most of the birds you shoot should be picked by yourself, and only the occasional one given to the dog to retrieve.

The first season with your dog has to be approached with care and consideration. Too much work in the field with some dogs can create problems that will override all the good habits you have imparted. Continue to develop your dog in stages; he is still not fully trained, and the good habits must be reinforced and built upon until they become second nature.

Never stop training your dog with dummies, as this will provide a continuation of the habits developed. Also, if your dog transgresses in the field, you can go back to dummy training in an attempt to overcome any problems that may be arising. Reminding your dog of what he has learnt is an important part of responsible gundog ownership.

BEATING IN THE LINE

Working in the beating line, driving the game over the waiting guns, is a sport in itself. A good dog under control can be of great benefit in creating an effective beating line, particularly when birds are sitting tight – a bustling spaniel can soon encourage even the most obstinate bird to take to the wing. But good dogs in the beating line are not common. Many of them push too far ahead, often flushing birds in too large a number or before required by the keeper. A good beating dog will hunt all the cover, channelling the birds ahead of him without chasing them. He will flush birds, again without chasing, and await your command to continue hunting within a controllable distance. I would suggest that you do not allow your dog to hunt further away from you than you would if you were shooting over him. In the beating line there may be ten yards between yourself and the other beaters alongside you, therefore hunt the dog between these two beaters, using each of them as the outer limits of your dog's quartering pattern.

The beating line is a very exciting and stimulating place for you and your dog. With a young dog it can be very nerve-racking, so it should not be tackled until your dog is under good control both with dummies and when rough shooting, where only a few people and probably much less game are present.

The noise of beaters and the bad example set by other dogs can influence your young dog. Concentrate on him all the time, and if you have developed a good hunting pattern with all the right reactions to the associated commands, you will be able to train him to be effective as a beater. Try to keep whistle blowing to a minimum and voice commands as quiet as possible; this will make the dog listen for you, and you will be able to raise the volume when required. If possible, keep him away from the other dogs in the beating line. If this proves impossible, continue to be the leader of your dog, and make sure that he does not begin to follow his newly found canine 'commando' friends.

To take a young dog out for a full day's beating is asking for trouble. Too much excitement and too long a period of control for a young dog will tire him, and he will go wrong at times when you can do nothing about it. Bad habits are easy to get, but difficult to remove, therefore don't hunt your dog on every drive. If you can, leave him in the car while you beat the occasional drive by yourself. If the car isn't available, then walk him through the drive on a lead – in neutral.

Some cover will be difficult for a young dog, and some will hide him from your view. Though he may have handled rhododendrons and other large bushes quite effectively and under control when out only with yourself, the beating line can add another dimension to the exercise. If in doubt, ask someone else to beat it out with their more experienced dog, or tap it out yourself with a stick, keeping your dog on a lead.

One situation where panic can set in, is when you yourself have to fight your way through heavy cover, even crawl on hands and knees. To put the dog on a lead is difficult, and in trying to get through such cover you cannot keep a close eye on him. Keep calm, however, and stop now and again to call your dog to you, reassuring

yourself that he is there and letting him know you are still in charge. Concern yourself with maintaining that contact. Once you are out of the cover, settle yourself and your dog, establish contact this time with the line, and carry on with an air of confidence.

The basics of good beating are having a well trained dog that is under control, concentrating on him all the time, keeping in line with the other beaters, and most of all doing what the keeper asks. A good keeper who respects what you are doing with your dog and wants a good dog for the future, will understand you are not taking risks. So if you are asked to do something beyond the capabilities of your dog, do not be afraid to explain the situation – a good keeper will find a more experienced dog to do the job.

PICKING UP BEHIND A GUN

If you have a good dog, then you should have no shortage of invitations to pick up. Picking up is enjoyed by many handlers as much as, if not more than, actually shooting, and invitations are much sought after. The aim of picking up is to find game that would be difficult to locate

A beater's dog has to have stamina, determination, game-finding ability and control.

A hard-working spaniel bringing back game that would have been difficult to find without a dog.

without a dog, such as birds that have fallen in heavy cover or a flowing river, and particularly wounded birds – the runners that have to be 'tracked', found, and brought back to hand where they can be humanely dispatched.

Picking up is an extremely useful transition stage for the novice dog that hopefully will become a no-slip retriever sitting by the Gun's side: he will experience a shoot day with all the associated atmosphere and noises, but the advantage is that you will be able to concentrate totally on him. During the day there will be opportunities to widen his experience in many ways: sitting through the drive he will hear beaters approaching, see birds take flight and falling to the accompanying fusillade of shots, and after the 'all out' is called for the end of the drive, watch other dogs retrieve, and carry out some simple retrieves himself. You will be able to check on his steadiness and calmness, and make further plans for training if problems arise.

Picking up is not easy to get if you are not known, therefore it is useful to have contacts in order to obtain an invitation. If you have a young dog that needs experience, it is a good idea to make the keeper aware of this, and offer

to pick up for free. Picking up is a good way of educating your dog, but the main aim is to do the job, so if you cannot fulfil an effective role, it is better not to take any form of payment.

According to the type of shoot it is, the keeper will know how many pickers-up he requires; if you are extra to his requirements, make sure you don't get in anyone's way. It is an advantage to be near an experienced dog, which can deal with any difficult retrieves, and even better if the handler of that dog is sympathetic to what you are trying to achieve and will help you. Put yourself in the hands of the keeper after explaining your situation; if you have a good older dog as well as your young one, this is better still.

Where you position yourself depends upon the type of shoot and the game being shot, and you would be as well to take the lead from more experienced 'pickers'. I would avoid standing next to a dog that squeaks or whines, because this bad habit can be catching.

Keep an eye on your dog during the drive, and be ready to calm and reassure him, and control him where necessary. Never be tempted to send a young dog for a runner during the drive unless you are well back from the Guns, out of

Build up the number of dogs you can work at any time. Here, top trainer John Halstead works nine dogs at the CLA Game Fair – all under control.

sight and sound; in fact during his first outings, if your dog has not picked runners before, it is better to leave this to a more experienced dog. Judge each situation according to its merits, however: if there is a weak runner down, then it may be a good bird to start on, provided your dog is up to warm game.

A Duck Shoot

I remember having a young dog out for the first time on a duck shoot. He was not experienced on runners, so at the end of the drive I sent my older dog for the two we had watched down that were alive. A third duck had fallen and was lying dead in the middle of the field; this looked the ideal novice retrieve. So following the older dog's work on the runners, through which the young dog had sat patiently, I sent him for this third one.

He went out to it directly, having watched it down and remembered its fall. But imagine my surprise, and his even more so, when this 'dead' duck suddenly sprang to life, quacked angrily

at him, and set off at a good waddle across the field! I called him off, a command he obeyed very willingly, and sent the older dog. It took a few more outings before he picked duck happily after that, and many more before he took to runners and divers. The moral has to be: send your young inexperienced dog only for birds that are *definitely* dead until you have been able to introduce runners gradually.

Select Your Retrieves

Where birds are lost in cover, it is good practice to hunt your dog close in order to find them. Much of picking up work involves 'sweeping' the ground with your dog to find the ones that have been missed; this will help him to develop his hunting technique, and teach him to look to you for assistance and guidance. Always be ready for the flush of live game, and stop your dog on the whistle when it happens. Give the command 'Gone away', and continue with the work.

Select your retrieves for a young dog during the development stage, but do not forget that all birds should be picked. Pick some by hand, enlist the help of an experienced dog, and if you cannot find a bird you know is down, let the keeper know what it was and where it fell. Try to mark, in your memory, each bird that has fallen. If there are a lot, it helps to make a small drawing and mark their fall on this.

One important point that can keep you out of trouble is to let the Guns pick their own birds if they wish; even without a dog, many will walk around and pick their birds by hand. Walk up to the Gun and ask if he would like your help, and what birds might not have been picked. Do not send your dog on a retrieve during the drive, where he may run amongst the Guns or trespass into the next drive. If in doubt, don't!

Another useful piece of picking-up work takes place the morning after the shoot day: this is called 'cold picking up', and involves looking for birds that have fallen and not been found, and birds that have been wounded, landed in trees and then fallen during the night. On some large shoots, the birds picked up the morning after can be numerous; I have picked up as many as eight to ten birds on a 300 bird shoot. Cold dead birds will have less scent than freshly shot ones, making your dog work that little bit harder. He will also probably flush live game, so the experience can be invaluable.

When working your dog for other people, a calm, quiet, respectful and understanding approach is the best one to take. Don't pretend to know if you don't know, and don't be frightened to ask if in doubt. Your young dog, as he develops, will catch the eye of Guns and keepers; if he catches the eye favourably you will receive more invitations. And don't be upset when they all think that your dog is a natural, that it is a good dog and you had nothing to do with it. Smile, say thank you for the praise, and rest secure in the knowledge that you really did it together.

KEEPING IT ALL GOING

You will have spent months educating your dog, teaching him what is right and wrong, and building that strong foundation of behaviour and habits that will last a lifetime. But your dog is a living creature, not a robot, and like many

of us animals, can slip quite easily into the more 'fun' bad habits. Eternal vigilance and reading your dog is the essence of keeping him on the straight and narrow. Never be too proud to go back to dummy training: in the out-of-season months, not only will it keep your dog fit and trained, but you will both enjoy it – both you and your dog should never stop learning. After a time he will work in such a way that you will be able to relax, knowing that he can be trusted. Like all old craftsmen, he has done the job so often and has so many experiences under his belt, that he does it seemingly without effort – a natural. But the craftsman can become careless with familiarity, and has to work at maintaining the original standards.

Keeping Your Dog Fit

A dog is for life and not just for the shooting season. Out of season he will give you a great deal of pleasure as a companion and trainee, and you should use these times to keep him in trim and fit for work. To leave him resting all through the summer and then ask him to do a day's work when the season starts is most unfair. Some dogs are given an 'injection' of keep fit and training just prior to the season; it helps, but why not provide a continuous regime of training and exercise throughout the year?

To face and deliver birds through this type of cover, your dog has to be fit.

Your dog should not need as much food in the summer months as in the winter, when he is working. Swimming, memory retrieves and other training exercises will keep him fit and maintain those strong foundations you have built. It will need only a few hours each week to do this, and what better way can there be of enjoying the countryside than being out with your dog preparing him for the times you both enjoy? Of course, during the summer months there will be the occasional pigeon and rabbit shooting, where you can again practise all that has been taught, but make your canine friend a partner for more than just the shoot.

The nights are drawing in, a chill hangs in the air as evening approaches, light mists greet the early morning, and once more the shooting season is upon us. Guns are oiled, cartridges bought in ready, shooting gear and camouflage prepared, and all equipment brushed up and ready to go. But what about our dogs? Are they ready for a hard day's work in all weather conditions, maybe in and out of water, and through the heaviest of cover that has not quite died down after its spring and summer lushness? What about muscles that have been relaxing in the back garden soaking up the sunshine, and a brain that has not been tested since last year? Dogs also get 'rusty', 'dusty' and, like ourselves, unfit.

Too many times I have seen dogs damaged physically, joints and muscles strained beyond their capabilities, and training ruined through bad preparation or, more often, lack of it before the shooting season. Just consider how many miles a beating or rough shooting dog must run in order to get those birds out over the guns. Watch a picking-up dog force its way through rough cover, get over streams, fences and ditches to bring back the bird, and then imagine the strain being put on muscles and mind. This is not ordinary work: this is the work of athletes, and dogs should be at their peak both physically and mentally to come through a day successfully. This is commando work, and failing to prepare your dog for the 'battle' ahead is tantamount to neglect. You owe it to your dog to prepare him for the hard season ahead, and also to make preparations that will eliminate or, at the very least, minimize any potential for physical damage or accidents.

Short walks do not get your dog fit for the season. Exercise and fitness routines need to be gradually built up until he looks, acts and thinks fit. There needs to be a spring in the step, a clarity in the eye, an enthusiasm in the brain, a shine on the coat and a figure that shows just the outline of rib, with a good tuck up in the lumbar region. Feeding and the correct exercise bring this about, and some of that exercise can be given during a brush-up training programme.

So often I hear the comment 'Oh, I like the dog to have a little fat on him at the beginning of the season; he quickly loses it, and looks great after a few weeks.' However, that little extra weight and lack of fitness can cause the problems that may mean your dog is out of action after a few weeks. Good quality food will keep weight on your dog through the shooting season if you feed him the right amounts, of the right type of food. In the summer I often reduce the protein intake of my dogs, but about six weeks before the season starts I put them on to a premium food with a higher protein and fat content. This does not mean they get fat just before the season: if you watch your dog you can regulate the quantities, and as you give him more exercise, increase it accordingly. Don't go by just what it says on the bag – use some common sense, because every dog is different.

Road Work

If you can give your dogs 'road work' safely, this is a good way of getting them fit. Why not take your mountain bike, or borrow one, and get off on the forestry or heathland tracks with your dog following? I know some trainers who use ATV three-wheelers and teach their dogs to follow them on that. I would not advise running them alongside a car, however, as you cannot easily see where the dog is, and accidents have occurred on a number of occasions where owners have done this. An ATV does make it easier, but the bicycle will help get *you* fit as well.

Swimming is another way of creating fitness, and does not strain the muscles in the same way as running. So where your dog is overweight, judicious feeding and some good swims will certainly help start the fitness regime; then move on to 'road work' or other forms of running exercise. To get pointers fit for the season in America, not only do they run them behind

*Partners and companions
— the perfect team.*

ATVs, but they also fasten them into special harnesses, to which they attach chains, the weight of which is increased as their muscles and fitness levels improve. In competition these dogs are often running up to three hours at one stretch, covering such great distances that the handlers follow on horseback to stay with them. Peak fitness for these dogs is therefore essential.

Memory Retrieves

I don't use a bicycle or an ATV, but as part of my training programme I build the memory and fitness of all my dogs through memory retrieves. I drop a dummy or ball, walk on, and then send the dog for it. Not only is it good training, but it also means the dog does three times the distance that I do, and for two of those

'legs' he is running. With my labradors I build up their memory so they can go back well over 300 yards. Three or four retrieves like this and a dog is beginning to get some good running and stretching out.

As the dog becomes fitter, why not leave the ball or dummy at the top of increasingly steep hills? Running up the hill will definitely put muscle on his rear quarters and develop stamina. I regularly watch with admiration people who want to get fit running up slopes and carrying backpacks with increasingly heavy weights. I often saw the Marines doing this. If you live near the seaside, running on a sandy beach and swimming in the sea is a fun way to build muscle and fitness – but don't forget to wash off all that sea water afterwards.

Hunting

With my spaniels and any flushing dogs, as well as swimming I like to get them fit through hunting and increase the time hunting gradually until they will work happily for up to an hour, without 'blowing' excessively. I want to keep pace in the dog, and I also feel that the brain gets tired well before the body. So with a flusher that covers a lot of ground I feel more comfortable and confident knowing they can give everything for up to an hour. When I am upland hunting or rough shooting I take more than one dog, and they work alternate drives, one taking a break either walking at heel or in the car while the other works. I guess I am building the sprinter, not the long distance runner, but that is my preference.

One way of getting plenty of hunting and exercise is to put in regular training sessions of rabbiting or pigeon shooting, and in America, having a visit or two to a game preserve. In this way not only can you get your dog fit hunting up the birds, flushing them and maintaining steadiness, but you are also polishing up his training. Simulate situations you are going to encounter in hunting – blinds, boats, sitting for longish periods, different types of cover – and prepare your dog for what he will have to deal with.

The best time to work on fitness and training is when the day is cooler, in the early morning or in the evening. But whenever it is, don't do too much, too quickly.

MAINTAINING CONDITION

Fitness and training is only part of the preparation. For example, I always check my dogs' vaccination records to make sure they are up to date; I also always carry a first aid kit for the dogs, with plenty of eye wash and wound powder plus a large field bandage in case of emergencies.

The other item I have found invaluable is a water container with a top similar to a dishwashing liquid bottle, so that I can give the dog a drink by squirting water into its mouth. I have a rectangular one pint bottle that I carry in a leather pouch on my belt; however, it would be just as easy to carry it in a pocket or in a game bag. The dogs become very adept at catching the stream of water, to which I add powdered glucose. I have seen a number of dogs collapse, including one of my own, with sugar deficiency. At the beginning of the season when the weather is still warm and the vegetation lush, it doesn't take long to burn up a lot of energy and deplete the sugar reserves to the point of collapse. So glucose in the water is just one way of keeping those energy levels up.

As well as refreshing the dog with clean water at any time, rather than just at lunch time, I believe that wetting the dog's mouth washes out the dirt and dust and provides lubrication for the mouth and rear nasal passages to absorb scent. This gives the dog a greater scenting ability. Now some of you may think this is a ludicrous idea, but I have done it and it does seem to help.

There are many little things you can do to make your dog's work so much more enjoyable and thereby reduce injury or illness. If your dog has a longish coat, trim between the toes so that grass seeds, mud and other debris do not get caught up in there, causing soreness. Make sure his ears are clean and free of any infection, because if there is the slightest hint of this, then all the dirt, dust, seeds and water will aggravate it until it becomes very unpleasant.

And if you really want your dog to feel on top of the world, give him a good bath and groom not only a few days before the first shoot, but also regularly during the season. It seems to perk up a dog, besides which, while doing it, I always seem to find those little bumps, cuts and scratches which I missed during everyday routines. It's a bit like the car: you never notice the rust spots until you wash it.

The health, fitness and training of your dog is essential if you want a good shooting season together – and let's face it, if he is going to give you so much pleasure, you surely owe it to him to make sure he is ready in every way.

Conclusion

From the moment the dog realized that working with man had its benefits, and man realized that a dog would be a great advantage in hunting and killing game, providing food for the family, a partnership has developed. Today's partnerships between dog and man should be based on mutual respect and understanding. To many people there is nothing more rewarding than working with an animal, dogs and horses being at the top of the list of animals that people most like to work with.

Working a really responsive gundog, where you are at one with each other – a team – is a most satisfying experience. Using the dog's natural abilities to the full, but with him totally under control and working with you, is something to be proud of. Furthermore, a good intelligent dog can bring more to the partnership: through practice and experience he can add that extra dimension to the work, and make you really appreciate and wonder at a dog's abilities.

I started off by stating that I hoped this book would get you thinking about gundog training – you should never stop thinking or learning. Nothing you do goes 'by the book' all the time, and you will encounter difficulties that I have not mentioned. Try to think them through. Why have they occurred? What is in the dog's mind? Have *you* done wrong, not the dog? Work out a way forwards, built on a positive approach to training and developing your dog and yourself gradually, step by step, stage by stage. Take stock of where you are, and what you have achieved, and read your dog. He cannot tell you in words how he feels, but he will certainly tell you more than enough by his actions.

Martin and partner Two Dot. (Pat Tricher)

Read yourself also, and ask for help when you need it. Read other books, watch videos on training dogs, attend training sessions to get other ideas and approaches. In this way you will develop your own abilities and also build up a pool of knowledge that you can dip into whenever the need arises.

The pleasure of shooting for me has always been working a good dog, so much so that I very rarely pull a trigger myself. My pleasure comes from working my dogs for others, and of course in doing so for myself. The pleasure of a shooting day can be enhanced or spoilt by a dog's behaviour; it is up to you and your training to build a partnership that will make every shoot day pleasurable. You should become 'partners in the game'.

Appendix

Training Exercises

To be successful, training exercises must be fun and only repeated enough times to show the dog a small step in the training program. Stop with a small improvement. Quit while you are winning. Watch your dog to see when he is beginning to be confused or bored. Take steps to avoid both. Try for gradual improvements with each step and each exercise. Be clear in your mind as to whether your dog does understand or is simply following a routine. Test for understanding and always believe your dog is trying to please you and get it right unless he shows completely the opposite.

From the exercises, graduate in small steps to the actual field work. Simply because your dog does the exercises it does not mean he will understand and do it in the field. Reduce distances, use support and help 'tools' and approaches. The thrower can be a great help and can also create big problems, therefore teach your thrower what to do and what not to do. They are important in the training of your dog. If in doubt, help your dog; your dog will then look to you for help and leadership when he needs it.

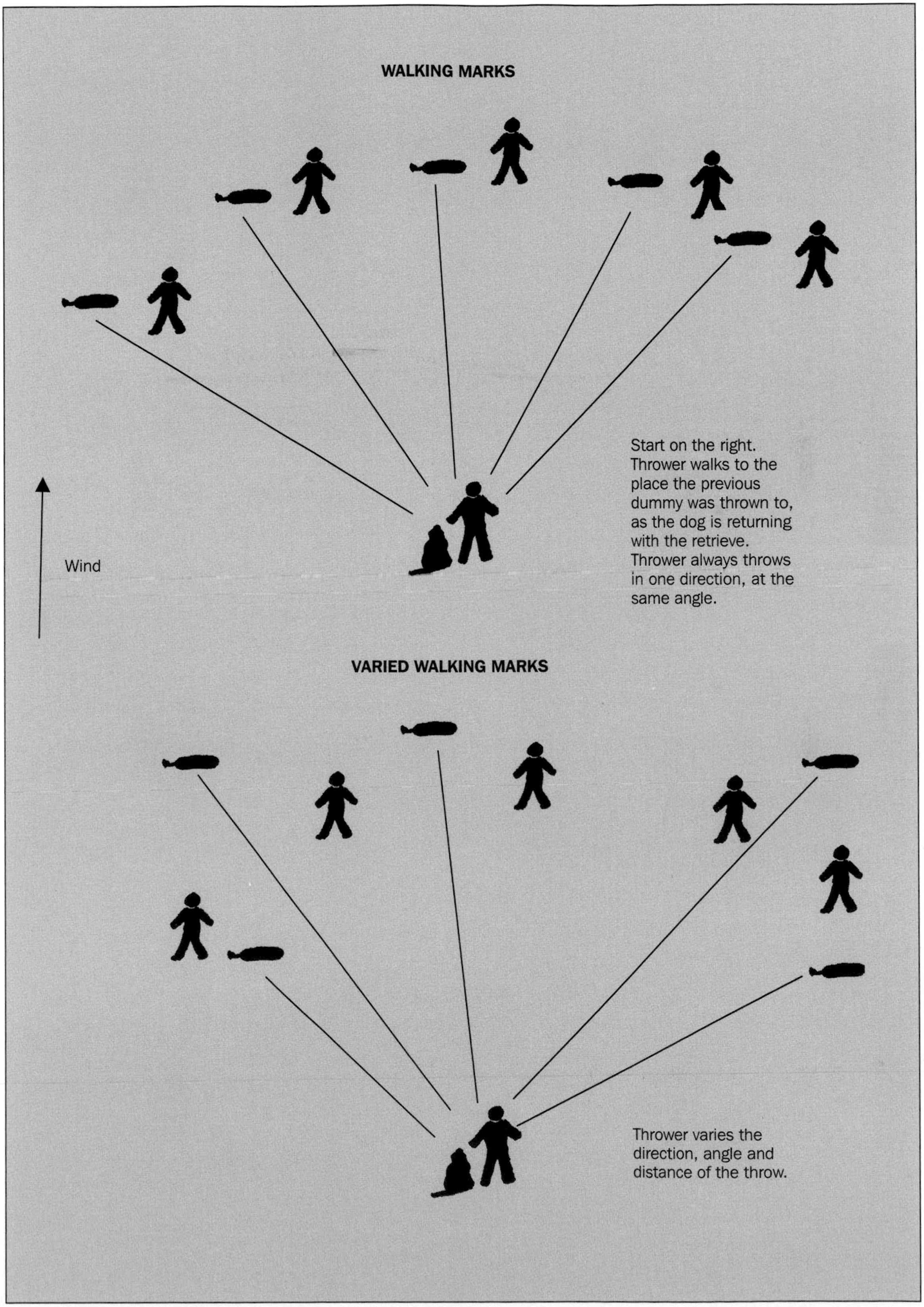

WALKING MARKS

Wind

Start on the right.
Thrower walks to the
place the previous
dummy was thrown to,
as the dog is returning
with the retrieve.
Thrower always throws
in one direction, at the
same angle.

VARIED WALKING MARKS

Thrower varies the
direction, angle and
distance of the throw.

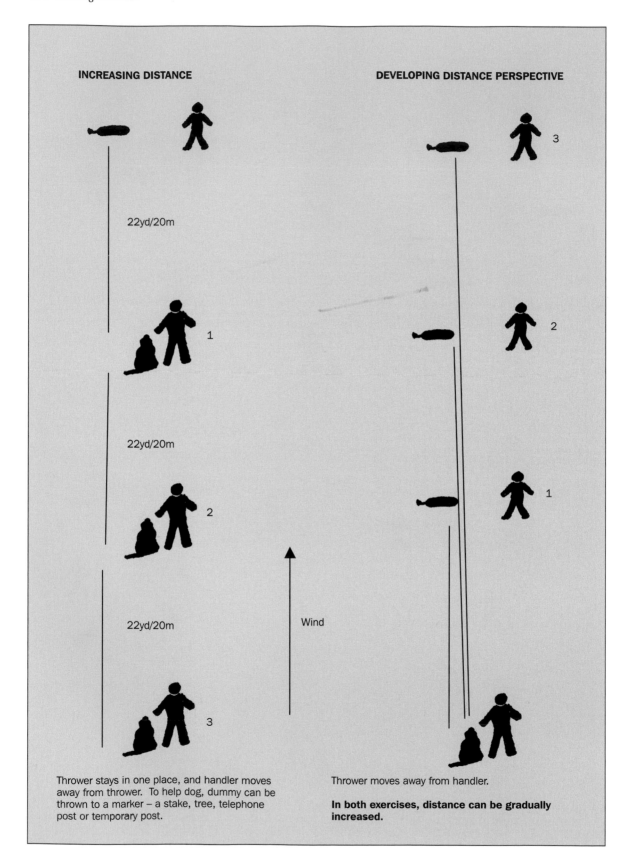

INCREASING DISTANCE

22yd/20m

1

22yd/20m

2

22yd/20m

3

Wind

DEVELOPING DISTANCE PERSPECTIVE

3

2

1

Thrower stays in one place, and handler moves away from thrower. To help dog, dummy can be thrown to a marker – a stake, tree, telephone post or temporary post.

Thrower moves away from handler.

In both exercises, distance can be gradually increased.

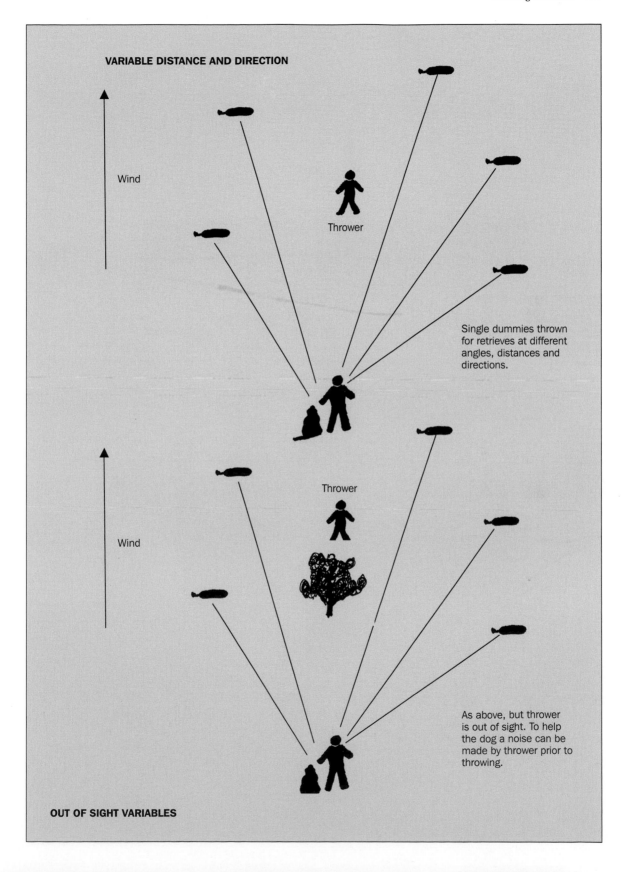

VARIABLE DISTANCE AND DIRECTION

Wind

Thrower

Single dummies thrown for retrieves at different angles, distances and directions.

Wind

Thrower

As above, but thrower is out of sight. To help the dog a noise can be made by thrower prior to throwing.

OUT OF SIGHT VARIABLES

With your dog by your side, face in the direction you are to throw the dummy. Throw the dummy, then turn to the next direction. Throw out three dummies initially at 90 degrees to each, and then build up to 45 degree angles. In this drawing, five dummies are down before the dog is sent.

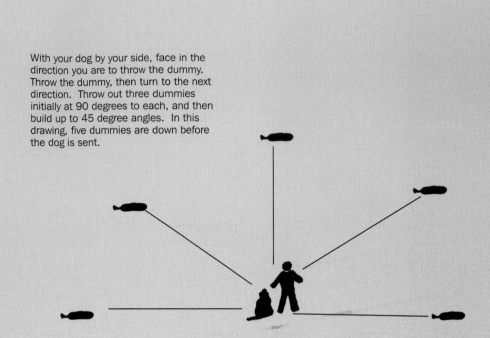

EVEN DISTANCE HALF CARTWHEEL

As above, but distances are varied.

STEPPED HALF CARTWHEEL

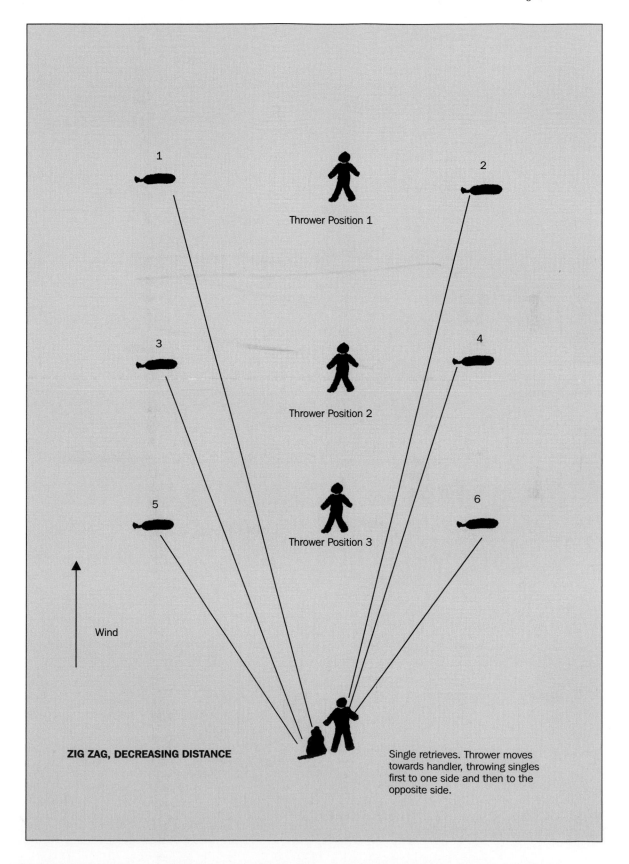

1

2

Thrower Position 1

3

4

Thrower Position 2

5

6

Thrower Position 3

Wind

ZIG ZAG, DECREASING DISTANCE

Single retrieves. Thrower moves towards handler, throwing singles first to one side and then to the opposite side.

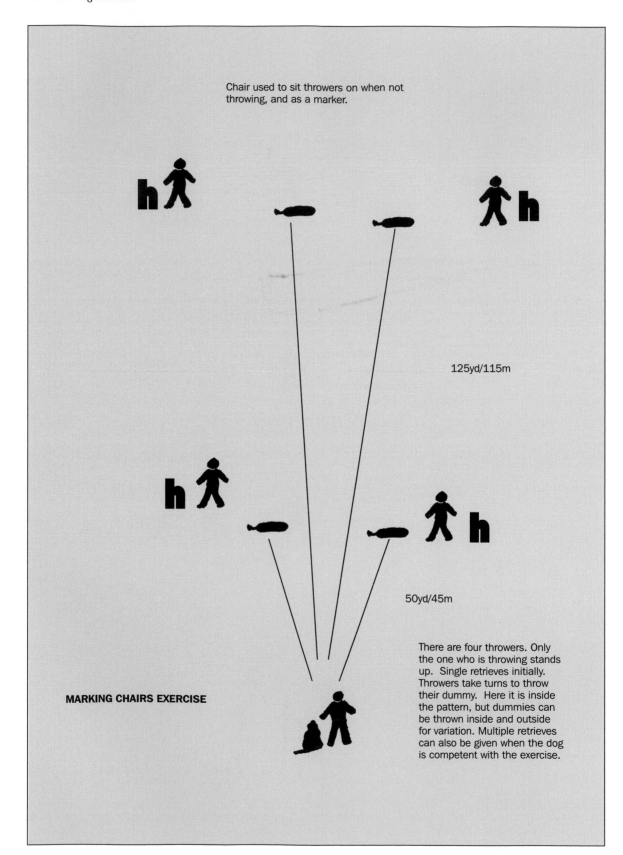

Chair used to sit throwers on when not throwing, and as a marker.

125yd/115m

50yd/45m

MARKING CHAIRS EXERCISE

There are four throwers. Only the one who is throwing stands up. Single retrieves initially. Throwers take turns to throw their dummy. Here it is inside the pattern, but dummies can be thrown inside and outside for variation. Multiple retrieves can also be given when the dog is competent with the exercise.

Same concept, similar layouts

THREE PEAT EXERCISE – MARKS AND BLINDS

Initially this exercise can be done as marked or memory retrieves. You can then move onto blind retrieves to help the dog 'focus' on a picture. Blind retrieves are placed in a familiar situation – between two trees, but different trees in different places. White dummies are used first, then orange ones. The places change but the picture becomes familiar.

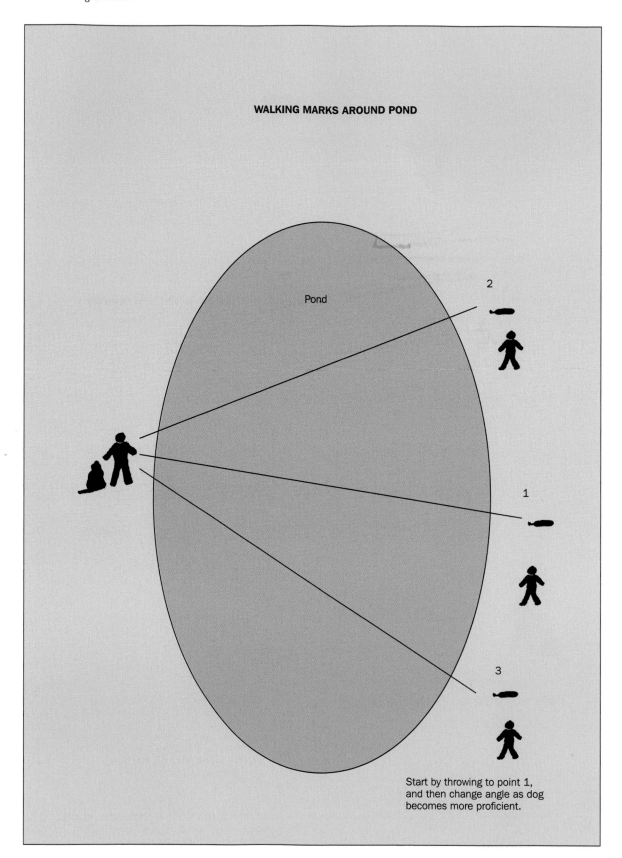

WALKING MARKS AROUND POND

Pond

2

1

3

Start by throwing to point 1,
and then change angle as dog
becomes more proficient.

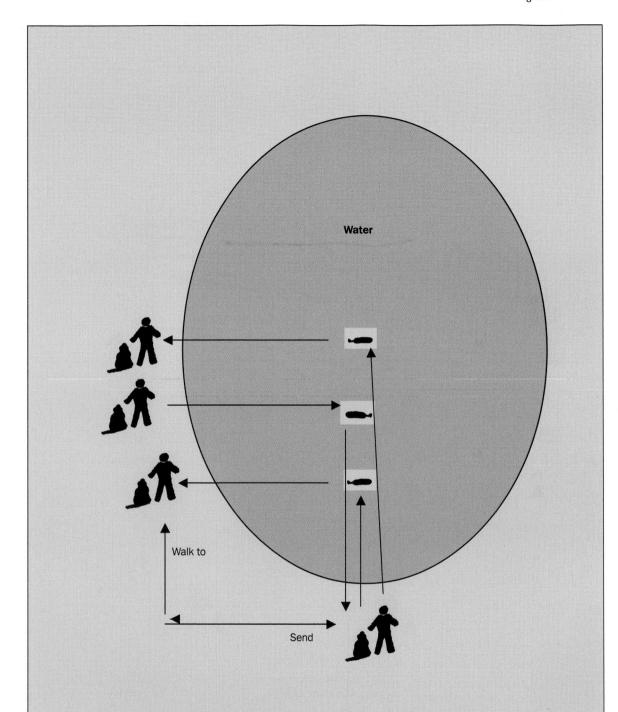

Water

Walk to

Send

BACK AND FORTH 'COME TO ME' EXERCISE IN WATER

To teach dog to come back by water. Throw dummy in and then change your position while he is swimming out to it. Call to catch his attention at the moment he picks the dummy.

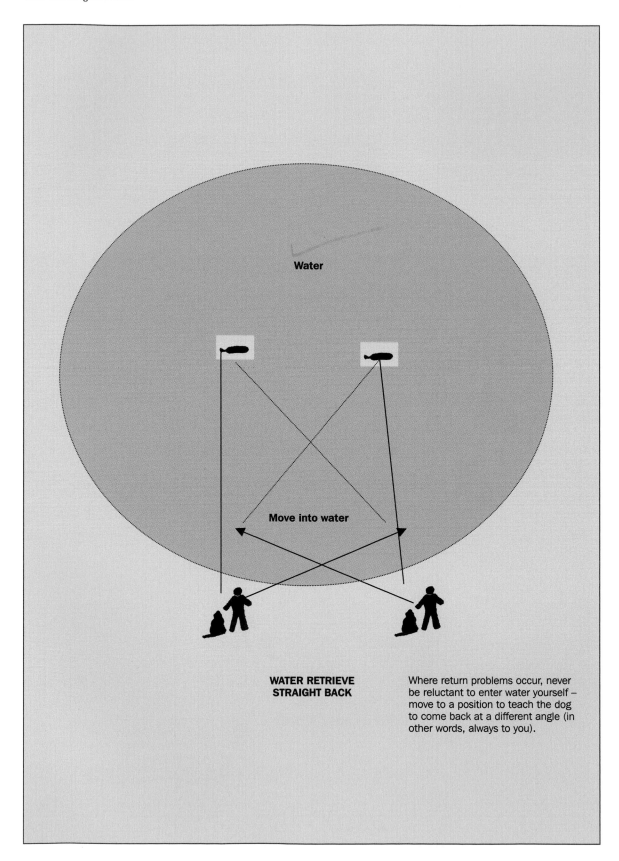

Water

Move into water

**WATER RETRIEVE
STRAIGHT BACK**

Where return problems occur, never be reluctant to enter water yourself – move to a position to teach the dog to come back at a different angle (in other words, always to you).

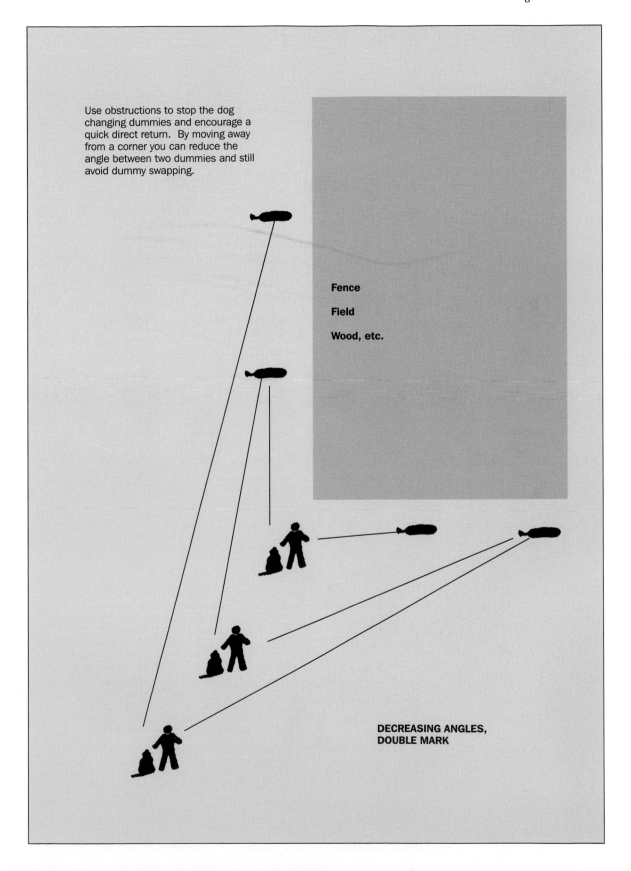

Use obstructions to stop the dog changing dummies and encourage a quick direct return. By moving away from a corner you can reduce the angle between two dummies and still avoid dummy swapping.

Fence

Field

Wood, etc.

DECREASING ANGLES, DOUBLE MARK

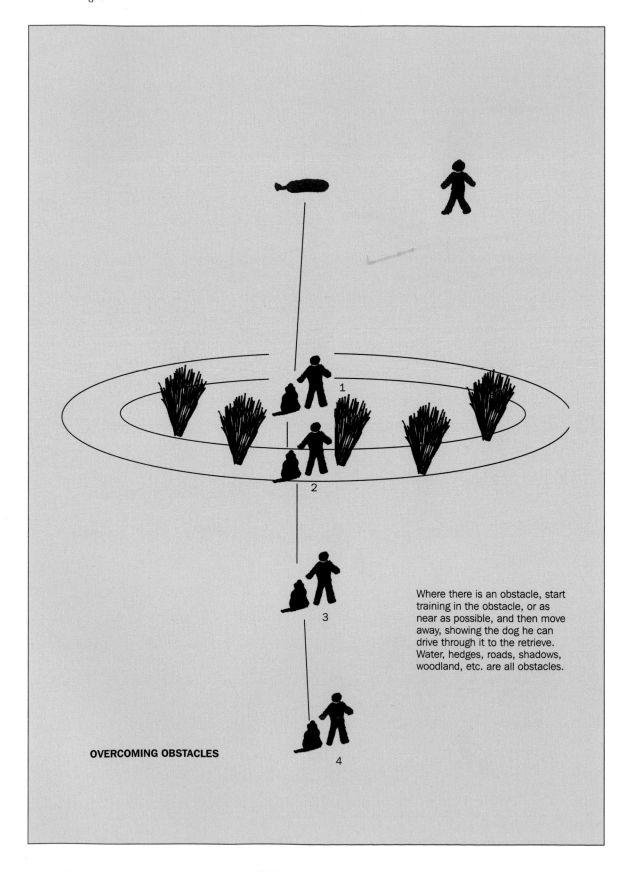

1

2

3

Where there is an obstacle, start
training in the obstacle, or as
near as possible, and then move
away, showing the dog he can
drive through it to the retrieve.
Water, hedges, roads, shadows,
woodland, etc. are all obstacles.

OVERCOMING OBSTACLES

4

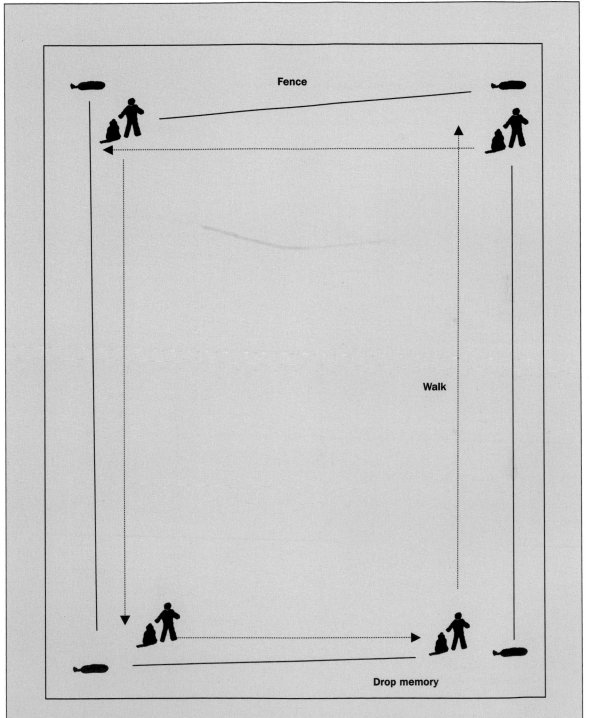

Fence

Walk

Drop memory

CORNER MEMORIES

Use fences and corners where he regularly retrieves dummies to create straight lines and confidence in memory retrieves, which lead to blind retrieves.

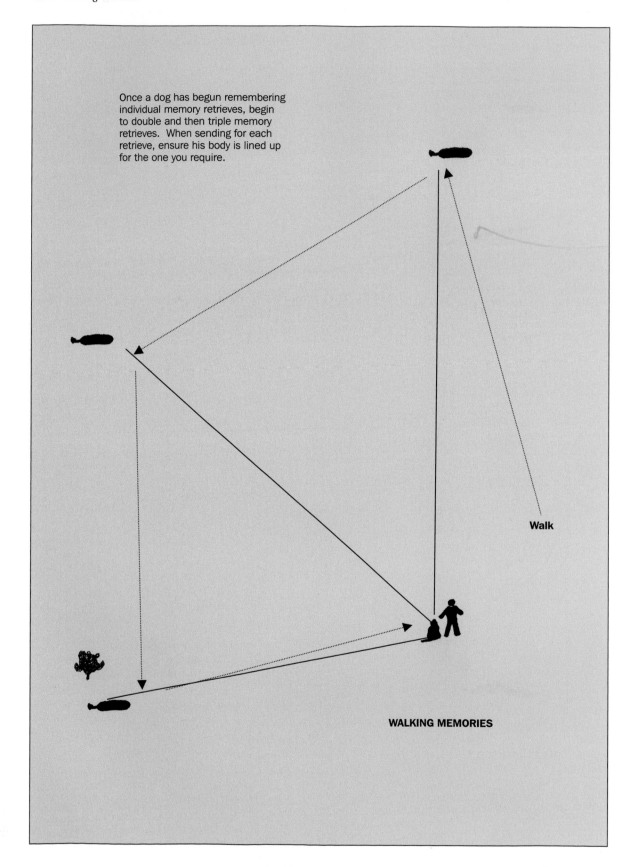

Once a dog has begun remembering individual memory retrieves, begin to double and then triple memory retrieves. When sending for each retrieve, ensure his body is lined up for the one you require.

Walk

WALKING MEMORIES

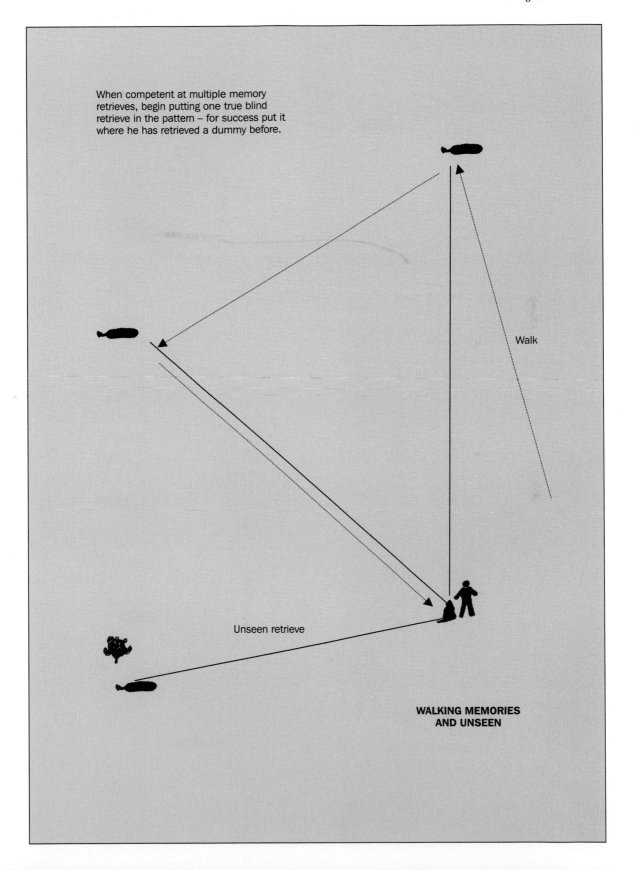

When competent at multiple memory
retrieves, begin putting one true blind
retrieve in the pattern – for success put it
where he has retrieved a dummy before.

Walk

Unseen retrieve

**WALKING MEMORIES
AND UNSEEN**

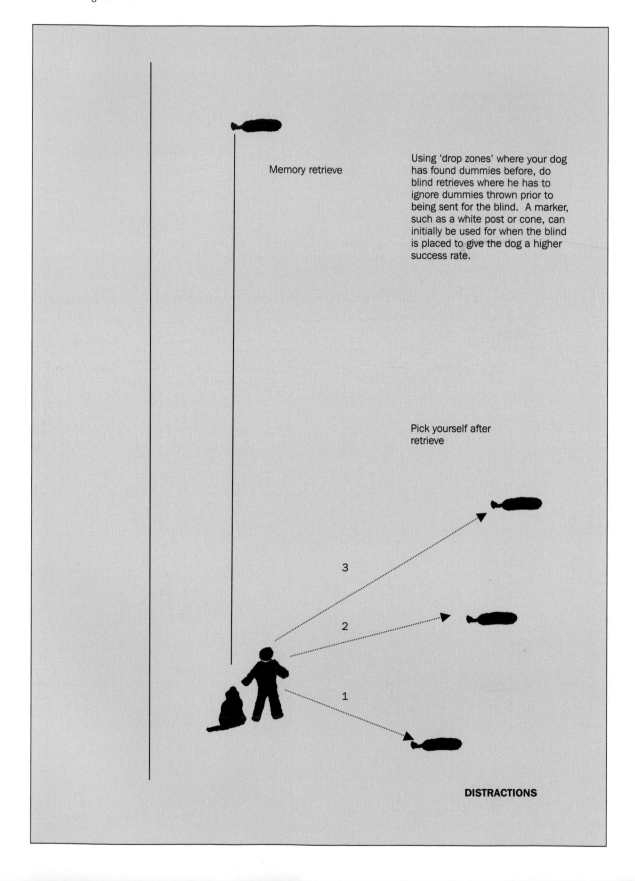

Memory retrieve

Using 'drop zones' where your dog has found dummies before, do blind retrieves where he has to ignore dummies thrown prior to being sent for the blind. A marker, such as a white post or cone, can initially be used for when the blind is placed to give the dog a higher success rate.

Pick yourself after retrieve

3

2

1

DISTRACTIONS

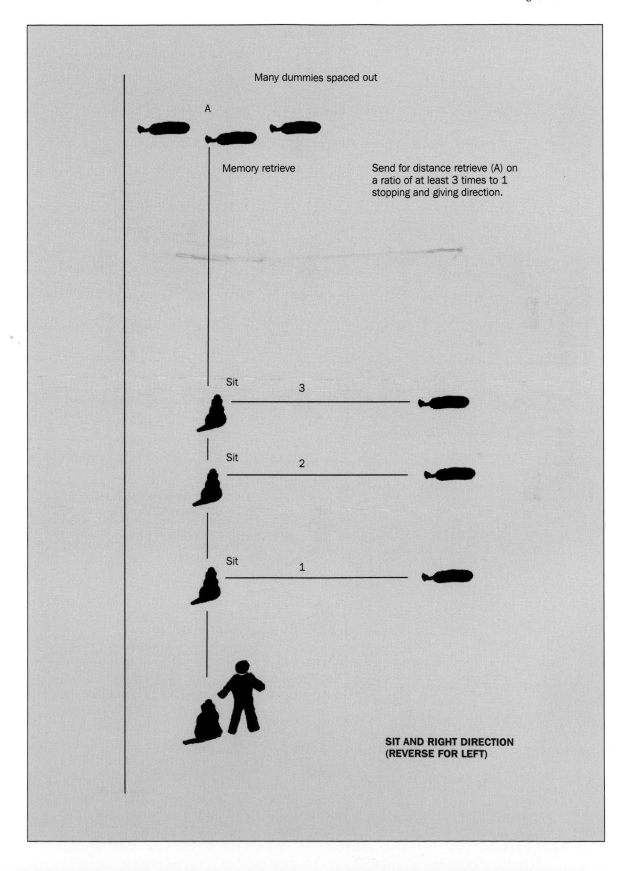

Many dummies spaced out

A

Memory retrieve

Send for distance retrieve (A) on a ratio of at least 3 times to 1 stopping and giving direction.

Sit

3

Sit

2

Sit

1

SIT AND RIGHT DIRECTION (REVERSE FOR LEFT)

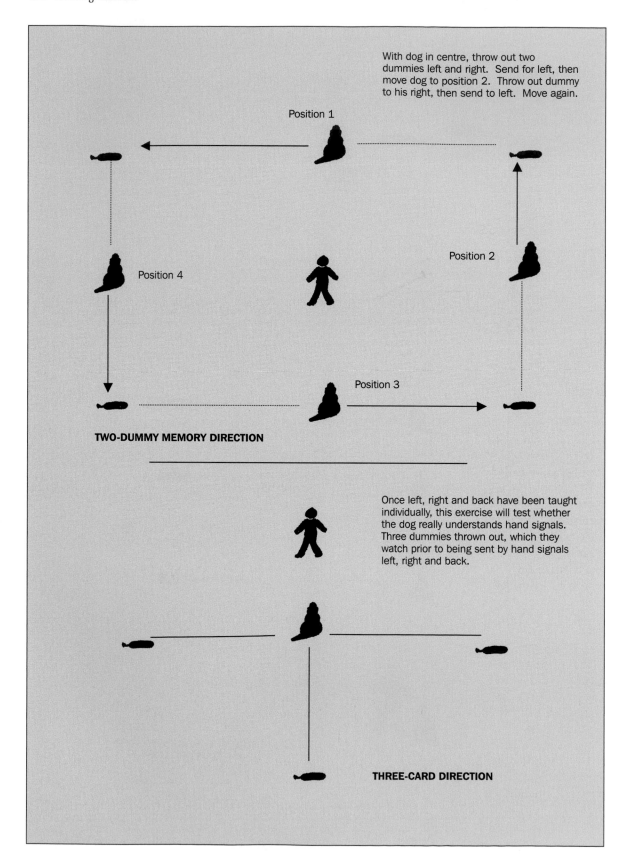

With dog in centre, throw out two dummies left and right. Send for left, then move dog to position 2. Throw out dummy to his right, then send to left. Move again.

Position 1

Position 2

Position 4

Position 3

TWO-DUMMY MEMORY DIRECTION

Once left, right and back have been taught individually, this exercise will test whether the dog really understands hand signals. Three dummies thrown out, which they watch prior to being sent by hand signals left, right and back.

THREE-CARD DIRECTION

Index